# The Meaning of Video Games

*The Meaning of Video Games* takes a textual studies approach to an increasingly important form of expression in today's culture. It begins by assuming that video games are meaningful—not just as sociological or economic or cultural evidence, but in their own right, as cultural expressions worthy of scholarly attention. In this way, this book makes a contribution to the study of video games, but it also aims to enrich textual studies.

Early video game studies scholars were quick to point out that a game should never be reduced to merely its "story" or narrative content and they rightly insist on the importance of studying games as games. But here Steven E. Jones demonstrates that textual studies—which grows historically out of ancient questions of textual recension, multiple versions, production, reproduction, and reception—can fruitfully be applied to the study of video games. Citing specific examples such as *Myst* and *Lost*, *Katamari Damacy*, *Halo Façade*, Nintendo's *Wii*, and Will Wright's *Spore*, the book explores the ways in which textual studies concepts—authorial intention, textual variability and performance, the paratext, publishing history, and the social text—can shed light on video games as more than formal systems. It treats video games as cultural forms of expression that are received as they are played, out in the world, where their meanings get made.

**Steven E. Jones** is Professor of English at Loyola University Chicago. He is co-editor of the *Romantic Circles* website and author of *Satire and Romanticism*, *The Satiric Eye*, and *Against Technology: From the Luddites to Neo-Luddism*, also published by Routledge.

# The Meaning of Video Games

## Gaming and textual strategies

Steven E. Jones

Routledge
Taylor & Francis Group

NEW YORK AND LONDON

First published 2008
by Routledge
270 Madison Ave, New York, NY 10016

Simultaneously published in the UK
by Routledge
2 Park Square, Milton Park, Abingdon, Oxon OX14 4RN

*Routledge is an imprint of the Taylor & Francis Group, an informa business*

© 2008 Taylor and Francis Group

Typeset in Perpetua by RefineCatch Limited, Bungay, Suffolk
Printed and bound in the United States of America on acid-free paper by Edwards Brothers, Inc.

*Library of Congress Cataloging in Publication Data*
A catalog record has been requested for this book

ISBN10: 0–415–96055–X (hbk)
ISBN10: 0–415–96056–8 (pbk)
ISBN10: 0–203–92992–6 (ebk)

ISBN13: 978–0–415–96055–7 (hbk)
ISBN13: 978–0–415–96056–4 (pbk)
ISBN13: 978–0–203–92992–6 (ebk)

To Emilia and Henry, Research Assistants

*My, Earth Really is Full of Things*

# Contents

# Illustrations

# Acknowledgements

Every book is a collaborative, social product, and that's especially true in this case. I want to thank, first, my students at Loyola University Chicago, particularly the members of an advanced undergraduate seminar on Video Games and Textual Studies in spring 2007, who read some of the following chapters in draft and whose discussions and group projects taught me much as I formulated the rest of the book. They are: Jeff Behrends, John Blyschak, Kevin Cioffi, Andy Dost, Betty Foley, Kristina Giovanni, Kristin Hertko, Tiana Jansen, Joe LeBlanc, Dan Lenzini, Peter Leonteos, Bryan McCutcheon, Dan Melnick, Punit Patel, Ryan Ptomey, and Elise Rombach. I also want to thank Doug Guerra, an exceptional graduate student with an interest in games and a history in Chicago theater. He loaned me PS2 games when I needed them, discussed them theoretically, and put me in touch with a colleague of his, Chloe Johnston, who played the voice of Grace in *Façade* (my thanks to her in turn, for answering my questions in email). Talmadge Wright, of the Department of Sociology at Loyola University Chicago, visited my class and was always happy to talk video games in the hallway between our two classrooms: what I liked to call material interdisciplinarity. Thanks to *Halo* players who shared their experiences with me for chapter 3, including two anonymous friends of the formidable Megan Milliken and two anonymous Loyola University students ("John" and "Dave").

In the game studies community, I'm grateful to Espen Aarseth, for a brief but simulating lunchtime conversation at an Association for Computers in the Humanities conference in Sweden; to Nick Montfort, for joining a panel I organized for the MLA and for his own pioneering interdisciplinary work. For helpful responses to my questions on *Façade*, my thanks to Andrew Stern. Among textual-studies colleagues, I'm indebted especially to G. Thomas Tanselle, David C. Greetham, Karl Kroeber, Suzanne Gossett, Neil Fraistat, Matthew Kirschenbaum, and, in particular, Jerome McGann, whose theoretical work on textuality helped to inspire my approach to this subject. Reports from anonymous readers at Routledge were very useful as I completed the manuscript, as was the editorial guidance of Matthew Byrnie. For permission to use the photo illustrating *Katamari Damacy* "cosplay" in chapter 2, I'm grateful to Kathryn Hill. For the photo of actors playing Wii in the British cinema in chapter 5, I'm grateful to Dean McKain of CommentUK.

Finally, I want to thank Henry and Emilia, who were only too happy at any time to help me with the research for this book, especially when it involved playing *Zelda*, *Okami*, *Wii Sports*, or the incomparable *Katamari Damacy*.

# Introduction

This book is about video games, a pervasive and significant form of expression in today's culture. It's based on the premise that video games are meaningful—not just as sociological or economic or cultural evidence, but in their own right, as cultural expressions worthy of scholarly attention. The growing number of game studies scholars and dedicated academic programs would seem to support this view. Game development and computer science programs now offer courses in the theory and interpretation of games to their students; communications or media studies programs include courses on games; sociology or anthropology departments occasionally offer courses on the significance of video games in society. This book aims to make a contribution to the study of video games from the point of view of textual studies, but it also aims to enrich textual studies with an exploration of the nature of video games. It's interdisciplinary, therefore, not only in approach but in spirit, a double, diplomatic effort.

I'm an English professor specializing in textual studies and digital media as well as Romantic-period literature. I work in a fairly typical English department, where I can wander the halls and find colleagues working on film studies, visual culture studies (including the semiotics of digital media and social networks as well as, say, photography), electronic editions of medieval and Anglo-Saxon texts, traditional print editions of Renaissance dramas by Shakespeare or Middleton, the history of popular religious movements in the nineteenth century, theoretical essays on hypertext and pedagogy, jazz and modern poetry—in addition to the traditional work of our discipline, studying and interpreting literary texts in contexts past and present. An English department these days covers a lot of ground, in many media besides literary texts, and yet I know that many of my colleagues are skeptical about the value of studying (and teaching courses on) video games, even though games are arguably the most influential form of popular expression and entertainment in today's broader culture. The usual cultural and aesthetic prejudices apply in this case, of course—prejudices against mere games, what are assumed to be at best mass-market commodities or mindless pastimes for children (of all ages), and at worst, training devices for misogyny, militarism, and violence. But I also think that the resistance runs deeper than these prejudices, that it touches my colleagues where they are often most sensitive—in their professional identities. Even among those with some experience with video games (in my age cohort and younger this is statistically pretty likely), there is a sense that what literary scholars *do* is at odds with what video games are *for*. We read, we interpret. We produce meanings by performing either close readings of verbal texts or somewhat more "distant" readings of the historical and contemporary contexts out of which those verbal texts are produced and within which they circulate. But how do you interpret a video game? Video games are to be played, my colleagues know. Their stories often appear to be based on clichés of genre fiction and the most popular titles are designed and made by large teams, for the most part. As formal systems they consist of fairly unpredictable behaviors in response to rules and events within the gameworld. It's hard for literary scholars to understand how they can truly be *meaningful*, any more than a soccer game is meaningful, I mean apart from what most of them perceive in advance would be superficial semiotic readings of the characters or mythical narrative structures of games—Mario as the Hero with a Thousand Faces, say.

Such trivial exercises in game interpretation are parodied in D. B. Weiss's 2002 satirical novel, *Lucky Wander Boy*. At one point the hapless protagonist, Adam Pennyman, who is writing an obsessive, sprawling, and interpretive *Catalogue of Obsolete Entertainments* on classic arcade-era games, is challenged by a female colleague: "Does everything have to 'mean' something? What do you think you are, some kind of writer?"[1] Pennyman proceeds to follow his obsession with games down the rabbit hole of "deeper" symbolic interpretations, and he goes insane. Nevertheless, one point of *Lucky Wander Boy* (as I understand the novel) is that video games *do* mean something, but in a different way than poor Adam Pennyman (and most literary scholars) might assume. They are meaningful less as narrative or symbolic "texts" to be interpreted than as complex forms for social activity. Pennyman remarks at one point that games are like "central switching stations through which thousands of our most important memories are routed" (7). He wrongly jumps to the conclusion that interpreters must dig for hidden meanings, assuming that meaning must lie below the surface of the games and becoming fixated nostalgically on adolescent "memories." Instead, I think the metaphor itself—"central switching stations"—is far more richly suggestive than Adam realizes in his interpretive monomania. It suggests that video games must be understood as parts of complex social networks, and that meanings flow *through* video games, and are produced at their prompting by communities of players. The meanings of video games are functions of their use within social networks, which link up to other forms of media, texts, institutions, and groups. The meaning(s) of video games are constructed and they are collaborative. They are *made* by social interactions of various kinds rather than *found* in the software and hardware objects themselves. The meanings of games are not essential or inherent in their form (though form is a crucial determinant), even if we define form as a set of rules and constraints for gameplay, and certainly not in their extractable "stories" (though the fictive storyworld matters in most games), but are functions of the larger grid of possibilities built by groups of developers, players, reviewers, critics, and fans in particular times and places and through specific acts of gameplay or discourse about games.

As I say, sociologists, anthropologists, cultural studies scholars, and media specialists have for decades now included video games among their objects of study. In my own university, for example, a sociologist colleague, Talmadge Wright, has done very interesting work on the social "meta-games" and "mediations" that go on in the background chat, as it were, during bouts of online play in the fan-created mod-game *Counter-Strike*.[2] During the 1990s, a number of humanists studied the proto-gaming virtual spaces of MUDs (multi-user domain, dimension or dungeon) and MOOs (MUD object oriented), as well as some early computer games, from the perspective of literary theory or cultural studies, alongside hypertext and other emerging forms of electronic textuality. (I contributed an early article myself, on the acclaimed first-person puzzle-game *Myst*, which I wrote in 1995 and published in the online journal *Post Modern Culture* in 1996.) More recently, industry-attuned programs in video game design and development have begun to include courses in form, genre, and the theory of games. Younger scholars who specialize in the study of games, many of them with game design experience, have begun to build and teach in and these dedicated programs.

Around 2001, a wholly dedicated academic area arose, much of it indebted to the work of Espen Aarseth, now at the Center for Computer Games Research, IT University of Copenhagen. Aarseth's influential *Cybertext* (1996) had examined what he called "ergodic" literature (requiring a "non-trivial effort to traverse the text," by which he meant more than the visual and mental effort of reading), discussing hypertext and some early computer games, in terms that emphasized the configurative work done by the user of such texts, in supposed contrast to the normal practices of reading traditional literary texts. This school, with which were associated Gonzala Frasca, Markku Eskelinen, Jesper Juul, among others, and whose work often appeared in the peer-reviewed journal in "computer game research," *Games Studies* (2001–), became known as "ludology," from the Latin word for game, in order to focus on its attention to play, rules, and constraints, when it comes to understanding games. The opening editorial article of the first issue of *Game Studies*, written by Aarseth, sounds the manifesto (complete with capital letters): "2001 can be seen as the Year One of Computer Game Studies as an emerging, viable, international, academic field."[3]

Ludologists deliberately placed video games in the larger family of games in general, cultural practices descended from go or chess rather than *Gilgamesh* or Chaucer. As discussion developed around definitions and taxonomies, some began polemically to downplay the role of "story" in video games, or to refute the usefulness of Aristotle's theory of drama, for example, for understanding games, since, they argued, a game is not a story or a drama but a form unto itself. They asked, for example: where's the story in *Tetris*? How can narrative or dramatic theory help to explain its form? Isn't chess still chess if played with corks or stones instead of kings and pawns? Does Laura Croft's sexualized body really matter to the essential experience of playing *Tomb Raider*? What is it, they asked, that these diverse games have in common, in their essence, *as* games? In part, ludology was an institutional reaction to existing interdisciplinary work on games by cultural studies and comparative media studies scholars such as Janet Murray and Henry Jenkins, who treated games as one among a whole range of cultural forms of media expression and, according to their critics among the ludologists, often from a perspective that privileged text-based or filmic presuppositions of meaning or aesthetic value.

In fact, the groundbreaking work of Murray and Jenkins, as well as others in related fields, was rarely as focused on narrative as some ludologists claimed. It was, however, comparative and interdisciplinary, and ludology sought the kind of disciplinary purity that would ensure autonomous departments, classes, and research funding and would allow specialists to concentrate their energies on games as a unique object of attention. Still, the cultural and media studies programs at MIT and The Georgia Institute of Technology, where Murray and Jenkins taught and mentored students (including some leading ludologists), have continued as strong centers for the study of video games. Georgia Tech, for example, was the initial host and institutional hub for the extremely important group blog, Grand Text Auto, whose collaborative authors have focused on games alongside other forms of electronic literature and avant-garde art. These include, notably, interactive fiction, a text-based game-like narrative genre analyzed thoroughly by Nick Montfort in his *Twisty Little Passages* (2003), and the interactive drama best exemplified in the experimental game, *Façade* (2005), created by two other authors of the Grand Text Auto blog, Michael Mateas (now at University of California Santa Cruz) and Andrew Stern.

For a brief time the exaggerated debate between ludology and other approaches to games (often referred to under the umbrella terms of "narratology" or "narrativism") took center stage. In its extreme form, one observer has

noted, ludology amounted to a reductive formalism.[4] Some ludologists sometimes ironically seemed prepared to recapitulate the history of twentieth-
century *literary* formalism, with "the game itself" replacing the New Critics'
"text in itself" as the hermetically sealed object of attention, rules and procedures replacing tropes and symbols as the features to be analyzed in isolation
of authorial, historical, or cultural factors. On the other hand, the ludologists
were right to point to the unique qualities of video games as a form of
expression, and they rightly perceived the continued danger, not so much of
narrative theory, but of a facile (and sometimes condescending) cultural-
studies or media-studies approach. The danger in this case was of the other
kind: that cultural studies would merely fit video games into earlier models
based on studies of TV and other broadcast media, or that it would generalize
games under a vague umbrella-concept developed in the 1990s, "cybercul-
ture." This kind of culturalism tends to treat games as just another "medium"
like other media, a product of the culture industry and a way of perpetuating
the dominant ideology or (in its postmodern version) substituting a simulated
reality for the material world. This is not to say that studying power and the
processes of ideological control is not important when it comes to video
games, just as much as with other forms of cultural expression. What McKenzie
Wark (among others) calls the "military-entertainment complex,"[5] for example,
a variation on Dwight Eisenhower's military-industrial complex, raises interesting questions for critique in the current era, though it also runs the risk of
contributing to the generalization of video games as mere instruments of the
culture industry. Nevertheless, there are real questions worth asking about
institutions of power and games, just as with any popular form of expression,
for example, how are video games affected by the funding from the U.S.
military in an era of "total war?" What kind of game, really is the military-made
*America's Army*? How do people actually play it? What specifically do video
games bring to the ideological transactions of our era?

One reason ludology arose in the first place was to address the question of
video games' unique features as a form of expression. The infamous game vs.
story debate was also about making sure analysis and interpretation had a
particular object in sight, that critics knew what was special about games as a
form before generalizing about their cultural significance as if they were merely
a more violent form of TV. Leading ludologist Gonzalo Frasca published a
piece in 2003 aiming to clear up the "erroneous assumptions" in the game vs.
story debate, which he calls a "tiresome topic," a debate which he argues "never
took place" in the form in which it got represented, in part, he claims, because
narrativists never showed up.[6] Frasca disavows the over-simple definition of
ludology that would pit it against the study of narratives in games. Ludology,
he says, was always about studying both game-form and story. But Frasca

underplays the degree to which some ludologists had in fact couched their theoretical positions in polemical anti-narrativist terms, and in doing so, had often cut off avenues for discussing the cultural significance of games, and the way their production and marketing might be affecting global culture. Markku Eskelinen, for example, sought in a 2001 essay in *Game Studies* "to annihilate for good the discussion of games as stories, narratives or cinema," and asserted reductively that stories were "just uninteresting ornaments or gift-wrappings to games, and laying any emphasis on studying these kind of marketing tools is just waste of time and energy."[7]

I have no desire to revisit the game vs. story debate (though it did in fact take place). I only mention it here and in the chapters that follow in order to provide a context for what I *am* interested in: a very different kind of "textual" approach (more about that in a minute), one that has very little to do with story per se and is, I think, in sympathy with the aim of ludology to do justice to the uniqueness of games as a form—but one that also refuses to cut games off from the larger culture. Thankfully, discussions in game studies have mostly shifted now in a more productive direction, towards embracing a more prag-matic eclecticism that avoids both the dangers of sterile formalism and of facile culturalism and that takes into account contextual elements in games such as story and diegetic gameworld, as well as abstract ludic structure. Recent work by Jesper Juul (for example, *Half-Real*, 2005) focuses on the role of fictional world as well as the "real" ruleset in the overall structure of a game. And scholars such as Stuart Moulthrop have argued for a more socially situated understanding of game dynamics.[8] Even more directly, Ian Bogost has expressed suspicion at "the zeal with which the burgeoning field has relied on formalist approaches to its object of study," and regrets that the field now "reaps what it has sowed—functionalist separatism."[9] Likewise, Rune Klevjer has rejected the formalism of the more radical ludological arguments, questioning their "self-contained arguments for advocating the purity of games" ("In Defense of Cutscenes," 2002). Instead Klevjer calls for greater attention to ways that the "alien" aspects of "cultural conventions" (story in particular) can actually be integrated into gameplay, arguing that scholars should pay more attention to "a typical textual practice, at once configurative and interpretative, both unique and intertextual."

Klevjer's focus is on "typical textual practice," on how video games are actually played today, rather than the abstract platonic ideal of gameplay that may underlie them. This usefully returns attention to the larger social context, where cultural and interdisciplinary approaches have much to contribute. Seeing games as "intertextual" reminds us that no game or instance of gameplay is an island; like literary texts, every game extends outward from itself in many directions. The relationship of text to context and intertext has after all been at the center of modern literary theory for decades. The term "intertextuality" was originally formulated by Julia Kristeva[10] as a way to express a fundamental quality of language as a system of signs, its dialogic "citability" and the way that all texts are always already referring to and incorporating other texts. Intertextuality is historically a linguistic concept, however. It describes a process of signification within language as a system. It's therefore probably more appropriate for describing verbal texts than the hybrid, extra-linguistic, open-ended, *configurative and procedural systems* that video games are. For that reason I prefer another theoretical concept from literary theory, one whose scope is more material and less exclusively linguistic: Gerard Genette's concept of the paratext.

Interestingly enough, Genette is known for his work in narratology. But the paratext is not a narratological concept. Properly understood, it's a bibliographic concept. It was most fully defined in a separate book titled *Seuils* (1987), or *Paratexts: Thresholds of Interpretation* (1997), in English. Elements of a book that are not its main text, the title, author's name, epigraph, preface, and so on, as well as jacket copy, even advertising and publicity, all make up the paratext or threshold, as Genette imagines it, between the text and the world outside the text, an area of "transition" and "*transaction*," serving the text's reception (2). Genette further distinguishes between the peritext (texts that actually accompany the text in its same bound volume) and epitext, at a level further outside the book, such as publicity, interviews, author's letters: "Paratext = peritext + epitext" (5). The paratext is a multilayered system of frames around a text that helps determine its reception, from naming the genre ("mystery") or implied audience ("trade paperback" or "bestseller"), to advance reviews printed as blurbs, or the footnotes and index, even an author's photo, all of which affect how the book is read and interpreted. The paratext is thus about the material conditions of a book's production, publication, and reception, how a book makes its way out into the world and comes to mean something to the public audience that receives it.

Genette's theory of the paratext thus shares a great deal with the field known as *l'histoire du livre* (or book history), which treats books as physical objects that have histories and are in turn part of cultural and social history, and with textual studies, which has always studied the production, transmission, and reception of texts, as well as theorizing the methods of producing scholarly editions. But even though he knows that the paratext depends on such factors as "period, culture, genre, author, work, and edition," Genette chooses to disregard the technical and historical distinctions that he sees as the special subject of textual studies and bibliography, facts of typesetting technology or book format, for example, or of differences among various editions and states of a text (3, 5n). And although he acknowledges the new kinds of discourse produced in the " 'media' age," kinds of discourse not known in earlier periods, he sticks primarily to verbal texts (7). Still, he (and we) can't escape the implications of his own theory: the paratext is a way of thinking about the material and cultural articulations of texts and contexts. Ultimately, he admits, "every context serves as a paratext" (8).

Genette may restrict his own analysis to verbal texts, but he knows very well that paratextual work may be done with other kinds of media: illustrations, typography, or even the basic facts surrounding publication (7). What Genette's theory suggests, then, goes well beyond his own apparent intentions to limit it to verbal texts: what he calls in the end the paratextual "field" clearly involves extra-textual and non-verbal features, such as the technologies and material means of printing, publishing, page design, illustration, but also, relatively seamlessly, the machinery of marketing, previews, and reception, the whole *social* realm in which texts are given meanings by the transactions between their producers and their readers and critics. This audience for a book, it's important to note, implicitly includes many who do not actually read it but who may react to an author's reputation, for example, or take part in a controversy over censorship. They too are part of the paratextual field.

The paratext is ultimately a way of describing what has always been under the purview of the fields known as textual studies and book history. And the interesting debates going on in game studies first came to my attention because I was a textual studies scholar working on digital media, attending interdisciplinary conferences. I was giving papers at the same events as some game studies scholars, as well as reading their publications, just as the field was emerging. Interdisciplinary work is sometimes what happens on the way to change within a single discipline. Significant changes within textual studies during the past two decades—namely, the increased centrality of theories of the social text, and the increased importance of electronic editing and text analysis—brought video games into focus for me. Textual criticism in the Anglo-American academy through most of the twentieth century was focused on author's intentions for a text and on systematic methods for recovering that intention in scholarly editions. Institutionally, the MLA's (Modern Language Association's) own Center for Scholarly Editions, which awards a seal of approval to editions that adhere to its published guidelines, for many years was governed by the theories of W. W. Greg, Fredson Bowers, and G. T. Tanselle.[11] To summarize briefly a complex history: the Greg-Bowers-Tanselle school of textual studies developed a series of principles and procedures to make it statistically more likely that an editor could reconstruct the author's intentions for a text. The whole focus was on isolating authorial intentions from the "noise" of textual transmission, the "corruptions" of history, time, human use, and decay. Since the 1980s, however, textual studies has experienced a paradigm shift, away from the relentless focus on the prior ideal of an author's intentions and in favor of focusing on the historical reception of texts, and on the "social text" (as theorized by D. F. McKenzie and later by Jerome McGann). This new school has focused more on the collaborative nature of all texts, and on the afterlife of texts in the world, as they are published, read, and often reconfigured by readers and interpreters. What's more, McKenzie had argued that the social text was a productive paradigm for understanding all sorts of cultural phenomena, from treaties to geography, to film, sound recordings, and (then just beginning to be evident) computerized media.

In 1991, echoing McKenzie, David Greetham described "textual scholar-ship" in a handbook published by the MLA, by acknowledging first that other media and forms besides verbal texts could be the focus of attention for textual studies, from painting to film, to "gesture."

> All these media have meaning or form, and it is in part the textual scholar's aim to preserve (or, if necessary, to re-create) this meaning or form in the face of the laws of physical decay.[12]

Sixteen years later, in a contribution to a collection on book history, he emended his summary in light of what had come since, pointing out that "casting physical change as 'decay' too easily plays into a Platonist view of the ideality of an irrecoverable originary form, from which all subsequent physical manifestations or embodiments are but shadows, lacking their own authen-ticity."[13] The work of Jerome McGann in particular, Greetham writes, has persuaded increasing numbers of scholars to focus on the whole social history of texts, on the "totality of cultural expression" of any work.

Several years ago, it occurred to me that video games were forms that vividly illustrated this kind of scope, the articulation of material form with larger cultural and social meanings. It's perhaps more intuitively obvious in the case of games than of texts, especially as literary texts have been interpreted and handed down to us over the past two centuries in particular, but viewed over their long history, something analogous is true of texts as well. A video game, however, is a system designed such that it only fulfills it potential for meaning when its specific technical features—from the code, to the interface, to the ruleset, to the player stats—are expressed as the game makes its way out into the world, when it's played. You don't have to be a ludologist to know that a game is always in the playing. But it's important to remember that the playing is always in the social world, always a complicated, highly mediated experience, never purely formal, any more than a text is purely a verbal construct. Players *make* games meaningful, make their meanings, as they play them, talk about them, reconfigure them, and play them again. They inevitably do so as members of various overlapping communities.

As Henry Jenkins argues, online fan communities are "self-organizing groups focused around the collective production, debate, and circulation of meanings, interpretations, and fantasies in response to various artifacts of contemporary popular culture."[14] And Jenkins fully understands the marketing and commercial aspects of this model, the interest of the game development industry, for example, in selling "experiences" rather than objects, and thus its interest in building communities of loyal users whose feedback will help to shape the "experiences" that are in turn marketed to them. This is one reason game companies make available the software engines with which they made the games, so that users can build and share levels, some of which may influence future versions of officially released games (148). But rather than reduce gamers to mere passive consumers, or naively assuming their complete autonomy, Jenkins attempts to analyze the give-and-take relationship of players and the industry, to look at the circuit of creative and revisionist energies flowing between those two poles (136).

Cultural expression is a dynamic event, what Genette characterizes as a "transaction," and thus it always involves more than the text (or game) itself. This helps to account for what every serious gamer knows: the fact that the full potential of video games is most fully realized by the kind of dedicated, meaning-making, community-based players who call themselves fans. And this potential always extends outward from the game itself into the real social world, the "media ecology," where technologies or expressions combine with corporate interests and audience demands, and the constructed "universe" of a game, including its paratextual materials (packaging, game guides, collectible objects, online stats), narrative elements, story and back-story, and imagined gameworld. It doesn't matter if any particular player is aware of every aspect of this extended "game;" it's a collective and *potential* reality, a transmedia, multidimensional grid of possibilities surrounding any given game.

Transmedia experiments in advertising, entertainment, art, and cultural expression are everywhere at the moment.[15] Anyone who has seen TV shows such as *American Idol* or *Lost*, with their tie-in cell-phone voting or web-based forms of response and "interaction," has a sense of this. Different platforms— broadcast television, the Internet, including fictionalized websites, "independent" blogs, official and unofficial podcasting, print, video games (mobile, online, PC), even live events—are for crossing and combining, according to the latest model of media "synergy" and "viral marketing." Marketers, on the one hand, and fan communities, on the other hand, are interested for different reasons in cultivating extensive feedback loops between users and products or forms of expression, interested in the idea of "user-generated content." All of this is old-hat to gamers because in fact a good deal of it is derived in the first place from video games and their robust and savvy fan communities, as I suggest in chapter 1. The rise in recent years of the ARG (alternate reality game), a transmedia form of fictional play that is often (though not always) tied into marketing campaigns, is the most vivid example of this development. In ARGs, players engage in an elaborate game of make-believe out in the world; they may use websites, TV shows or ads, payphones, text-messages via cell-phone, even mailed physical objects, as tokens and forms of expression and communication. The gameworld in this case is the real world, encodable as GPS coordinates, for example, and as public as an actual mall or a city square or a phone booth. This form of viral gaming, which is often mixed with viral marketing and relies on existing social networks to spread itself and become realized, may seem like an exception, but I would argue that it's only a more extreme case of what is becoming the rule across the media spectrum.

The new era in transmedia marketing in the age of social networks was the subject of William Gibson's 2003 novel, *Pattern Recognition*, which explored the blurry line between art and commerce, entertainment and advertising, collecting and gaming. That book may well have influenced and been influenced by some of the ARGs taking place as it was being completed, discussed online by the author and fans, and then published. Gibson coined the term "cyberspace" (before there was a World Wide Web) and popularized the idea of the future global network as an alternative, parallel universe. His most recent novel, *Spook Country* (2007), explores the actual application of that idea in recent history, a moment in which cyberspace is "everting," being "turned inside out" and mapping itself onto the external material world. The new network is the grid imposed on the natural world by GPS satellite data, for example, linked up via RFID (radio-frequency identification) tags and Wi Fi. This is paradoxically a less idealized version of reality than in the film *The Matrix*, for example, or Baudrillard's shadowy simulacra. This "everted" network has the matter-of-fact, plastic feel of the material world as artists experience it, as a possibility space. The primary artistic medium of the novel is locative art, which makes use of "spatially tagged hypermedia" to create "annotated environments" by overlaying crafted images and data onto geographical locations. The plot turns on a major political demonstration/prank that looks like an act of terror but turns out to be more like a work of performance art. An ad hoc group of interested parties with various kinds of expertise, mental as well as physical, "geohacking" as well as martial arts, come together and cooperate in order to "mark" by irradiating a shipping container full of cash by shooting capsules into it at long range. That's the goal. It's of course blocked by many obstacles (including homeland security laws) and requires the use of special tools and skills, and, in fact, the more you begin to think of it this way, the "prank" at the heart of Gibson's novel appears to be a kind of game. At one point, the protagonist imagines a powerful character watching the action via satellite and surveillance camera on a "huge screen in his office. The world as video game."[16]

Recently game theorist McKenzie Wark has identified the same situation in a different way, emphasizing gamespace instead of cyberspace: "The real world appears as a video arcadia divided into many and varied games," he says, "from work to politics, to the economy."[17] The stark logic for understanding the link between game and world Wark describes as "allegorithmic" (2.30)—an allegorical correspondence controlled by rules-driven processes, algorithms. This can be seen as a revision of Jean Baudrillard's theories of simulation and simulacra, but one that recognizes computer games as the dominant metaphor today for organizing experience. Gibson, however, begins from a perhaps more skeptical perspective, from an interest in street-level uses of technology, hackers' and artists' appropriations, and the possibilities for creative expression and community implied within the otherwise bleak prospects of an "everted" network, the world as a gameworld or grid of possibilities as well as (or instead of) a matrix of control.

In a sense, in this novel Gibson is catching up to actual practice in the computing and gaming cultures that helped to inspire his early cyberpunk work. He has said that the idea of "cyberspace" came to him while watching "the body-language" of kids playing early video games in a 1980s arcade, leaning into the consoles and—so Gibson assumed—longing to "reach right through the screen and get with what they were playing with," to merge with the game, to inhabit the *Tron*-like virtual space behind the glass.[18] The iconic *Neuromancer* (1984) was about human and artificial intelligence, both forms of consciousness, inhabiting the global network, and its vision of the "bodiless exultation of cyberspace" became a widespread cultural cliché.[19] But the idea of arcade players as disembodied, totally immersed in the virtual space of the game "behind the screen," while based in a feeling many gamers have experienced of being "lost in the game," is actually a misleading partial truth. Gameplay (especially in an arcade) is a hybrid experience, as much bodily as mental. Many videogames these days directly involve and foreground the player's body movements: dancing on electronic pads, manipulating a plastic guitar, pulling physical triggers, simulating skiing or driving or kung-fu fighting. Even using the conventional joystick and button combination controls requires a physical as well as mental form of engagement, and it is common to see players at home or in arcades twisting and leaning into their consoles or control pads, dancing or playing drum- or guitar-controllers. Gibson's muses, those arcade gamers, were just as likely trying to master the wood and glass and plastic consoles whose buttons they were pushing as they were to be seeking some sort of transcendence, to escape from their bodily existence. After all, the observation began with their body language, and quickly shifted to the dis-embodied "space behind the glass." Video gameplay in many popular accounts (Gibson's is only a very famous early one) is often depicted as entirely dis-embodied when compared the real thing,[20] which actually requires a mixed form of attention, "cool" in its detachment and aware of both the game and its always partly haptic or somatic interface. Gibson invented cyberspace as a form of virtual-reality transcendence inspired by observing gameplay but downplay-ing the savvy physical side of actual gaming. It's only right that the repressed material reality, the somatic-and-mental experience of video games, would return in Gibson's recent fiction, in the form of cyberspace turned inside-out, leaking out into the physical world. This way of seeing the real world as overlaid with a projected abstract grid of possible moves and outcomes, a gameworld superimposed on a real world, is pretty much the norm, taken for granted as typical, in video games. As Jesper Juul says, video games are always half real.

Consider another example, the acclaimed fall 2006 episode of the animated TV show *South Park*, set almost entirely within the real MMORPG (massively multiplayer online role-playing game), *World of Warcraft*.[21] After it aired, it instantly became a big hit on the Internet, in part because gamers recognized how well (like any good satire) it knew its topic. The makers of the show even collaborated with Blizzard Entertainment, the game company behind *WoW*. The show used "machinima" techniques, or the making of movies using a game's software engine and set inside the game's world, combined with other scenes created in its usual style, to follow the characters' avatars as they played the game and cooperated to fight a "griefer," someone who was randomly killing other players' avatars in unfair attacks. The episode demonstrated an insider's knowledge not just of the game, but of the culture surrounding it, including videos made in-game and posted on YouTube. The boys log on and use voice chat to communicate with each other, occasionally getting inter-rupted by someone's father coming into the room, for example. As their mission becomes an obsession, the boys ruin their health with junk food and all-night sessions. But the line between their physical reality in the world and their in-game reality is never really unclear for them, even when they are playing obsessively. They just deliberately neglect their health to sit in front of their screens, eating junk food and getting no exercise. The irony of course is that the "real world" of South Park is depicted in a deliberately primitive, flat style of animation. The 3-D in-game scenes therefore look more "real" than the show usually does. But the episode treats with respect the ability of gamers to move in and out of the gameworld—in fact, to be both in and out at the same time, as when, during chat, they talk about snacks or going to the bathroom when they are supposed to be "in character." In this it resembles an earlier audio (later video) comedy sketch about a *Dungeons & Dragons* RPG (Role-Playing Game) session in which players move in and out of character while discussing the fine points of the rules, laughing at each other, calling on one another to roll the dice, arguing over the rules, or looking for the Cheetohs.[22] This kind of divided attention is, I think, the norm in playing video games, the statistically typical style. Successful gamers have to remain partly in the game and partly in the world (if only to monitor their health meters or how the console setup is working), have to play comfortably at the "threshold" of game and world. For video games, paratext is integral to the experience of play, manifest in something as familiar as interface conventions, or in gamer community interaction. The space of play is not impermeable, hermetically sealed.

It has become common for game theorists, especially ludologists, to cite *Homo Ludens: A Study o the Play Element in Culture* (1938) by Dutch historian, Johan Huizinga. Huizinga's book takes a broadly anthropological approach to the role of "play" in culture. Its title suggests that the human species can be defined as much as "man the player," as (is traditionally said) "man the tool-maker," for example. "All play means something," he says on the very first page, and it's clear why ludologists would find this valuation of play helpful in establishing the significance of their object of study. But on that very same first page, Huizinga also makes a telling assertion about his view of the nature of play in culture: rather than the meaningfulness of play grounding games in everyday human culture, his formulation actually implies for him "a non-materialistic quality in the nature of the thing itself" (1). The assumption seems to be that meanings are inherently non-material (rather than that material realities can have meaning). A strain of Romantic idealism colors the entire book.

Play, Huizinga says, is not part of "ordinary" or "real" life (8). Now, anyone who has put aside other activities to play a long game can attest to the basic truth in this assertion, but Huizinga's idealization goes much further. It's true that we set aside a special space to play unhindered, but does that mean, as he asserts, that play is "connected with no material interest, and no profit can be gained by it" (13)? If play (or a game) sets its own boundaries and rules, inside what he famously calls a "magic circle," drawn around themselves by exclusive social groups, those in the game, does that really mean the circle has no traffic with material realities? For me, as a literary scholar, Huizinga's chapter on play and poetry is the most revealing of his fundamental Romantic idealism, in its celebration of the otherworldly at the expense of material existence. Poetry is a form of play, and takes place in a space apart (119). Poetry, because it is play, is not serious; it is associated with the "primitive," with children and animals, "the savage and the seer," and so on (119). Dreams, otherworldly "enchantment," and childlike simplicity characterize the magic circle of play (119).

In my field, this is known as the Romantic Ideology, an idea of the poet and poetry as otherworldly that arose during the Romantic period and became accepted as natural and universal truth.[23] Although Huizinga suggestively refers to poetry as a "cultural game" and "a social game" (122–4), and other of his insights are often highly resonant for the study of games, his theory of play is finally so deeply tinged with Romantic primitivism that it ends up unintentionally condescending to play, reducing play to a space apart from the world, a magic circle not of this world, a haven for eternal children or poets. Too often the magic circle sounds like a fairy circle in a primitive forest of the mind, rather than a robust and knowing, socially collaborative, cultural construct that affects and is affected by material reality.

We might do better to imagine the space set aside in a game in more material, less magical terms, perhaps an actual chalk circle drawn for a game of marbles, for example, or the mutually-agreed mapping out of imaginary territory that takes place prior to a game of "war," or even the digital maps, sometimes "modded" by fans, that define a campaign level of a video game. The point is that the delineated space of any game is necessarily a social convention. That makes it very much part of the real world. Players come together and agree to stay inside of the circle, as it were, in so far as they remain players, abiding by the rules and working toward the objectives of the game. Clearly this does not imply that gameplay has nothing to do with the real world, even the often vulgar world of commerce—in fact the contrary is perfectly clear to anyone who has encountered a virtual billboard or other instance of branding inside a video game, or has played an ARG out in the streets nominally sponsored by ABC TV or Sprite.

A useful, less Romantic alternative to the concept of the magic circle is something game designer Will Wright likes to call a "possibility space," and we can think of it as he does, as an array or a grid, a mathematical visualization of actual possible moves and states within a defined game. Such an unromantic grid of possibilities offers the relative freedom of play within its own defined constraints, lines that are drawn and can be redrawn. Developers and players and various hybrid combinations of the two must agree to trace and then play within such a space (or test its outer limits to see if they'll break, which is probably more common). It's not nature, it's art (or engineering). It's socially co-constructed, and you have to agree to "see" it as the space of the game, for the duration of the game. Maybe another time, you'll modify or reconfigure it, because that possibility too is always inherent in, built into, the kind of constructed spaces that define games.

All play means something, yes. In this I fully agree with Huizinga. But the meanings of play—of video *gameplay* in particular—are ultimately connected to social and material realities (rather than offering merely a means to escape from those realities, as it's widely believed). Playing usually involves remaining simultaneously aware of both the gameworld and of the real world, of yourself and of other players as performing at the boundary of the two, while you go online to search the boards for a helpful "cheat," for example, or consult a printed game guide, and then follow up by looking at a fan-authored article in a dedicated wiki. It seems to me that the job of scholars looking at video games should be to illuminate those connections and boundaries, to trace the material and cultural determinants, from software code to design, to marketing, social networks of players and fans, and to wider cultural fictions and key texts, that help to shape the production, distribution, and reception—which is to say the meanings—of video games. One very promising recent development in games studies is the announcement of a new forthcoming series of books at MIT Press, edited by Nick Montfort and Ian Bogost, called *Platform Studies*. The first book in the series, by the two editors, will be a detailed study of the Atari 2600 (VCS) system as a platform—a way of looking at the relation of hardware and software design to the creative works, games and other forms of media, produced and inspired by this system. One should always hesitate before identifying a disciplinary convergence, but this series, emerging from the discipline of game studies, sounds to me perfectly in tune with the aims and methods of the most advanced developments in textual studies. In fact, a potential future contributor to the *Platform Studies* series is Matthew Kirschenbaum, one of the leading textual studies scholars of his generation, whose own theories of "textual forensics" cover an array of digital objects, including games.[24] My own present book—with its emphasis on theories of material textuality, the production, distribution, and reception of the social text, and the paratextual relations between forms of expression and the world in which they are made meaningful —aims to contribute to this emerging interdisciplinary possibility space.

Chapter 1 begins with a look at the hit TV show and transmedia phenomenon, *Lost*, which I argue is formally based on the conventions and structures of video games, and which has resulted in one official game already (with another on the way) and an ARG, *The Lost Experience*. I compare *Lost* to an early and significant PC game, *Myst*, with which it shares settings and structural devices. The connection to games is one feature of the extensive paratextual field surrounding the show, especially the way its creators have tapped the energies of the fan community and have drawn on literary conventions along with game conventions. Chapter 2 focuses on the cult hit for PS2, *Katamari Damacy*, which serves as a useful test case for the idea that video games are primarily for "fun" and considers the question, what does fun *mean*? This odd game also demonstrates the centrality to games and game culture of the act of collecting. Points, levels, scores, objects, paratextual paraphernalia—most of all knowledge about the gameworld—gaming is always on some level about collecting. And

collecting is a form of meaning-making. *Katamari Damacy* makes this the deliberately simple central figure for the entire game, which you play by rolling
up everything in the gameworld into a giant ball. It taps into the widespread
fan interest in collecting Japanese culture, which I triangulate with reference
to eBay and Walter Benjamin's theories (and his own practices as a scholar-
collector).

*Halo*, the blockbuster space epic for PC and Microsoft's Xbox, is the focus
of Chapter 3. As with *Lost* in the first chapter, here I trace the dimensions of the
massive paratextual universe extending outward from the *Halo* game(s). From
the use of artificially intelligent NPCs (non-player characters), to the role of
the back-story, to the conventions of the FPS (first-person shooter), to the
quintessential ARG, *I Love Bees*, which was created to introduce *Halo 2*, I
examine formal and technical features of the game as they influence the game's
reception, and as they lead outward into the larger universe of the game's
potential meanings. The genre known as "interactive drama" is the subject of
Chapter 4, as demonstrated with a detailed look at the best example to date,
the independent PC game, *Façade*. Given the history of controversy surrounding this genre, one purpose of the chapter is to demonstrate that *Façade* is
indeed a game, and that so are any number of forerunners and precedents for
interactive drama, from the fictional *Star Trek* holodeck to the established
theatrical practice of improvisation. Indeed, the theatrical tradition of improv, I
argue, is already profoundly gamelike, as is *Façade*. Comparisons to more
conventional commercial games, such as the acclaimed *Kingdom Hearts* series,
with its Disney characters interacting with *Final Fantasy* characters and its
highly dramatic cutscenes, further call into question the hard and fast line
between drama and games, showing that improvisation in response to artificial
intelligence is built into almost all modern video games.

One of the hypothetical examples offered in the prospectus to the *Platform
Studies* series is Nintendo's Wii, code-named by its developers "Revolution."
My chapter 5 is not a full-fledged contribution to platform studies, but it aims
in a preliminary way to examine the meaning of platform in the case of the
Wii. The chapter focuses on the marketing of the system, its innovative interface, and the marketing of that interface, exemplified in the new Wii controller, which uses motion-sensing accelerometers to map intuitive player gestures
into games. I look at the particulars of the technology involved, the way the
platform has situated itself in the market by appealing to casual gamers or non-
gamers, and what all this reveals about the culturally constructed meaning of a
game platform.

The final chapter is about *Spore*, a new game that doesn't exist yet, or at any
rate, has not been released, but has been previewed, presented, analyzed and
demoed for several years. I look at the hypothetical structure of *Spore* as well as

the "pre-game" phenomenon of its advance marketing. *Spore*, created by the iconic game designer Will Wright, is a game of evolution on a cosmic scale that aims to be a meta-game incorporating a number of game genres. It was at first code-named "Sim-Everything." But its most significant feature is its planned content-generating system, allowing users to make creatures and other objects that will be procedurally animated and placed in the games of other players. Maxis and Electronic Arts are planning a massive network over which players can share their created content, not live and online but in a time-shifted upload and download system. I explore the way this system seems to have been modeled on one of Wright's obsessions, the SETI program (the Search for Extra Terrestrial Intelligence). *Spore* too is a kind of search for intelligent life in the (game) universe—artificially intelligent and humanly intelligent—with which to play. In this way, *Spore* will (if it is realized as planned) embody the ideal of a game as a possibility space—in this case, modeled on space itself—within which to collaborate and compete with others in both making the game and making it meaningful.

# Chapter 1

# The game of *Lost*

You find yourself marooned on an apparently deserted tropical island. You have to solve a series of puzzling mysteries in order not only to survive but to reveal the story behind the island itself, the meanings hidden beneath its surface (literally, it later turns out). Along the way you encounter a series of unexplained phenomena: voices in the trees, cryptic documents, films and videos left behind by previous inhabitants, what seem to be invisible monsters in the jungle and powerful anomalies of nature everywhere. You have to use the available tools you find around you to overcome obstacles and solve whatever puzzles you encounter. At one point, for example, you use salvaged dynamite to blow open a locked hatch you discovered earlier in the jungle, in order to go down the hatch and see what's in it, look for further clues, further meanings. You listen to a cryptic radio signal and try to decipher the series of numbers being broadcast. Levers and buttons and caves and tunnels abound. The process seems open-ended if not never-ending, but every so often you solve an important mystery and reach a new level. Then, you continue to explore the island world in order to find out where you are now, what to do next, and who or what is behind it all—what it all means.

## The game of *Lost*

That sounds very much like a description of a video game, but it's actually a summary of the hit TV show *Lost*, which debuted on ABC in 2004, a serial drama about the survivors of the crash of Oceanic Flight 815 on a mysterious island somewhere in the South Pacific. I might just as well have been describing a video game, especially a game of the puzzle-adventure or action-adventure genres. That *Lost* draws upon video-game conventions and structural devices is not exactly a secret. Lynette Porter and David Lavery, who wrote the unauthorized guide, *Unlocking the Meaning of LOST*, note that the show's narrative progress is based on video games. Just as in a video game, with *Lost* the characters on the show and the viewers have to acquire the tools they need—weapons, texts, skills—in order to solve the mystery of the island. Significantly, the authors point out, this leveling up depends as in video games on making use of the "collective knowledge" of others posted online.[1] For their part, the writer-producers of the show speak about their experiments in "nonlinear storytelling," which, all the debate in the games studies community aside (over the role of narrative in gameplay), they understand simply as a synonym for game-like storytelling: as starting with a well-stocked fictional world containing potentially meaningful objects, tools, codes, "hints and clues."[2] An executive consultant for the show, Jeff Pinkner, said in an interview on the DVD of the first season that "exploration" of the island would drive the story, would amount to "a mystery and adventure unto itself," and that "the island would in a way be a dramatic version of a video game . . . [you could] find the hatch but it could take you several weeks before you had the proper tools to open the hatch." With the support of a major TV network owned by Disney, the creators of the show may have begun by attempting to fictionalize *Survivor*, fundamentally a team-based reality game show, set in its first season on a tropical island.[3] But they did more: they adopted the world-building gestures of videogame design. This is much more than simply planning for the future release of tie-in games; that has, of course, become standard practice for many films and TV shows these days. The writers actually seem to have based the formal structure and narrative possibilities of the show itself on video game conventions, and they've done so in part in order to better create the kind of networked community or fanbase usually associated with games—a potential audience ready not just to watch but also to "play" *Lost*.[4]

Though there are predecessors among earlier TV shows set on Islands—consider *Gilligan's Island*, for example, or an even closer analogue, *The Prisoner*—the visual experience of watching *Lost* is fundamentally more like a video game than like any of these TV precedents. Steadycam shots through the jungle or down the beach create a dynamic first-person point of view that alternates with wide shots and stylized, fuzzy or slow-motion transitional "cutscenes," with background music and providing quick visual exposition. The use of the Hawaiian locations makes the natural seem virtual (and vice versa), to the extent that CGI (computer-generated image) palm trees can easily be mapped onto actual footage of the jungle, and the elemental sets, the beach, the horizon line at sea, a giant rock formation, a pillar of black smoke, could in many shots, as far as the viewer can tell, be either computer-generated or filmed. Consider the crucial importance of mapping and world-design to the show, the gradual revelation of meaningful geography on separate "levels," above and below ground, at sea level and in the mountains. Making iconographic maps of various kinds, maps that help characters interpret the island as well as navigate it, occupies a number of the characters (Kelvin, Locke, Rousseau, Ben).

The writers have said that they consider the island itself a character, almost as if it were a non-human artificial intelligence—or a computerized game engine. During season 2, an old-fashioned tape-drive computer in an underground bunker (the Hatch) literally controlled the action of characters, who had to input a series of numbers and push a button every 108 minutes in order to avoid a possible (and long unspecified) disaster. In fact, the Hatch computer controlled that season's story as a whole. We eventually learned that this Hatch (and others like it on the Island) were part of a shadowy project called the Dharma Initiative, either a Stanley Milgram-like psychology experiment or post-apocalyptic survivalist training—it remained (and, as I write, still remains) unclear. But something like the mid-twentieth-century cold-war military-industrial complex would seem to be responsible for the technology of the underground geodesic-dome roof and whirring tape drives and green-screen input terminal. By the end of season 2 an "electromagnetic anomaly" is revealed, in a building reminiscent of nuclear silos, complete with a failsafe switch and an explosion that fills the sky with bright light. Throughout the season, some hidden force (apparently whoever created the Dharma Initiative, perhaps the Hanso Foundation) seems to lie behind or literally beneath the surface of the island, a set of concealed intentions driving the events and experiences of the castaways, who must make sense of what they encounter, piece together fragments of meaning, even though they have no direct contact with the mind(s) and intentions behind the whole. On one level this is a metaphor for how the viewer relates to the team of writers behind the scenes of the mystery show, who are producing meaning week to week (and rumor has it, sometimes on the fly, in response to fan feedback). But on the other hand it also describes how any player approaches most video games, and especially games of the puzzle-adventure genre: by exploring the world and its objects (often with tools or weapons in hand) in search of patterns, hidden meanings, a way out or over or to safety, the reason for the overall design or intentions behind the place and whatever pieces of the puzzle you encounter along the way.

The human castaways on *Lost* in effect play against this shadowy underground intelligence, the island itself with the Dharma Initiative behind it, in the life-or-death game. But the fan-viewer also "plays" *Lost* at home. Just as there are avatars in a multiplayer RPG (role-playing game) or FPS (first-person shooter), the characters in the show serve as surrogates for the viewers as players. And most of *Lost*'s principal human characters can be mapped onto recognizable genre types—the sexy female action-heroine (Kate), the violent redneck (Sawyer), the Asian gangster (Jin), the drug-addicted has-been rock star (Charlie)—the kind of hip personae that are common in hit games from

*Tomb Raider* to *Grand Theft Auto*. They repeatedly go on quests or "missions" (a game term often used in the show) brandishing torches, selecting weapons—and sometimes shooting them—as part of the puzzle-solving action. *Survivor*-like teams maintain camps on opposite sides of the island, the "Losties" or "Lostaways" (as fans came to call them) and the at-first mysterious Others, and it was repeatedly suggested during the first three seasons that there might be all-out battles between these tribal "teams," a promise fulfilled in the finale of season three. The fake "primitive" yurt encampment and dress of the Others even looks at first like a vaguely medieval RPG—at least until it's revealed as a kind of set (hatch doors open onto a stone wall, beards and costumes are fake-rustic), which, more than puncturing the fourth wall for the viewer, actually suggests even more strongly that the castaways are engaged in playing a kind of game, where identities and props can be adopted in order to gain an advantage, then put away when the game moves on to another level (a new season).

This is not to say that the show is undramatic in traditional ways, or emotionally uninvolving on a psychological level. Much of the writing focuses on the (often interconnected) personal back-stories of the castaways, told through frequent flashbacks, as well as their on-island relationships. But these are interwoven into complex, long story arcs and connected plot lines, in the sort of game-like structure that Steven Johnson has recognized as crucial in today's successful TV series.[5] Though some viewers surely watch *Lost* more passively, just as a kind of prime-time soap opera, it's hard to imagine how they overcome their frustration at the show's mysteries and science-fictional, video-game-like elements. For those in the know, the viewers who become fans, the whole point is to exceed the weekly story, to extend the universe of *Lost*. Back-stories are filled in and interconnected by postings on numerous Internet message boards, blogs, and downloaded podcasts, both fan-created and official ones sponsored by the show, providing a more complex knowledge that helps them fill in the gaps and solve the overarching puzzle of the island's meaning. This doesn't preclude emotional involvement with the characters; quite the contrary. But it does imply a larger, rules-based, goal-oriented, methodical, obstacle-overcoming style of "watching" the show that is more like playing a game.

Perhaps aimed at this game-savvy kind of viewer (and as a private in-joke among the writers), the scripts for *Lost* self-consciously and repeatedly call attention to the theme of games and the game-like nature of the show. Literal games are everywhere. This has led at least one serious fan to create his own website (in 2007), Lost is a Game.com, which argues for a comprehensive theory explaining the whole show in terms of the premise that "Lost is a game with 6 levels," with "specific objectives for each level . . . time limits . . . numerous roles . . . points that can be earned . . . specific instructions/rules for the game . . . game prompts that lead the player through the game."[6] The creator of the site catalogs all instances of references to games in the show, including to my mind some that seem to be merely coincidental references to toys or "play" or "points." I don't share the general theory if it's to be interpreted literally. It's too close to the hackneyed TV trick known as "it was all a dream." I suspect instead that what is discernible in all of these references is the conscious and unconscious modeling of the show on video game conventions. But at this point in the series, which is scheduled to conclude in 2010, who really knows? It could turn out to be a giant Sim Island after all.

Among the references to games (all of which, and many more, are noted on Lost is a Game.com) are included the fact that Locke educates Walt during a game of backgammon, which he says is based on a 5,000-year-old game using bones for dice, "one light, one dark," an obvious allegory for the meaning of the *Lost* story as a whole, at least from one point of view. In a flashback we learn that Locke was an avid player of tabletop war-game simulations; he also used to work in a toy store, where we see him playing the contraption-based board game, *Mousetrap*; when dealing gingerly with dynamite, he mentions the game *Operation* and Jack asks: "You like to play games, John?" "Absolutely," he answers. In a different flashback we see Walt playing with a handheld Game Boy console in the airport before the flight. Hurley builds a golf course on the island and it distracts everyone for a time with its free-zone of gameplay, but in another episode Hurley shouts metatheatrically: "This isn't a *game*, man!" Referring to the raft Michael builds to attempt an escape in season 1, Sawyer asks, "You gonna vote me off?"—a winking allusion to the "reality" gameplay on *Survivor*. At the end of the season-2 finale, two hired explorers in what appears to be Antarctica (they are speaking Portuguese) are playing a game of chess when they detect the electromagnetic anomaly that may reveal the island to the outside world. The list could go on (as it does on Lost is a Game.com).

My point is that *Lost* is a self-conscious product not just of video game conventions, but also of gamer culture as a whole, and that it has become a hit in a popular media culture in which video games are now the dominant, paradigmatic form. This becomes clearer when we look not just at its themes and formal devices but also at its mode of production—the way the show gets written, produced, and marketed to its layers of fans and more casual viewers. *Lost* is the first major-network show to employ the formerly independent strategy of deliberately cultivating its own interactive fan culture, using the web and fan conventions and related publications, official and fan-created podcasts, a dedicated wiki (the Lostpedia), and, most of all, a far-flung viral marketing campaign based on pervasive gaming, a truly transmedia phenomenon.[7] The core of this strategy was the multifaceted ARG (alternate reality game), played mostly during season 2, called *The Lost Experience*, which emerged from the crossroads of fan-base community-building and collective gameplay, as exploited by marketing.

I'll have more to say about the nature of ARGs in chapter 3, but in this case it is important to understand that in *The Lost Experience* participants played a sprawling pervasive game across the borders of the TV show's fictional world, a number of related fictional worlds, and the real world. Players watched for clues inside and outside the show, including telephone numbers listed in fake commercials shown during broadcasts, editorial ads printed in newspapers, and fake websites for the fictional Oceanic Airlines and the nefarious Hanso Foundation. Manipulating the Hanso websites using clues from the ads, for example, yielded "Easter eggs"—extra clues, sometimes concealed in images or employee profiles on the company site. All of this was discussed by fans at length on both official and unofficial blogs and threaded discussions, and in real-sounding entries in Wikipedia, for example. The official sites were sometimes sponsored by the show and on these, the show's writers and producers sometimes took part online. The duo most associated with the show, executive producers and writers Damon Lindelof and Carlton Cuse, provided content for a regular podcast posted during the TV season. In it they offered behind-the-scenes insights and answered some fan questions from online discussions. In one instance, they responded to a threat from the fictional Hanso Foundation as if it were real, in effect playing along with the ARG.

The writers of *Lost* have from the beginning played with intertextual allusions and clues to interpretation by way of books planted within its storyworld. One strand of the second season's finale focused on Desmond Hume's always-postponed reading of Dickens's last major novel, *Our Mutual Friend*; the strange instructional movie in the Hatch is hidden behind a copy of *The Turn of the Screw*; glimpses of an obscure 1967 (completed 1940) experimental detective novel, *The Third Policeman* by Flann O'Brien, fueled sales of the book—and months of speculation about parallels with the show, especially the idea that the castaways, like the characters in the surreal novel, might be already dead and in some kind of purgatory. Sawyer reads *Watership Down* and a character makes an allusion to *Lord of the Flies*—and the fans started reading, searching for clues, and sharing the results on multiple online forums. A sign out on the dock reads "Pala Ferry," and fans quickly noted the reference to the island utopia in Aldous Huxley's 1962 novel, *Island*, a posting sure to have spawned many searches and postings following that thread. The curious might notice, for example, that Huxley's novel opens with a man shipwrecked on an island, finding himself unexpectedly lying in the forest "like a corpse in the dead leaves, his hair matted, his face grotesquely smudged and bruised, his clothes in rags and muddy. . . ."[8] This scene bears an obvious resemblance to the abrupt opening scene of the pilot episode of *Lost*, in which Dr. Jack Shephard wakes in much the same state in a similar setting. In general, the writers have used glimpses of or allusions to books in order to send (real or bogus) encoded messages to the always-vigilant fans, creating a kind of shifting asteroid belt of texts always circling around the TV narrative, for those in the know. In this way, watching the show often feels like following hypertext links on the web.

In one sense these are examples of what literary theorist Gerard Genette has called the paratext, an element attached to any text—for example, title, subtitle, dedication, preface, even cover, binding, illustrations, epigraph, or note—that somehow comments on the text and shapes its reception, that prompts the reader's interpretation by situating the main text in some way.[9] The paratextual elements of *Lost* work in just this way, as Porter and Lavery have suggested, becoming significant clues for hard-core viewers at least, those "engaged in active interpretation of the 'text' "(176). The concept of the paratext helps to make sense of the effects of the ARG, which often includes intertextual literary allusions, across the borders of show, game, and the external world. Genette defines the paratext as a "threshold" device (the French title of his book is *Les Seuils*, or *Thresholds*) the formal mediation between the inside and the outside of the text, between the text per se and the rest of the world. Paratext is not just about predetermined authorial meanings for a text, but is also about a strategy for determining the reception of a text. Genette breaks down the paratext further into the separate functions of the *peritext*—the extra texts or bits of text or physical features that are physically appended to the main text in a book, say—plus the *epitext*—elements that stand *outside* the physical boundaries of the main text itself but also shape its reception and interpretation. This epitext includes, for example, author interviews and other forms of marketing that bear on reception, which is the pragmatic sense in which paratexts indicate a *transactional* space where paratextual cues to interpretation overlap with, and I would say are today often indistinguishable from, "PR," the various organized means of advertising a work.[10] Genette's additional analytical division between public and private epitexts (an author's TV interview versus his correspondence) does not always hold: the boundaries separating these threshold elements themselves often become blurred or confused (1997, 344–403).

Paratext is the more general category out of which Genette further distinguishes peritextual and epitextual functions. But the point, especially when it comes to thinking about video games, is that these are artificial distinctions, parts of a continuum of "threshold" effects active in any textual or other expressive object with a life in the world.[11] Consider blurbs printed on removable jacket covers, early reviews solicited from celebrity authors or others. These are primarily peritextual elements—appended texts that shape the reception of the book. But they may also be part of larger ad campaigns and are meant to serve as headlines in catalogue copy—in which case they become more epitextual in their aims. The really interesting paratexts are usually hybrid elements, at some socially constructed boundary between the text proper, its physical packaging, and the world outside both, what we might think of as the text-world (on analogy with the term gameworld). What is most important to realize is that all forms of cultural expression make their way into the world by way of threshold devices of various kinds, where they prompt the construction of meaning(s) by an audience who can in turn move back and forth across the work's thresholds in the process of making meaning(s). Especially when it comes to today's popular media, it's necessary to treat a print-culture construct such as paratext as a helpful but inevitably limited, slippery concept. Think of an author's blog, for example, which also often includes a comments section containing instant correspondence with readers; or the regular podcasts by the writers of *Lost*, listened to by an individual fan on her iPod, or postings by the authors on fan discussion boards, especially those in which the writers confess to an editorial or production error, or reveal personal reactions to their own work. By definition these are public epitexts, but they represents themselves as relatively intimate in their effect on the individual fan's or small community's reception of the show: we might think of it as a "semi-private" epitextual effect.

Perhaps the most striking example of paratext in *The Lost Experience* ARG was the ghost writing (in more than one sense) and publication in 2006 of a real mystery novel by Hyperion Books, another company owned by Disney: *Bad Twin* by "Gary Troup" (whose name, the fans quickly pointed out online, is an anagram for "purgatory"), an author said to have gone down in the crash of Oceanic Flight 815. Executive Producers Lindelof and Cuse reportedly came up with the idea as an antidote to the usual marketing device of paperback "novelizations." So instead they concocted a novel that was *both* inside and outside the fictional frame of the TV show. An ABC executive repeated the fan rumor that the author Gary Troup was the anonymous passenger sucked into the severed jet engine on the beach in the pilot episode. In an episode soon thereafter, Sawyer is seen reading Troup's manuscript of the book on the beach. In May 2006, near the end of the second season, the actual book (in fact the work of practiced ghost writer Laurence Shames) entered the *New York Times* bestsellers list. Amazon.com posted short video interviews from a fictional talk show appearance, with an actor playing the author, talking about his book and the Hanso Foundation, as well as a suppressed earlier book about a mysterious mathematical formula. The novel itself is a conventional-enough detective story about murder, mistaken identity, and inheritance, but its fictional world overlaps with that of the show, since it concerns a wealthy family, the Widmores, and their corporation, which has a connection to (what else?)

the Hanso Foundation. The plot of the novel suggests that the Hanso Group, through its representative Mittelwerk (who showed up on the ARG websites as well), is "dangerous—ambitious and brilliantly two-faced, a man acting out an agenda of his own."[12] There are references to joint ventures and environmental violations, and earlier, Paul Artisan, the detective, goes to the Widmore Building in New York and accidentally gets off the elevator on the floor apparently leased to the Hanso Foundation. There he glimpses somewhat "robotic" people in lab coats working secretively in cubicles. A plaque extols the mission of the Foundation, "at the vanguard of social and scientific research for the advancement of the human race" (31–2). Real newspaper ads were placed in spring 2006 as if from Hanso, condemning the book as a smear campaign, and these were matched by ads by Hyperion pretending to defend the book against the foundation.

The novel, *Bad Twin*, is fascinating as a case study. It's reflexively situated at the paratexual border of even its own fictional worlds, since it purports to be the work of an author killed in the crash: are we to assume its story is based on "real" characters (within the *Lost* universe) like the Widmores and the members of the Hanso Foundation? In the season 2 finale, viewers were introduced in a flashback to a character on the show named Penelope Widmore (the same name as the Hanso-related corporation in the novel), whose boyfriend is Desmond, the caretaker of the Hatch when the later castaways discover it. In the jarring conclusion of the episode, Penelope is glimpsed taking a bedside call from hired explorers who have detected the electro-magnetic anomaly coming from the island at the time of the explosion.

Part of the fun of such intermediation is the viewers' or players' pleasure in following the official "hacks" or media repurposing, crossing the threshold between text and outside world, seeing different media crossed and re-crossed in order to use the media network as the "platform" for a larger, unstable structure, even if we know that structure is at bottom (at the bottom line) a marketing device for an entertainment product. The whole point is that the marketing is simultaneously entertainment, that an ARG such as *The Lost Experience* earns the attention it gets by telling complex stories and engaging players in a real game, a series of sometimes shared, pleasurable acts of puzzle-solving and meaning-making. The pleasure, in other words, is about playful, transmedia threshold-crossing, like the older campaigns involving real decoder rings for radio shows, or for that matter (since we are dealing with Disney after all), seeing onscreen cartoon characters walking around in the physical space of a theme park, or recreated through "animatronics," where entertainments are immersive, physical, virtual reality rides, the result of "imagineering." It comes from seeing the media crossings of fictional creations take place in real time and physical space—watching Sawyer read a manuscript on the show (on the island as it were) and at that moment, watching TV with a laptop in front of you, being able to find the material, hardcover book and traces of its author in the real world, at Amazon.com—but also the next day in a brick-and-mortar retail store; and then seeing that semi-real novel's fictions referred to in newspaper ads as if they were real.

Such crossings retain a distinct aura characteristic of early RPGs, such as *Dungeons & Dragons*, where people act out imaginary gameworlds in physical space, guided by on-the-fly writer-directors known as gamemasters. The pleasure of such reality crossings is diminished therefore when cruder forms of *mere* product placement intrude, as they did with the use by *The Lost Experience* of tie-ins such as the Sprite "subLYMONnal" website (tagline: "obey [your thirst]"), to which a number of fans reacted negatively. At least these pages attempt self-conscious irony about the attempt at the subliminal tie-in. Much worse was the Jeep CJ7 ad that one reached from Jeep-themed product-placement clues on the Hanso website and which rewarded viewers with a very brief visual clue at its conclusion (signaled with a beep). The whole experience too closely resembled the websites that force the user to watch a brief video ad before opening their content. All of this suggests that a viral marketing campaign that is like a game is one thing; fans will play along so long as the ARG is not perceived as having crossed the fine line between game and *mere* marketing—or, rather, so long as it does not call too much attention to how fine the line actually is. After all, *Myst* and *Lost* are entertainment products as well, purchased on CDs, or watched on commercial network TV, or downloaded for $1.99 from the iTunes Music Store. What exactly is the difference between being shown a Jeep ad while playing the ARG and watching ads at breaks during a network broadcast? It seems likely that the ARG is interesting to some players precisely because it moves back and forth across the border between game as art or as entertainment and marketing, thus probing and mapping the contours of those shifting borders.

At its best, *The Lost Experience* ARG, with its focus on the Hanso Foundation and the Widmore family, doesn't *merely* market the show or its sponsoring products, but also feeds back into the storyworld of the TV show. The writers commented in the final official podcast of the second season (May 26, 2006) that this coda scene represented the first time in the show's run that (flashbacks excepted) viewers had "left the island" and confirmed the existence of the world beyond. In the literal sense, the book and ads and websites are outside the show's fictional world, of course, so references to them are to a relatively external reality. The writers used the ARG to create this sense of an "outside." They represented the Widmore plot twist (and cliffhanger) as a way to "blow up" some theories of the show that proposed that the island was a remnant of the world destroyed at the moment of the crash (more or less as in *Lord of the*

*Flies*, another often-cited source text for the show), or a metaphysical purgatory where the victims were trapped in a twilight zone doing penance for past
crimes, or a collective hallucination. The character Desmond himself professes
such a theory during the episode, exclaiming at one point: "We are stuck in a
bloody snow-globe. There's no outside world, there's no escape!" This remark
probably alludes to an infamous TV finale, for *St. Elsewhere*, in which, absurdly,
the hospital where the series had taken place is revealed to have been inside
a child's snow globe all along. At any rate, the final scene served as notice to
the viewers that *Lost* would not be resolved (or completed or won) that easily
("it was only a dream" or, I would add, "only a [literal] video game"), that its
"play" would not be so narratively self-contained. It seems a tacit acknowledgment of the multi-platform, transmedia field of play that is the *Lost* phenomenon, a self-conscious reference to the arbitrariness of the island as a fictional
limit or bounding horizon for the show, which as a cultural product is anything
but an isolated object, cut off from the world. Viewed in formal terms, *The Lost
Experience* ARG is only part of a larger intermediated network with *Lost* the
show as its central node. This kind of production raises key questions, especially about academic assumptions concerning the unity, integrity, and the
isolated individuality of any work of cultural expression. It serves to remind us
that no TV show or video game or text is an island. On the contrary, it's
normal for cultural products to resonate with special significance precisely at
the places where readers (or viewers or players) encounter them and bring
them into existence in the world, at the always-forming pathways of emergent
(and unstable) information-becoming-meanings.

## Return to *Myst* Island

The transmedia, paratextual nature of virtually *all* forms of cultural expression
(apparent to varying degrees) comes into focus when we compare *Lost*—so
much like a video game—to a specific video game it strongly resembles, the
1993 puzzle-adventure game for PC, *Myst*, created by Cyan and published by
Ubisoft. In May 2006 it was announced that an actual video game version of
*Lost* would be published in 2007—also by Ubisoft—for multiple platforms,
portable, console, and PC. The mobile version, a classic RPG for cellphones
and iPods, was released in May 2007 by Ubisoft's Gameloft division. With this
release it has become possible to download both TV episodes and the game and
"play" both the show and the game on the same fifth-generation iPod 2.5-inch
screen, for example. The Gameloft website offers this teaser:

> What if you woke up on the beach of this famous, mysterious island after
> your plane crashed? Try to save the lives of passengers at the accident site,

set up a camp, learn to live among the rest of the group, explore the jungle, hunt, witness unexplained phenomena, and avoid the bizarre traps scattered around this hostile environment. . . . attempt to crack the secrets of the island![13]

Gameplay for the mobile RPG is surprisingly compelling, with oddly realistic-feeling mostly overhead-shot 3-D graphics, locations such as the jungle, the beach, the Hatch, the cages at the Others' research station and a mix of necessarily sprite-like avatars in wider shots and close-ups of characters when they are speaking. The famous whispers in the jungle appear as tiny text-words in the foliage, as well as sounds on the soundtrack (which includes a background musical score). There are weapons for your inventory, power-ups (fruit, a first-aid kit), and a status bar for health. You control actions such as lifting objects or tuning in a radio receiver, as well as navigate, by scrolling the iPod clickwheel, and you use the select button for shooting or stabbing boars or interacting with NPCs (non-player characters). You have to find your way through a maze of jungle foliage, for example, while fighting off squealing boars and avoiding sinking in the swamp.

The fact that *Lost* feels like such a natural fit for such a game from the start (playing as Jack, you run onto the beach and begin helping the survivors amidst the plane wreckage), even in the limited mobile format, only calls attention to the way the show has from the beginning structured its sets and situations to resemble "maps" and "levels" and gamelike missions and challenges.

An executive producer of the show was quoted in the game announcement as saying, "Many of us on *Lost* have been hardcore gamers for years and the chance to work with Ubisoft, a company behind some of our favorite titles, has excited us to no end." He was probably thinking of more recent titles as among the Lost team's "favorites," but it's possible he had in mind *Myst* as well, since the game was so widely known in the mid-1990s' era of home-computer gaming. Either way, the producer characterized the forthcoming *Lost* game as "a wonderful opportunity to organically extend this creative phenomenon into an interactive consumer experience," a nice bit of public relations for the deal with Ubisoft, yes, but the fact is that *Lost* has from the beginning been conceived of as an "interactive consumer experience." The show is already a video game at one remove; turning it into an actual video game is simply the final step in actualizing its potential as a cross-media form of expression, a puzzle-adventure franchise.

Just before the *Lost* game announcement was made, on an art student's blog in spring 2006 a homemade user-icon mashup combined the logo for *Lost* (in bold capitals) with the famous image of an earlier mysterious island, the surreal primary setting of *Myst*.[14] This photoshopped parody image combining worlds vividly represented a significant connection that some viewers had already noticed, between the now-classic best-selling video game of the 1990s and the game-like hit TV show that debuted just over ten years later. Both works are set on mysterious islands and require castaways to piece together clues to discover where they are and what it means. Both demand that players or viewers (vicariously, in this case, through the actors) solve puzzles and figure out how to work complicated technological contraptions. And both turn out to be games about discovering the mysterious underground source of an author's *intentions* for the worlds in which they take place. But beyond these resemblances, taken together, *Myst* and *Lost* tell us significant things about the intermediated and social nature of games and other, related forms of cultural expression, including TV shows and printed texts.

The original *Myst* was played at a stately pace on a PC using a single CD-ROM. The game opens with a cutscene in which a silhouetted body falls through a "fissure" in space, soon followed by a tumbling book that, when opened, reveals a movie on the blank recto: a fly-over of what we later learn is Myst Island. In retrospect this opening looks significantly like a declaration of the cross-media aspirations of the makers of the game—books, cinematic effects, and adventure games are all combined from the start. From there the gameplay proper begins and you play in immersive first-person mode (on your PC screen you see only a pointing hand, like a conventional cursor icon, in lieu of the weapon of FPSs); you click to move around and explore the island environment, as well as to zoom in on objects, pull levers, open boxes or doors or books, and pick up anything that you can pick up. You eventually learn that movie-containing books of this sort, which you'll encounter at various locations around the island, are actually portals, "linking books" through which you can teleport to interlinked "ages," separate but linked worlds (or levels) in other parts of the space–time continuum, like parallel universes. But you learn this only by exploring, by clicking your way through numerous settings and solving puzzles on the apparently deserted but strangely haunted-feeling island. As is the case with most games of this type, you play *Myst* by figuring out how to play *Myst*. As Steven Johnson has pointed out, this sets video games apart from traditional board games, say, in which the rules must be crystal clear from the start.[15] With video games, you have to explore and "probe the depth of the game's logic," through trial and error, playing in order to learn how to play. This, "the ultimate mystery [that] drives players deeper into the gameworld," is the question of how the game is played (42–3). Gameplay is in this sense itself a quest to solve a fundamental mystery at the heart of the quest: this is the route, rather than through its thematic story elements, to begin to understand what a game like *Myst* "means." By the same token, this formal or ludological quality is intertwined with the fictional gameworld elements, including the story of

Atrus and his competitive sons. (In *Myst* that story is itself all about open-ended world making, so the relationship of story and formal gameplay is rendered explicit.)

Similarly, the makers of *Lost* have said that the origins of the show's story (represented in the opening of the pilot) lie in a start-screen image: a well-dressed figure finds himself dropped into the jungle on what he soon discovers is a mysterious island; he wakes up and begins to run (as if someone had picked up a controller and thumbed the joysticks), immediately trying to figure out what has happened and where he is. Even the opening music of the show, an ominous layered glissando chord that imitates the whooshing sound of the jet engines (and is also used to close scenes where commercial breaks are cut in), has a precedent in Tim Larkin's celebrated ambient score for *Myst*, in which an ascending electronic chord marks the first and each subsequent transition via linking books. Both the game, *Myst*, and the show, *Lost*, are based on open-ended exploration of apparently isolated island worlds, but both works also end up having hidden agents manipulating events, and forward momentum in each case relies on hidden portals as transitional links, elements that take the player or viewer, as well as the fictional characters, beyond or outside the apparent limits of those island worlds, to what amount to new levels with new, increased challenges. And, interestingly enough, in both works, fetishistic books, charged with indeterminate significance by writers who often seem more like game-masters, serve within the game as literalized paratexts, thresholds to linked worlds.

There are a lot of books on both *Myst* and *Lost* islands. In *Myst*, besides entering the game through an antique leatherbound book (with "MYST" embossed on its cover), you find that the island contains a library whose shelves hold books with handwritten texts and pictures, full of clues as well as back-story narratives. Framing these shelves are two large books sitting on lecterns, each a trap for one of the two sons of Atrus, the island world's creator, who you later learn, like Shakespeare's Prospero, created these worlds by writing them. Around the island and in the other "ages" to which you can travel, you find torn-out pages that litter the landscape or are stashed away in drawers; the endgame turns on choosing and putting these retrieved portions of books into the outstretched hand of the father/creator/author figure of the island you have been exploring. In the end, Atrus is found seated at his writing desk in an underground cave of "D'ni" (like the Hatch in the second season of *Lost*). From there you are returned to the library, the node of branching inter- and paratextuality, from which you are set free to continue to explore the island and its connected ages. Even before you reach this endpoint, however, you hear in the soundtrack and sense in the found pages and other clues a shaping intelligence behind the apparently deserted island. Like Friday's footprints in the sand in *Robinson Crusoe*, there are tantalizing signs everywhere of an over-arching plot or underlying back-story behind the mystery in *Myst*. In fact, a novelized prequel was published after the game appeared, in a hardcover edition by Hyperion Books (coincidentally enough the same publisher as *Lost*'s *Bad Twin* and the official "companion" book, *The Lost Chronicles*; the game and the show share media-company parentage along with gamelike DNA). *The Book of Atrus*'s glossy boards are covered in photo-process faux-leather, complete with peritextual "water stains," "scratches" and raised and textured "gilt" corners, and its main title is represented as "stamped" or "burned" into the cover, with its subtitle apparently scribbled beneath with a pen, just above a mandala or rose-window emblem. Inside, the pages are artificially yellowed, the illustrations deliberately primitive pencil or charcoal sketches from the protagonist's notebook. Clearly, this book means to stand for books as cultural artifacts and symbolic "portals" to connected meanings. As a prequel to the game, *The Book of Atrus* (Miller et al. 1995) ends literally where the game of *Myst* begins, its first-person Epilogue repeating the Prologue cutscene voiceover one hears at the beginning of the game, explaining that a lost book dropped into a volcanic fissure earlier in the novel is, in fact, the very same small book that plops down into the darkened, starlit space of your computer screen when you first open the game of *Myst*. Like *Bad Twin*, but in more explicit fashion, *The Book of Atrus* is a cross-media spinoff and guide to the game; both books contain clues that feed back into watching the show or playing the game. But of course both works, game and show, also contain numerous intertextual allusions to books from which they draw themes, plot devices, and supplemental meanings.

The immediate textual inspiration for *Myst* was Jules Verne's *The Mysterious Island* (1874).[16] Rand and Robyn Miller, the brothers who created the game, said in numerous interviews that they were longtime fans of Verne's fiction. This classic Victorian science fiction novel is a techno-adventure work, an example of what some have called the "Robinsonnade"—deriving from Defoe's *Robinson Crusoe, The Swiss Family Robinson, Treasure Island*, and including, some might say, *Lord of the Flies*—the story of castaways who must fend for themselves, reconstructing their lost civilization on a primitive desert island. This is a broad genre into which *Lost* can be fitted as well. Along the way, the novel's adventures often seem mere excuses to showcase ingenious gadgetry and complicated machines—which are all constructed out of the raw materials of nature, like precocious solutions to difficult engineering-school puzzles. Bridges, tunnels, ships, gunpowder, metal alloys, pulleys, elevators, windmills, dams, and machines of every sort are designed, built, and then explained in detail.[17] "From nothing they must supply themselves with everything," we are told of Verne's castaways. In answer, a shipwrecked sailor cheerfully remarks:

"there is always a way of doing everything" (37, 26)—which might stand as the motto of any optimistic gamer facing a new gameworld.

Behind all the adventures and puzzle solving, there is a nagging mystery to be solved. The castaways in *The Mysterious Island*, like players of *Myst* and the plane-crash victims of *Lost*, discover traces of a hidden presence, signs of an anonymous, paternal, yet invisible hand, which offers provisions and needed equipment, intervenes at moments of crisis, and—significantly—leaves written, textual clues to guide and encourage them. At one crucial moment in the Victorian story, Verne's castaways discover and salvage barrels of supplies that have washed up on the beach, seemingly by chance. These include an "inventory" (later to become a key term in all kinds of games) of "tools," "weapons," "instruments," "clothes," "utensils"—and books. The inventory of books is short but it includes an atlas, dictionaries, and a Bible, as well as three reams of paper and "2 books with blank pages" (186). It's hard not to see these blank books as the tempting intertextual *tabulae rasae* on which *Myst* the game was "authored" by Rand and Robyn Miller and their team of programmers, inspired by their discovery of Verne's text. But it is the English Bible (inevitably) that becomes the central logos, the text with an unseen author through which the invisible genius of Verne's island speaks to the colonists under Nemo's secret direction. Upon opening it at random one Sunday evening in a traditional game of prophetic fortune telling, the castaways find a passage marked with a penciled cross: "For every one that asketh receiveth; and he that seeketh findeth" (188)..

The hidden author who annotates and then plants the inscribed Bible for Verne's colonists to discover is Captain Nemo. We know him from the earlier Verne book, *Twenty Thousand Leagues Under the Sea*. As his name in reverse indicates, he is the omen of meaning revealed in the mysterious island's "text." He a kind of programmer before the fact, the inventor of futuristic devices and a techno-wizard, a maker of worlds. Nemo has constructed a little self-sufficient world under the sea in his submarine, the Nautilus, complete with its Victorian library, electric lighting, and a pipe organ—as well as a subaqueous and subterranean cavern in which the colonists finally discover him. These spaces anticipate the Hatches on *Lost*, but they also obviously inspired the endgame of *Myst*, in which the user finally meets "face to face" with the "author" of *Myst* Island and its connected worlds. The castaways in *The Mysterious Island* only discover Nemo through persistent exploration and puzzle solving, activities that sound a great deal like gameplay or textual editing *and* interpretation. As one of the leaders says,

> We will begin our researches as soon as possible. We will not leave a corner of the island unexplored. We will search into its most secret

recesses, and will hope that our unknown friend will pardon us in consideration of our intentions. (379)

Actually, "intentions" are precisely what are at stake, here, both the explorers' and the "author's." And Verne's novel serves as an important reminder of how both *Myst* and *Lost* work, as meaning-generating entertainments, puzzles around a central mystery, whose solution is postponed in order to allow for exploration. In both game and show represented "authors," as well as actual game-creators or TV writers (the lines between these levels of authorship are deliberately blurred in both cases), are seen primarily as sources of clues that serve as cues for further production of meanings, in other words, as occasions for interpretive play. In this way, once you begin to notice it, it is clear that Verne's novel, the game *Myst*, and the TV show *Lost*, with its linked ARG, all turn on the ancient problem associated with interpreting texts of all kinds as well as playing many kinds of games: the problem of the author's (perceived) intentions—and what one can *do* with those intentions.

## The game of author's intentions

In textual studies, the branch of literary studies concerned with the material production, reproduction, and reception of texts, the goal for much of the twentieth century among mainstream practitioners was to recover the author's intentions for a given work (often in order to produce a new scholarly edition that best represented those intentions).[18] The nineteenth-century's higher criticism of the Bible and classical philology focused on Greek and Latin texts began by confronting the mystery of missing or disputed sources. Modern textual criticism descended from these practices and started from a similar premise: that an author's final intentions for a work, the meanings he or she intended to convey, had once existed (like the ur-texts or manuscript sources of classical and biblical scholars), but would necessarily have been obscured ("corrupted") by the media through which they got communicated—the necessary passages of the work over the thresholds of language, writing, print. The very thresholds by which the work enters history became in this view the obstacles to a textual scholar's knowledge of the author's intentions for the work: the passage of time, publishing practices (where scribes or typesetters or editors intervened in the text), or chance itself (a lost manuscript, misaligned or damaged type, a plane crash that killed the author before he could correct proofs). The textual scholar's job, according to the traditional method that dominated Anglo-American practices for most of the previous century, was to overcome these obstacles in order to "recover" (or at least "reconstruct") the elusive author's intentions, an ideal standing behind the messiness of historical transmission. The scholar gathered and sifted all available "witnesses," including manuscripts, printed texts, historical documents, any relevant textual fragment, and adjudicated among them and their variants in search of the logical relationships (often expressed genealogically, in trees of descent) that allowed them to select particular copy-texts or base texts, and often to combine words and punctuation ("substantives" and "accidentals") from different sources, in this sense to construct an eclectic text, in order to improve the odds of achieving a simulation of what never existed in any real, material form: the author's ideal text of the work in question.

This may well seem like a pretty Romantic, even quixotic, ultimately impossible quest. And in fact in the past several decades textual studies has undergone a sea change, a paradigm shift away from that elusive idealist goal and toward the messier project of producing historical accounts of works and texts in all the instability of their material existence. Authors usually do have intentions for imaginative works, but it is now recognized that these are frequently multiple intentions, sometimes inchoate intentions, and, most important, they are almost always only one force interacting with chance, material conditions of the media, publishing institutions, the horizon of expectations in which the work is to be read or performed (received), including readers' intentions, and the general social and political and material contexts of the time(s) and place(s) into which the work emerges and continues to be experienced and interpreted. In other words, the dominant strain of textual studies now takes as its object of study the complex phenomena of the social text—a complex event-horizon, a cluster of dynamic interactions among various determining forces, agents, intentions, and chance occurrences. No text, in this view, is an island, much less an island ruled by a single author's unitary intention.

This shift toward studying the material conditions of the social text is most often associated with the work of D. F. McKenzie and Jerome McGann, theorists who focus not on imagined static verbal constructs, the isolated text, but on dynamic discourse fields composed of interacting forces: verbal, graphical (or bibliographical), cultural, ideological, and social. The social text is like the crossroads of these forces, the place where meanings get generated. Before McGann's *Critique of Modern Textual Criticism* in 1983, McKenzie was the first to argue for a broader definition of the social text, as any recorded form of "verbal, visual, oral, numeric data, in the form of maps, prints, and music, of archives or recorded sound, of films, videos, and any computer-stored information . . ." (13). McKenzie famously studied not just the text of a treaty with aboriginal peoples, but its embeddedness in the larger "text" of the physical landscape itself as it was mapped and interpreted by competing parties to the treaty. The object of bibliography and textual studies was for him a universe of textual events taking place in the world: "physical forms, textual versions, technical transmission, institutional control . . . perceived meanings, and social effects" (13).

More recently, Jerome McGann has become the foremost proponent of the social-text theory, beginning with his *Critique*, which shifted the focus to multiple versions of texts, shifting, multiple intentions of authors and others, and in general, "the dynamic social relations which always exist in literary production" (81)—explorations he has extended in recent years into the realm of digital textuality. In *Radiant Textuality* (2001), he advocates a focus on "quantum poetics" in which texts are not "discrete phenomena" but are non-self-identical events that include the position and engagement of the scholar.[19] Achieving this new focus on the dynamic social text as quantum event-horizon, McGann predicts, will come about not only by "exposing the fault-lines of interpretational methods that implicitly or explicitly treat any part of the study process as fixed or self-identical," but also by developing new kinds of interpretive practices and tools. Somewhat surprisingly he then concludes that "Models for these kinds of tools descend to us through our culture in games and role-playing environments" (164). Games are the newest best examples for the nature of all kinds of textual interpretation in part because they help us to understand in relation to new media a very old truth about texts, one obscured by their recent tradition of reception (for the past two centuries). McGann observes that "[e]very poem comprised in our inherited Western corpus could fairly be described as a nonlinear game played (largely) with linear forms and design conventions, but often with nonlinear forms as well" (148). This is more than the old poststructuralist position that language renders meaning a matter of the free-play of linguistic signifiers; it is an acknowledgement that interpretation is always a social act, actually an ongoing series of social acts of dynamic meaning-construction. There is nothing new in *that* concept for dedicated gamers (or fans of new-style shows such as *Lost*). In this sense, and not in the reductive focus by some in the media on their "interactive storytelling" or narrative "immersion," video games are the quintessential *social texts* of our present cultural moment. This is made vividly clear in the work of an important younger scholar in the field, Matthew Kirschenbaum, who as a matter of course includes games among the digital objects to which he applies the methods of a materialist textual studies.[20] A similar promising development applies methods like those of materialist textual studies to the specific material embodiments of games in Nick Montfort's and Ian Bogost's *Platform Studies* series.[21] What these new endeavors share—and I join them in the present book—is the recognition that a scholarly attention to details of material production, transmission, and meaning making can be fruitfully applied to video games. Moreover, rather than ask the tired questions of how games might become more like traditional conceptions of literary texts, or auteur-directed films, or *Hamlet*; or, conversely, how we might "read" games as self-contained formal narratives (for example), literary and cultural scholars would do much better to ask instead what video games (and game-like shows such as *Lost*) have to teach us about all kinds of texts, old and new, but as only part of the larger set of interesting objects of cultural expression.

## No Text (or Game) is an Island

What we see in the arc traced through the points represented by *Myst* and *Lost* is an increasing acceptance of the idea of "dispersed authority" when it comes for cultural expressions, and of emergent, user-driven, collaboratively constructed meanings when it comes to games and game-like entertainments. But the dynamic of dispersed authority has to some degree operated for centuries in the production and reception of texts of all kinds. A casual viewer of *Lost* (who plays video games) recently remarked to me that I and all the other fans of the show were just "looking too deeply into it," that there was "nothing really there." I recognized in his remark the same kind of reflexive skepticism many university students express about literary texts, a nineteenth-century novel, say, or a supposedly well-known seventeenth-century text by John Donne: "No man is an island, entire of itself; every man is a piece of the continent, a part of the main." Behind such skepticism, I believe, there lies a deep-seated form of Romantic intentionalism. The students want to know whether Donne (or, in this case, the writers of *Lost*) really put that particular meaning in the text, or, as they suspect, did he mean something else (or nothing at all) and these interpretations are just being read into texts by English and cultural studies professors? Some of these same students might be surprised to realize how much the reconstruction and filling-in of authorial intentions for centuries-old literary texts itself resembles a kind of serious game, a quest for meanings in which scholars overcome obstacles, solve puzzles, make conventional moves within certain rules of discourse and interpretation, and attempt to understand the patterns of the particular cultural expression—normally through a process of community collaboration (from research to peer review). The literary text, too, can be understood as a series of dynamic interactions between reconstructed intentions—authors' and others—and later acts of transmission and interpretation. In this view, meanings emerge not from some unitary source beneath the surface of the text but in the process of those countless dynamic interactions; this includes author's intentions, in so far as they can be determined, but certainly does not stop with them. Given this view of textuality, the textual-studies scholar's job becomes mapping the history of the complex relations of the social text.

Consider for a moment the well-known John Donne text I mentioned above, "No man is an island." One finds it quoted everywhere, along with its even more famous excerpt from the same source: "Ask not for whom the bell tolls, it tolls for thee." Sometimes one finds the lines broken up and printed as "poetry," but textual scholars know that they were originally written as part of a prose meditation, a conventional form of religious devotion (and of course they were not spelled in the modernized form in which I have quoted them). One literary critic, Stephen Greenblatt, takes the "bells" that "toll" in the passage as referring to the doctrine of purgatory, which was of course highly disputed in seventeenth-century Protestant England, where the traditional practice of ringing bells for the dead in order to call for prayers to help speed them through purgatory was viewed as dangerously Catholic.[22] No man is an island, no man is trapped alone in purgatory, because we are all part of one continent, "the shared community of the living and the dead," as Greenblatt reads it, and so our purgatory is here, in this life. The very idea of an island of penance for the dead, a purgatorial snow globe, is an error, an illusion. But note as well that this version of John Donne's reconstructed meaning is only one version among many; moreover, this reading is much more than a matter of Donne's intentions as an individual author; Greenblatt's reading of the (no) island image is based on exploring and decoding the complex social forces operating upon the production and reception even of Donne's spiritual devotion as a *social text*, one with partly obscured but still vitally important *contexts*.

This becomes even clearer when we look at the history and form of production and publication of later, more popular literary texts, those closer in every way to the media and forms of expression and entertainment of our own time. Think, for example, about the ragged, rubber-banded copy of the book that shows up in the final episode of season two of *Lost* (titled, "Live Together, Die Alone"), Charles Dickens's 1864–65 novel, *Our Mutual Friend*. The multi-character novel contains possible thematic and narrative parallels for *Lost* and *The Lost Experience* ARG, including concealed identities, arranged marriage, and a disputed inheritance, but it also literally "holds the key" to the technological meaning of the Hatch, since Desmond uses it as a hiding place for his failsafe key. It also contains a letter from Desmond's long-lost love, Penelope Widmore, the textual "key" that connects the world of *Lost* to the paratextual world of *Bad Twin* and *The Lost Experience* ARG in general. In this sense the novel contains proof against Desmond's despairing theory that he is in a hermetic purgatory— that the island is the only isolated place left on earth (a theory shared by and perhaps introduced by some of the show's fans). Instead Dickens's Victorian novel in effect "tolls the bell" for Desmond's release, signifying a way out of his "snow globe." It serves as a kind of *Myst*-like linking book, crossing the barrier of the island's isolation, and it leads to the final cliffhanger of the season, thus suggesting that the story can be linked to a new "world" of narrative, come next season.

But even more than the themes, plot, and characters of the novel, it is its textual history, its production and reception, that makes for the most interesting parallels with *Lost*. Most people are aware of Dickens's system for the serial publication of his fiction, eventually producing installments of paper-wrapped parts of a novel for a shilling each, twenty parts over eighteen or nineteen months. Clearly, this is one reason the writers of a TV serial drama made the allusion to *Our Mutual Friend*. Like them in a general way, Dickens was engaged in a broadly popular form of fictional entertainment. In one interview, Carlton Cuse noted that Dickens "was writing chapter by chapter for newspapers. We often think: 'How much did Dickens know when he was writing his stories? How much of it was planned out, and how much was flying by the seat of his pants because he had to get another chapter in?' We can respect what he went through."[23] In fact, we know something of Dickens's system of outlining. He usually planned the skeleton of a serial novel and then wrote individual numbers in "real time," more or less as they were due; he even preferred, like TV writers today, to get five numbers written before publication began, so he would have a head start on his reading public. The parallels with how episodic TV is produced are obvious. For a show such as *Lost*, which depends on keeping its viewers in the dark and only gradually revealing its mysteries, there is no better Victorian precursor. Dickens himself referred to overcoming the narrative difficulty of gradually revealing a mystery, a difficulty "much enhanced by the mode of publication"—of unfolding the story over nineteen months (798). What Dickens "went through," as Cuse puts it, in the case of *Our Mutual Friend* is, it turns out, even more relevant to the show, since he was under pressure to complete the final installments on time and compressed them; at one point he lost track of the process and had to write quickly in order to produce the correct number of chapters at the end.

But the production history of *Our Mutual Friend* overlaps with the themes of *Lost* in an even more dramatic way.[24] Dickens was nearing completion of *Our Mutual Friend* in June 1865 when he took a brief trip to Paris. On the final leg of the return, a railway trip from Folkstone to London, the train he was on ran over a 42-foot gap in a viaduct (then under repair) over the river Beult, just out of Staplehurst. Part of the train leapt the gap but some cars plunged into the riverbed below and ten passengers were killed. Dickens's own car hung suspended over the abyss, but he climbed out and worked for hours among the tangled wreckage of the disaster, aiding the injured and tending to the dead, reportedly carrying water in his top hat and a flask of brandy. Just as he was finally preparing to leave the scene, he suddenly remembered something, returned to the crashed train, and climbed inside to retrieve his almost-forgotten manuscript, the installment in progress of *Our Mutual Friend*, book IV, chapters 1–4 (840n). The transportation disaster, the crowd of survivors, the manuscript recovered from the wreckage—it would seem that the textual history of Dickens's novel, even more perhaps than its thematic contents, may have inspired the creators of *Lost*. Dickens's own version of events was written in a postscript to the finished novel—a classic example of the paratext (peritext). In it, the world of make-believe crosses into the real world to jarring effect, with the fictional characters of *Our Mutual Friend* imagined as victims of the real-world Staplehurst disaster. Mr. and Mrs. Boffin, in what Dickens suggestively calls their "manuscript dress," escape only because that manuscript—and its author—escaped. This was the cliffhanger to beat all cliffhangers, of course, and Dickens makes a kind of game of the dark paratextual possibilities of his near-death experience. If his car had not hung there above the cliff, we would not be reading the novel in our hands. "I climbed back into my carriage—nearly turned over a viaduct, and caught aslant upon the turn—to extricate the worthy couple. They were much soiled, but otherwise unhurt" (800).

Dickens's postscript makes a useful parable for would-be interpreters of all kinds of social texts and objects of cultural expression, of the hazards they face coming out into the world and the necessity that they do so if they are to mean something in the culture. Though it might seem to be about his authority as creator of the Boffins and their story, once it is published at the back of the bound novel it becomes the quintessential paratextual cue—an opportunity for readers to experience the novel in a new light, assuming they play along. The most interesting parallel between *Our Mutual Friend* and *Lost* is not the concealed identity of John Harmon, or the arranged marriage of Bella Wilfer, or even the shipwrecks and floating corpses, but the almost incredible facts of the novel's publication history and what Dickens does to emphasize the threshold where the fiction enters the author's representation of the real-world drama of the railway disaster, and thus the readers' sense of their own real worlds. The paratextual postscript of the novel resonates with what *Lost* tries to do *formally*, in its own forms of threshold-crossing play. Some casual viewers of *Lost* might have encountered the appearance of *Our Mutual Friend* as a simple allusion; but engaged fans and players of *Lost* and *The Lost Experience* ARG would have seen it as the paratexual portal it was, opening onto new levels of meaning—in the gamer's sense of level: a new contextual world containing different puzzles, challenges, obstacles, and goals.

Dickens's monthly numbers were eventually collected and bound into the whole codex book that we now think of as the novel, but as they were appearing, each installment of the work broken into twenty parts (the final number was a double, not unlike the final two-hour episode of a show such as *Lost*) was a discrete moment in an ongoing, dynamic publishing event. As Robert Patten has explained it, having each serial installment reviewed kept the novel before the public for an extended period and generated more attention for it (what would today be called "buzz").[25] But the serial structure also fed back into the shape of the novel as it emerged, as Dickens suggested in his postscript. The cliffhangers, huge cast of characters, major and minor, and multiple narrative threads (two major plots intertwined and often multiple background plots or subplots) were all narrative innovations that grew out of the serial form, the fiction's life in the world, among its readers. Dickens is famous for cultivating an interactive relationship with his readers. He received letters from them and would sometimes adjust the stories in response (to the frustration of strict intentionalist interpretations of his authorship), and he performed in public, reading his own texts for live audiences. Jay Clayton argues that Dickens's invention of and control of the material form and medium in which his works appeared in the world amounts to an example of innovative "nineteenth-century information technology," one that combined cultural expression with economic opportunity.[26] Clayton reminds us, as well, that Dickens oversaw the placement of illustrations and advertisements (even some of the ad copy) for consumer goods that appeared wrapped with his monthly numbers, and he took a keen interest in spinoffs (though they were not licensed and he received no royalties for them)—for example, going out of his way to visit a tavern named Our Mutual Friend. He "understood the publicity value that came from their wide diffusion" (153).

This was an entrepreneurial move on the part of the career-savvy Victorian author, a bid for greater financial control, sure enough, but I think it was also a way for him to extend the discourse field of his fiction, to promulgate his own kind of dedicated fan base. In its way, Dickens's mode of production and dissemination was a kind of precursor to the mixed art and marketing phenomenon of our time, the ARG. In both cases, despite the impetus of commerce, the result is also a formal extension of the discourse field or the arena of the cultural expression outward into social space. Dickens's publishing practice depends on, even while it attempts to exploit, a model of user-shaped and sometimes even user-generated "content." Jay Clayton senses this at work when he speaks of Dickens's "restless technocultural creativity" and his "craving for cultural bandwidth" (200). The writers of *Lost* do much the same when they produce ARGs (including publication of paratextual books such as *Bad Twin* and multi-layered allusion to existing books such as *Our Mutual Friend*), publish podcasts, and—perhaps most notably—follow the boards, keep in touch with, and to some unknown degree (it is the subject of much speculation online) shape their work interactively in relation to what the fans are posting on the Internet. What Robert Patten says of Dickens's serial publication rings true as a description of game-like new media, as well: separating the story into twenty entertaining parts encouraged readers to "inhabit" the novel's world. This is of course precisely what is said about today's games and game-like media: that they allow users to inhabit or become immersed in the world surrounding the imaginative work. As Patten says, Dickens's form of serial publishing

> blurred the distinction between reading a book, a closed container whose contents are enjoyed in a private space and time separated from diurnal activities, and reading an installment that is simultaneously circulating, through reviews and conversation, in the public world of daily events.

We might say that Dickens's texts, like *Lost*, and like almost any popular video game, are always already predominantly paratextual. That is, the formerly limited role of the paratext, to serve as a threshold or transactional space between the text and the world, has now moved to the foreground, has become the essence of the text. Once you look at today's games and game-like media entertainments, it's *all* paratext, in concentric circles rippling out into the world.

## The parable of the *Myst/Uru* diaspora

In 2004, roughly ten years after the publication of *Myst*, the game had produced five sequels for PC, with several versions of some, and a live MMOG (massively multiplayer online game), within the mythology of the *Myst* universe, called *Uru*. With something like 10,000 players, *Uru* contained the kind of beautiful graphics and comprehensive mythology (and highly scripted back-story) that had inspired fierce loyalty to *Myst* for a decade. Then in February, for financial reasons, the game server was shut down and *Uru*'s players were turned into "virtual refugees." That term, and the ethnographic way of looking at what happened in the case of *Uru*, I take from Celia Pearce, whose doctoral dissertation research on game culture (as excerpted in published articles) is the source of the account that follows.[27] What Pearce discovered is that groups of refugees, members of what she calls "the *Myst/Uru* diaspora," migrated to existing online virtual worlds, about three hundred of them in *There* and two hundred or so more of them in *Second Life*, and, like immigrant communities in the real world, they brought with them their *Myst*-based culture. The "Uruz" crafted objects and buildings and settings replicated from the *Myst* universe, and in this sense "ported" the remnants of the lost game to the virtual shores of their new worlds. Pearce went inside the virtual worlds using her own ethnographer-avatar to study this phenomenon, and her research details the rich and complex recreations of *Myst*-based culture, the sometimes hostile reactions of established residents of the online worlds to these organized groups of "others" (20), and the *Myst/Uru* groups' internal conflicts over just how they should continue to play the game in these new spaces.

For example, some traditionalists wanted to follow strictly the official mythology, the back-story of which established that only the people of the original D'ni (pronounced "Dunny") culture had the power to create new worlds, new "ages," by writing them in books (20). Others engaged in making cultural hybrids, or, we might say, mashups, building *Uru*-like objects that fit into *There*, say, and selling them to players not limited to the *Uru* community. Varying degrees of replication of the original MMOG were therefore created by different players and groups within the new environments. But the world-making premise of *Myst* itself was tempting, and some among the former players of *Uru* took a more revisionist view. Eventually, as Pearce says, a collective group of players of *Myst* and *Uru* built their own carefully crafted original "age" inside *Second Life*. This amounts to a new game in the franchise, really, a fan-created addition to the *Myst* universe (22). Pearce's work is remarkable in a number of ways, but for our purposes it points to significant evolutionary changes in the form of a particular very popular game, namely, the increasing socialization of the *Myst* universe, driven not by the game's creators or publishers but by the community of dedicated fans and players who literally constructed the gameworld, and then reconstructed it when its original "authors" abandoned it (and them).

The original 1993 PC game is a notoriously lonely experience. You explore the island and linked "ages" of *Myst* on your own, unable even to see your own avatar's body, represented only by a pointing-hand cursor. The game seems deserted, and indeed is thematically based on the eerie pathos of discovering a depopulated culture. Eventually you win contact with videos of characters in the game, but they are, significantly, trapped in books or hiding underground. As the *Myst* sequel games evolved, they reflected changes in gaming culture, with enhanced graphics (a version of the original recreated with 3-D graphics was released as *Real Myst*), and more cutscenes with film-like interactions with costumed actors playing in-game characters. The first sequel, *Riven*, was delivered on six CD-ROMs as a result, which the player has to change periodically as he or she moves from one segment of the game to another. The most significant watershed, however, was the leap online into the MMOG world with *Uru*. The Miller brothers had always seen themselves as authors or film directors in the auteur tradition, operating from a traditional intentional-ism that is also built thematically into *Myst*'s back-story, centered on Atrus, the writer/creator of worlds. But of course *Myst* also tells the story of errant brothers and of splinters of the original civilization traveling to new worlds, new "ages," that are by their very nature infinitely multipliable. A kind of cen-trifugal chaos inherent in the game pulls the gameworld away from its original authorial center, and it is not surprising that players jumped at the chance to go online and explore the beautifully crafted *Myst* environments, live and simultaneously, with other players. It was essentially the emergent momentum of this outward-pulling social urge, I think, that drove the "Uruz" to strike out on their own after the official game was shut down.

Pearce situates the rebuilding by the diaspora in relation to a "postmodern sensibility" in recent popular culture that places value on acts of appropriation (18). In this climate, game players are motivated to reconfigure gameworlds (18). The activities of fans as "textual poachers" have been thoroughly explored by Henry Jenkins, who looks mostly at the example of TV shows and draws on Michel de Certeau's notion of cultural poaching to describe the appropriative and reconstructive energies of fan culture.[28] But I would suggest that the source of these fan appropriations, by the 1990s at least, was less a general, overarching "postmodern sensibility" and more the specific culture of video games and gamelike expressions of popular culture, as these thrive on the Internet. This general ethos is apparent in "Web 2.0" technology develop-ments—podcasts, blogs, Wikipedia, Flickr, Google Maps, Facebook, social tagging, social software applications of all kinds, all with user-created or user-aggregated content. Earlier forms of fan culture, first of course pre-digital and later using message boards, mailing lists, and websites, were precursors (and arguably sources) for these developments. Steven Johnson refers to the tie-in fan-based websites for TV shows, "online media that latches on to traditional media," using a term that connects suggestively with what I have been saying about paratexts, as "para-sites."[29] Arguably, such community-driven fan media reached a critical mass among gamers, who were among the first in digital culture to appropriate and repurpose the cultural products around which their community was formed, by modding the games themselves, adding custom levels, and producing paratextual media objects such as machinima films made within the gameworlds using the game engines.

But by now, I think, such acts of appropriation and repurposing—or I would say instead, paratextual extensions of the universe—of a cultural product appear increasingly like the norm in popular media.[30] In a recent article (2003), Henry Jenkins rightly suggests that ours is an era of media "con-vergence," enabling a "flow of content across multiple media channels" or platforms.[31] Jenkins wrote this a year before the debut of *Lost*, but his general assessment of the new climate for "transmedia storytelling" reads like a matter-of-fact prophetic announcement of *Lost*. The gamer generation, he says, is going to expect its TV shows to afford similar pleasures. *Pokémon* is a universe of meaning stretching across multiple media platforms, games, books, car-toons, films, and fans act as "information hunters and gatherers, taking pleasure in tracking down character backgrounds and plot points and making connec-tions between different texts within the same franchise" (Jenkins, see Note 31).

It's a milestone in media history, therefore, when ABC TV/Disney mounts a transmedia ARG not just to promote a hit TV show, but also, more accurately, to fulfill the basic formal implications inherent in that show itself—which clearly took its form in the first place from games and the cross-media fan cultures that surround them. The result is no longer random acts of fan appropriation (the term now seems quaintly subcultural by contrast) but more like a teeming cloud of dynamically intermediated paratexts. The social text has been subsumed by the game-like cross-platform culture of today's media, and in that climate, multiple intentions interact as a matter of course, making meanings in an arena from which textual studies scholars can learn a great deal about texts as well as games.

In spring 2006 it was announced that an official Cyan Worlds version of the MMOG *Uru* would return online, this time as part of the proprietary Turner Broadcasting game network, GameTap.[32] In fact, before the *Myst/Uru* diaspora, the game was kept alive as a saving remnant on authorized distributed private servers run by players themselves. This now looks like a bridging move, a kind of life-support system for the game between 2004 and 2006. But it remains to be seen whether the new official version or *Uru* can really match the creative energies of the fan-based cultural diaspora. At the very least, it's clear that the GameTap version had better take those energies into account. If we plot the points of *Myst* (1993) and *Lost* (2004–), they allow us to trace a certain trajectory in the game-like products of popular culture, marked by an exponential increase and normalization of fan-based, user-created, socially-constructed forms of cultural expression. At a higher resolution, we see that the trajectory also arcs through the best-selling computer game in history after *Myst*, *The Sims* (2000), another gameworld built with fan-created content, and, from there, continues forward until it connects with the next logical point in game history, the much-anticipated latest product by *The Sims*'s legendary creator, Will Wright, *Spore*. This extremely ambitious and much-anticipated game is literally about world building (or terraforming), but it's also about the meshing of multiple intentions, cooperative and competitive intelligences, to construct the meanings of particular objects of expression. I'll come back to *Spore* at the end of the book, in chapter 6. Meanwhile, the next chapter continues the discussion of the powerful energies of fan culture, energies one might well characterize as "editorial" in the textual-studies sense, by focusing on a console game in a very different genre—indeed arguably in a genre all its own—*Katamari Damacy*.

# Chapter 2

# Collecting *Katamari Damacy*

Fan culture—and especially game-fan culture—is collecting culture, as the examples of *Lost* and *Myst* in the previous chapter indicate and as any gamer knows. In most games one collects inventoried objects in order to manipulate the gameworld to advantage. Marking one threshold between the game and the world, paratextual and merchandised objects, paraphernalia associated with fan-supported works become collectibles: books, comics, DVDs, CDs, MP3s, MP4 videos, action figures, plush toys, trading cards, album art, autographs, animation cells, actual rare objects used as props, instruments, T-shirts, tattoos, posters, multiple versions, outtakes, pirated copies, variant artifacts, links to websites, but ultimately, and most important of all, lore itself: knowledge about a show or book or game or band, knowledge about what is invariably referred to as the "universe" within which the cultural product (as well as the fan) lives. Specialized lore is subcultural capital, and the more arcane the better, because arcana is by definition exclusive knowledge, the source of the "cult" in popular "culture."[1] Fan cultures are made not by their shared style, or even their shared inventories, but by their shared passions, obsessions, knowledge. The collections of objects that would at first appear to be what unites and defines fan cultures are in practice always dynamic, always in flux, with the emphasis on the collecting rather than the collection. The aura and history of individual objects, which we are used to thinking of as the driving force behind serious collecting, floats free of those objects in the case of fan culture, and is in fact as much a function of the culture itself and its activities as it is of any particular action figure or copy of a rare comic.

Games involve collecting, and collecting is itself a game. It's often competitive (whether or not one literally competes against other collectors in auctions), a repeated quest to gather the stuff of an arbitrarily-defined universe, to overcome obstacles, to trace a provisional constellation of meaning out of individual points of light, acquired or found objects and recovered fragments, to strive within a rules-governed realm to reach specific, if never wholly stable or final, goals. And just as is the case with gamers, real collectors scoff at the vulgar idea that mere acquisition, much less completion, is the true object of the game, the thing that gives it meaning. Even so-called completist collectors are usually serial completists, moving from one collection to another. Like game players, most collectors value the process as much as the objects, the pursuit, research, bidding—the social interaction—as much as the acquisition. After acquisition, competitive sharing and collaborative hoarding of particular knowledge, backstories, provenance, lore, become in effect bridges to new levels of the game.

## "My, Earth really is full of things"

What could be simpler? Just roll up everything you see. One video game in recent years in particular vividly exemplifies and makes its theme—and the central formal feature of its gameplay—the powerful drive to collect, and can immediately be recognized as a witty procedural parody of the whole idea of collecting objects in video games and elsewhere: Namco Bandai's cult hit for PlayStation 2, *Katamari Damacy* (2004).[2] The fractured fairy tale of a back-story sounds absurd—about as absurd as a yellow disk making its way through a maze pursued by ghosts and devouring pellets along the way (Namco's earlier arcade-era smash hit was *Pac-Man*). In this case you play as a tiny cosmic Prince whose father is the well-meaning but intemperate and self-centered King of All Cosmos. The King has destroyed the stars in the night sky (apparently on a drunken spree), and you must now go to Earth and roll up everything you can collect into a giant multicolored sticky katamari (Japanese for clump or ball of stuff). If you collect enough stuff to make a big enough katamari in the time allotted, the King accepts the gift and fires it into the skies to make a new star or constellation (or, failing that, stardust at least). Cutscenes in which the King either praises your achievements or (more often) abuses you with ridicule alternate with a separate series of cutscenes in which the children in a Japanese family (they look like stylized plastic Playmobil or Lego toys) learn from watching TV of the loss the stars and follow the process of the skies' replenishment, despite their mother's blissful ignorance, finally ending up rolled up themselves, happy together at a family vacation . . . on the moon.

But mainly, you roll and then roll some more. Using the twin analog sticks on the controller almost exclusively, since in this game to navigate is also simultaneously to target or "attack" and to collect, you simply roll up ever bigger objects into ever bigger katamaris in various brightly colored 3-D environments or levels, which themselves scale up as you succeed. (Two-player competitions can take place on another world, the Space Mushroom.) The graphics are whimsically reminiscent of Peter Max and the Beatles' *Yellow*

*Submarine*, as well as Japanese pop culture, full of rainbows and mushrooms and pandas and sparkling fabrics. The landscapes, objects, and figures are deliberately blocky or polygonal, sometimes tributes to classic 8-bit images, always anything but realistic. The music is retro-flavored Japanese pop, often with a swinging sixties or seventies feel, with mixed Japanese and English lyrics. The landscape is littered with all manner of decontextualized everyday objects: tacks, pins, coins, mah-jongg tiles, erasers, pencils, bowling pins, candies, cookies, chopsticks, lucky-cat figurines, various dolls, telephones, toy cars, Lego blocks, flowerpots, vegetables, fruits, ducks, swans, mermaids, fish, cats, dogs, cows, bears, pandas, turtles, pigeons, mice, snails, crows, balloons, cars, crowns, teddy bears, eggs, wrapped presents—anything at all in various and usually bizarre juxtapositions. One of the ritually repeated lines of the King of All Cosmos (when he speaks, you read text in word bubbles and hear a sound like vinyl records being scratched on turntables) is: "My, Earth really is full of things," a hilariously literal understatement in the context of the game's overstuffed dreamscapes. The game's physics allow for each katamari to be different, to emerge as a result of your actions, and for each object in each katamari to actually be counted and represented in the inventory of the rolling clump. (But real-life physics are otherwise overridden in many ways.) Part of the surreal fun of the game is creating weird juxtapositions, making emergent dada-like constructions of found objects, as things you pick up glom onto other things in the katamari, pigeon wings flapping, for example, even after the birds have been caught in the rolling juggernaut; long-handled garden tools protruding awkwardly from one side (and hobbling the rolling motion); giant buildings or rainbows sticking out of their katamaris just as forks and golf-balls do; even mice or little humans with their limbs flailing wildly and comically, once you are able to roll them up.

In fact, parts of the game would be considered quite violent, in the context of American culture, especially if they were more realistic, not so cartoonish. Comic "violence" is definitely part of the fun. And there are some potentially uncomfortable moments when schoolgirls (or "girls" in general, in the Virgo level) are being rolled up, squealing loudly, or (in the sequel) when you roll through a school "collecting" students, who run away from you screaming, but mostly such moments are rendered funny by their stylized silliness. Classic Tom & Jerry, not to mention their parodic avatars, Itchy & Scratchy, from *The Simpsons*, are far more disturbing. Especially when it grows huge, the katamari is often like a campy version of giant monsters in classic Japanese science-fiction films, rampaging through city streets as the police fire on them and crowds flee in terror. Looked at from another angle, the rolling katamari resembles the scenes in old cartoons where giant snowballs roll up everything in their downhill paths, or even the "fight cloud" in old comic strips, the cloud of dust with only limbs and hats and sticks protruding to indicate a confused imbroglio.[3] More generally, a certain scary psychedelic attitude (sometimes drawing on popular conceptions of Zen Buddhism) lurks just behind the bright colors, manifest in the capriciousness of the King (who may seem at times to stand in for the game's designer), adding an edge to the player's experience of the gameworld. Cute teddy bears stand alongside giant mousetraps, much larger than the tiny Prince avatar, for example; luridly painted, limbless and eyeless Daruma dolls show up everywhere; and some human figures wander the streets or the beach like zombies, sometimes wielding sticks in mechanical chopping motions and emitting monster-movie screams when rolled up. The darkly funny oedipal back-story is also not without its own air of violence, as the King (who once went on a cosmos-destroying bender) berates your character, his son, as small and weak and ineffectual, the kind of taunting one expects from adversaries in boss battles or in the dialogue in martial-arts fighting games. When things go especially badly, he causes thunder and lightning, and in the sequel he absurdly shoots laser darts from his eyes (you can move your Prince character around to evade them, as in classic arcade missile-shooting games such as *Space Invaders* or *Centipede*).

You might be excused for thinking the back-story is beside the point in a game this visceral *and* nonrealistic, with gameplay arguably closer to *Pac-Man* than *Final Fantasy*. The relationship between story and gameplay, the focus of so much discussion in game theory a few years back,[4] is deliberately simple in this case, and is self-consciously arbitrary and gratuitous, but even in this case the effects of the relationship during gameplay can be subtly complex. Though you encounter it mostly at the beginning and end of levels as cutscenes, the story (when it's invoked, when the player doesn't skip past it) frames the mood of the gameplay, dividing it up into formal, rhythmic structures, and it helps to create the playful atmosphere of psychedelic whimsy that carries over into the rolling-up action in the various levels. The fantasy tone of the story arguably enhances the sense of freedom of play, even if it may do so by bringing out a rebellious streak in the player (as you react against all the comic abuse in the early levels). In the end the very arbitrariness of the relation between story and game is rendered part of this game, is parodied, not semantically, by textual commentary or symbolism, but procedurally, by the configurative actions required of the player.

Even the game's thematic elements that seem transparently absurd or meaningless, gratuitously linked to gameplay, contribute to the carelessly arbitrary feel of the game. In one speech to a game developers' conference, the game's creator Keita Takahashi declared that "games can be as stupid as they like as long as they're fun."[5] He even suggested in the same speech that games are in the end essentially "meaningless," but then went on: "because games are essentially meaningless, don't they need to be stimulating and embrace this meaningless-ness in a punk rock style to remain entertaining?" The pursuit of punk-rock style fun is anything but meaningless, I would say, and *that* is perhaps the ultimate meaning of *Katamari Damacy*.[6] One set of characters you can collect in the game are "Punks" with blocky pompadour haircuts, some labeled "Playful Punks" and some "Double Punks." The connection to an imagined aesthetic of "punk rock" is telling: irreverent, sometimes playfully nihilistic, deliberately simple, engaging in play as a form of parodic rebellion defiantly in the face of the meaninglessness of everyday consumer life. What Takahashi has created is a game against interpretation (as such), a collecting game whose meaning is the need to make one's own meanings from what you collect, to make collecting meaningful, to make your own fun. Anticipating by a couple of years the highly-publicized release of Nintendo's Wii console and its surrounding ad campaign, Takahashi's stress on simplicity and fun as elements missing from most of today's games gestures toward non-gamers and casual gamers in a kind of populism. Before the Wii, especially, this was necessarily an oppositional position in a developer community that has until recently catered to hardcore players with increasingly difficult gameplay, while saying publicly they were in pursuit of better stories, deeper characters, and ever-more realistic cinematic graphics. Trained as a sculptor, Takahashi likes to point instead to everyday hands-on kinetic experiences such as bike riding and skipping as his inspir-ations. At one point in the training level in an open arena, the King of All Cosmos comments on his having gone to all the trouble of making the training space "just so you can roll a katamari," an obvious self-reflexive comment on the process of making the game itself, a complex software space in the service of the simplest kind of fun. That apparently wasteful (time-wasting) ludic gesture, creating an arena for surface play for the sake of play, is the point.

Video games can be situated along a continuum, with relatively more story-based or cinematic games at one end and more visceral and kinetic games at the other. What makes a game a game, what separates it from a novel or a movie, according to the ludologists, is something altogether different than its story, something more fundamental, closer to a ruleset.[7] The "story" of chess, for example (two armies fighting it out in a slow campaign), is not essential to the game. What matters most at the abstract level of gameplay patterns are the rules-based, obstacle-overcoming moves by chess players, unfolding dynamic-ally, complex events arising from simple rules. That's why it's possible to play with marked corks or bottle caps. This ludic core, the rules-based but often emergent gameplay itself, is what should be the focus of true game studies, according to ludologists. These theorists have objected to the colonization of game studies by literary and cultural studies scholars, seeing as one sign of disciplinary colonization the desire to "read" games as "texts," to reduce them to narratives, and especially the assumption that the development of games is necessarily moving toward more immersive stories or cinematic experiences. One leading ludologist famously exaggerated the definitional distinction in this way: "Luckily, outside theory, people are usually excellent at distinguishing between narrative situations and gaming situations: if I throw a ball at you, I don't expect you to drop it and wait until it starts telling stories" (Eskelinen, 36). In this context, *Katamari Damacy* feels like a punk intervention: the story's premise is a more or less transparent pretext for gameplay that is non-narrative with a vengeance—you just roll a ball. It serves as a procedural parody of the very arbitrariness of backstories and cutscenes, making that arbitrariness part of what this game *is*. If you're going to enjoy this story as well as rolling the katamari, then you're going to have to do so in the face of its over-the-top gratuitousness. And many players do enjoy it on those terms. If I throw a ball at you, you may not drop it and expect it to tell a story, but if I roll a katamari at you (or, better yet, give you one to roll), you'll surely become interested in what becomes attached to its surface along the way, by chance or intention, and, significantly, in what can be made of it all. Your gameplay will enact a procedural parody of rolling and collecting. Meanwhile, you'll also likely notice and become at least somewhat interested in matters of scale and proportion played with in the fictive, make-believe gameworld.

Considered apart from the framing and atmosphere-establishing effect of the story of the King of All Cosmos (along with the parallel subplot taking place on Earth), the rolling is a literalized metaphor for the simplest kind of gameplay: rolling a ball. It is also a literalized metaphor for a fundamental activity in almost all video games: collecting stuff. *Katamari Damacy* foregrounds, exaggerates, and parodies this activity, so important in such a wide range of games, from *Pac-Man* pills to *Pokémon*, in this case making collecting not so much an instrumental action that allows you to complete a mission, or win a battle, or gain an economic advantage within the gameworld, but the very gameplay itself. One English-professor colleague, watching me play *Katamari Damacy*, asked impatiently what I could *do* with each of the objects I was rolling up. The answer of course was usually nothing—except increase the bulk of my katamari and roll up more objects, and (oh yes) in the end store the objects in a database to be sorted in various ways and, simultaneously, convert their collective mass into the signifying objects of the constellations. Fun. In *Katamari Damacy* collecting is a kinetic, visceral, and surprisingly emergent activity, as big things (rolling up houses, trees, buildings, and rainbows, and eventually recreating stars, constellations, the moon) arise from the cumulative effect of numerous, tiny gameplay decisions executed with your thumbs on the analog sticks: veer left, avoid the kicking leg, reverse direction, skip the too-big milk bottle but pick up that Japanese coin.

McKenzie Wark reads *Katamari Damacy* as an "allegory" of the relation of the "analog" to the "digital" (80).[8] Moving the thumbsticks, according to this allegorical reading, represents the analog "labor" of reshaping the world to fit the new digital ontology (80). Ultimately Wark's topic is a larger kind of symbolic violence: the increasing domination of analog existence by the regime of the digital as manifest in the "military entertainment complex" (93): "the digital now distinguishes itself sharply from the analog, subsuming the analog difference under the digital distinction . . . a transformation not merely in forms of communication or entertainment, not even in forms of power or of topos, but a change in being itself" (81). This is a dystopian technological vision (though Wark actually refers instead to the "atopia" because of the tendency of the digital to subsume everything) in the line that includes, for example, the work of Jean Baudrillard on the video-game-like qualities of the Gulf War of 1991.[9] The digital totality is the result ultimately of a "boredom that, seeking respite from nothingness, projects its lines across all space and time, turning it into commodity space and military space" (89).

While interesting as a philosophical and political argument, as an allegorical interpretation of *Katamari Damacy* this leaves something to be desired. For one thing, it undervalues something absolutely fundamental to the gameplay experience: its wicked humor. It's telling that, while Wark recognizes as among the "charms" of the game the fact that it foregrounds "the labor the gamer performs" (100), he deliberately overwrites "play" (which is what benighted gamers *think* they are performing) with "labor." I would argue instead that katamari rolling is less an allegory of labor and more a *parody* of labor, a substitution of play for labor. The game is a highly self-conscious expression by Keita Takahashi and the development team, including the art students who helped to create the feel of the game. It explores with irony various possibilities for subversion in power relations like those represented by the Prince and the King, and presumably, by extension, by the citizen and the "military entertainment complex." The point is that *Katamari Damacy* is a tendentious work of popular art that "argues" with a shrug for the value of play as a kind of potential resistance to pompous claims to dominance, that explores what cultural studies critics have called a zone of relative autonomy within the very kind of omnivorous digital structures Wark theorizes. Ultimately Wark recognizes this intention in Takahashi; he closes the chapter by noting that the creator of *Katamari Damacy* is a sculptor who doesn't take games very seriously. But then he interprets Takashi's punk attitude as a more or less unconscious Luddite "longing," itself an allegory of the domination of the analog by the digital. Takahashi longs to return to art "as an analog pursuit" but in vain, Wark claims, ignoring the persistent practices of artists all over the planet (99). This seems to me oddly condescending, and itself symptomatic of critical theory's tendency to underestimate the agency of fans and players (as well as artists and game designers), and of the tendency of allegorical interpretations in general to render abstract and fixed the dynamic particulars of gameplay, especially when it comes to the troubling excess of potential and unstable meanings produced by satire, parody, gratuitous humor, and fun.

On the other hand, Wark's focus on the relations between the digital and the analog is a helpful reminder of something important in *Katamari Damacy*: its treatment of the interface as a subject of exploration as well as a part of the game, though I think the interface, including the conversion of analog to digital, is best seen in more particular, material terms. Not just *Katamari Damacy*, after all, but all video games—and computers in general—are based on the dynamic transformations of analog into digital (and, often, back again). This is not an allegory but a material reality and a determining condition of the experience of gameplay. The ADC (analog to digital converter) is an actual device built into almost every game controller, as well as other everyday appliances. A joystick's physical movement generates analog electrical signals that are translated by potentiometers into digital code. One vivid example is Nintendo's Wii console, released in late 2006 and, like *Katamari Damacy,* positioned as a "pure fun" alternative to most console gaming. I'll have more to say about this platform in chapter 5, but it's another example of "simplicity" being enabled by complex technology. Players leap around and swing their arms as the controller, with its accelerometer and gyrometer as well as button-controls, translates those analog movements into code that translates into digital representations on the screen of swinging tennis racquets or slashing swords. When you strike something in the game, the haptic interface vibrates the controller in your hand.

The leap "above" this material level of conversion and feedback to an idealized allegorical and amorphous realm of digital control is what seems less than helpful in Wark's reading (as opposed, for example, to some particular critical analysis of the U.S. military's use of force-feedback systems in popular games such as *America's Army* to train potential personnel as cyborg soldiers). As Matthew Kirschenbaum has shown in his own textual-studies work, the apparent "immateriality" of the digital realm has always been a "premeditated" and deliberately produced effect of computing. The "illusion" of digital "immateriality" is an effect which "exists as the end product of long traditions and trajectories of engineering that were deliberately undertaken to achieve it."[10] Now, this line of analysis might well support Wark's general view of the "military entertainment complex," but my point is that *Katamari Damacy* is not a simplistic or unwitting allegory of power. Few games represent more self-consciously (and humorously) the processes of transforming analog acts of play into digital expressions of meaning than *Katamari Damacy*. And few games more effectively represent those processes as effects of the player's creative agency as meaning-maker, even over and against the demands of a self-important, idealized, arbitrary and capricious power in the heavens above the world of things. The sculptor turned game designer knows very well that the "analog," the bodily, is always already inscribed even in the heart of the most totalizing but illusory domination of the digital.

Games have a long history of being bound up with developments in HCI (human–computer interface) design, including the translation of analog to digital (and back again). Most modern game controllers, for example, vibrate and make sounds in response to the digital display, thus reconverting the digital back into an "analog" experience in the body. Interface always looks two ways at once. Think of the mouse, invented by Douglas Englebart in 1964 as a small wooden box with metal wheels underneath: like the Prince rolling his katamari, the user literally rolls the mouse around an empty surface that corresponds metaphorically to the digital display. Using a mouse, you *roll over* stuff—icons or buttons or text or windows on the virtual "desktop," traversing the imaginary topography of the screen by rolling physically over a material, literal desktop. Thus you don't so much convert one into the other as link analog and digital in a feedback loop, and this is all the more the case when it comes to game controllers and interfaces.

*Katamari Damacy* begins in a sophisticated self-conscious understanding of the interesting material relation of digital processing and display with various kinds of input—including the blatantly analog or physical input of pushing thumbsticks. But the game only begins there. *Katamari Damacy*'s meaning lies in its implicit parody of the idealization of such activity, its parody of the sense that gameplay must, in order to count as significant, conceal more abstract latent meanings ("a change in being itself"), meanings metaphorically "deeper" than the self-evident "surface" fun of magpie collecting.

Almost every video game, across genres, involves collecting things of one kind or another: tools, weapons, keys, armor, clothing, magical objects, creatures, health points or packets (and ultimately lives), experience points, currency (scrip, gold, jewels, shells), not to mention the more obvious numerical scores. Inventory is one of the key measures of progress or status in a game, as well as a fundamental step toward overcoming obstacles and achieving goals within rules-based environments. In classic adventure games, you collect mostly tools to enable you to do certain things later on in gameplay, a key that will eventually allow you to open a grate in a tunnel, a slingshot or sword that will allow you to fight a demon, or a lantern that will allow you to find your way in the dark. In some games, you collect jewels or coins in order to purchase these kinds of tools, or markers of increased power, various weapons or ammunition or health points. In *Katamari Damacy*, by contrast, the objects themselves are instantly converted to fodder for scaling up the rolling katamari. Still, as in a good number of games, in this game what one collects is accessible as inventory, a "Cool Collection" arranged in the rows and columns of arrays (or in the sequel, *We Love Katamari*, in katamari-shaped radiant wheels) with data attached, viewable according to the fields of object type, location, size, name, or picture, so many "snack" items, say, or "people," or "plants," or "Japanese culture," and the percentage of each category in one's database. The visual tabular array itself is accessible at any stage, with placeholder question marks for kinds of objects for which one has no instances—empty sets. Browsing the database of objects in one's collections feels especially integral to gameplay when the gameplay is all about collecting in the first place. The formal transition from the chaos of the katamari—in which individual objects are only imperfectly distinguishable from the rolling, twitching mass of dada incongruity—to the constellations in the cosmos, ancient symbols of the human imposition of meaning on chaos, is simultaneously a transition into an ordered database: neatly arranged columns and rows of the Cool Collection, where all that stuff gets sorted, classified, counted, and statistically accounted for (even after being converted to stars, it is accessible as this collection of discrete objects), which only enhances the sense that collecting is meaningful in itself—if you make it meaningful. *Katamari Damacy* collections look and feel like database arrays with no serious purpose beyond themselves, or better yet, like tabular web-page collections on eBay.

## eBay and emergent collecting

Collecting on eBay, which author William Gibson has called "basically, just a whole bunch of *stuff*,"[11] is a significant analogue for the experience of playing *Katamari Damacy*. A number of scholars in recent years have looked at the cultural significance of eBay, including, for example, how its auctions allow for the selling not just of objects but also of "memorable experiences."[12] The buyer's pleasure often comes not exclusively from acquiring objects but "from closer association with the channels of desire urging its acquisition" (Hillis et al., 2). eBay itself markets the idea of dedicated collecting as the heart of the site's culture, even exaggerating the statistical importance of such fan behavior, according to Mary Desjardins.[13] Interestingly enough, Desjardins considers traditional media fan cultures and concludes that the "ephemeral temporal structure" of eBay bidding and its "competitive set of interactions and transactions work against some of the constituent elements of fan culture" (33). I would suggest, however, that this is not the case if we consider game culture, where timed and competitive "interactions and transactions," what might be called acts of "emergent collecting," are the norm. The resemblances of eBay collecting and gameplay are highly significant. A game such as *Katamari Damacy* merely exaggerates the connection, but it is with good reason that competitive, timed bidding at online auctions resembles the sort of gambling (which also often involves bidding) one normally refers to as "gaming."

Especially on eBay, as Desjardins points out, where an apparently infinite and ever-renewed field of play is open to the collector, collectors "express their desires for material objects serially," or we might say continuing to "roll over" and aggregate one object (copy, instance, variation, edition) after another (31). But, the logic driving their collecting is not usually completist, however much it may appear as such to outside observers. What is at work is more often a series of emergent reactions to what appears online, creating an "indefinite" or open-ended "seriality," a constantly deferred completion of the series, "since completion would mean a kind of death" (37–8).

This view of eBay culture connects collecting to the logic of fetishism and the fetishism of the commodity as Marx first described it. And the figure who most thoroughly explored this connection in the history of commodity culture and popular entertainment is Walter Benjamin. His famous unfinished *Arcades Project* sketched a picture of great detail of the covered malls of nineteenth-century Paris as resonant symbolic embodiments of capitalism and modernity in general. Besides displays of goods for sale, the entertainments in the arcades included panoramas, dioramas, and other precursors to video games. Benjamin offers game theory some historical analogues in his views on the "shock" effects of modern entertainments, on the decontextualized nature of capitalism's fetishized objects always being added to the great heap of commodity culture, and his grasp of the dynamic nature of modern experience—exemplified most famously in his view of the *flâneur*, the aimless stroller, as a kind of nexus of all this stimulation and representative of the subject-position it helps to construct. The figure of the strolling *flâneur*, moving along the maze-like arcades past accumulated and surreally juxtaposed collections of fetishized objects, is, when you think about it, an extremely gamelike figure, an image of what we might call a first-person-consumer game, a game of endlessly stimulated and deferred desires.

This collecting of decontexualized objects in the arcades Benjamin sees as in contradiction to an older form of connoisseurship, a contradiction he confronts in a famous essay on book collecting, "Unpacking My Library."[14] In the latter case, he says, "The most profound enchantment for the collector is the locking of individual items within a magic circle in which they are fixed as the final thrill, the thrill of acquisition, passes over them" (60). The possession of an object is rendered pleasurable because one possesses the aura of the history of the object along with it: "for a true collector the whole background of an item adds up to a magic encyclopedia whose quintessence is the fate of his object"

(60). But this kind of collector, Benjamin admits with wry wistfulness, is probably going extinct in the late industrial era in which he writes: "time is running out" for the type. The arcades of the previous era, the nineteenth century, had foreshadowed the future of collecting (a type already starting to dominate Benjamin's present moment): a panoramic and surreal series of jarring juxtapositions, an endlessly flowing stream of decontexualized objects as commodities, rolling along, separated from their use value and made available in the arcade of the modern marketplace. In this new regime collecting is exemplified in shopping, even that kind of virtual shopping known as window shopping, strolling along the arcades of today (the malls) glomming onto whatever one sees, one thing after another.

Can Benjamin's view of the Paris arcades usefully be juxtaposed, by way of historical analogy, with the phantasmagoria of video arcades—or, rather, the persistence of the cultural image of the video arcade even in today's more dispersed-platform *gameplay* environment? The game of collecting is one instance of games in general (and is like *Katamari Damacy* in particular). Interestingly enough, Benjamin's term for the space of collecting, the "magic circle," is the same metaphor applied by Johan Huizinga in *Homo Ludens* to describe the space of play: in this case the "magic circle" of voluntary submission to the rules of a space not part of real life but "a temporary sphere of activity with a disposition all its own," the gameworld.[15] In this context it's easy to read *Katamari Damacy* as a very late (and accidental, unintentional) parodic commentary on Benjamin's kind of troubled contradiction when it comes to cultural collecting, a commentary that in true punk fashion plunges into the midst of the contradiction with a shrug: his "magic circle" becoming the Prince's rolling ball of stuff; his "magic encyclopedia" becoming the radically atomized database of the game's Cool Collections—only thinly veiled with the transparently constructed significances of the constellations in the night sky of the cosmos. The little Prince, in fact, is an apt emblem for our own era of the *flâneur*: not a distanced and dandified aesthete (that sounds more like his vain father, the King), but an energized game player with a lot of ground to cover and a lot of stuff to collect. The *flâneur* has in our own time been replaced not by the passive consumer but by the active, meaning-making, culture collector whose epitome is the game fan.

### Lucky Wander Boy and otaku collecting

In D. B. Weiss's 2003 novel *Lucky Wander Boy*, the game-company cubicle-worker antihero Adam Pennyman is obsessed with the (fictional) classic arcade-era video game of the title, which is creator associated with Nintendo classics, obvious precursors to *Katamari Damacy*.[16] Adam sets out in his spare time to write his own "magic encyclopedia" of classic arcade-era video games, a collection of arcane game lore, the *Catalogue of Obsolete Entertainments*, on games such as *Pac-Man, Donkey Kong, Super Mario Bros*, and *Frogger*. Like the emulators that allow people to play old arcade games on their PCs, Pennyman's reference work is a nostalgia machine and an act of fanboy devotion. By definition, it takes itself too seriously in its immersion in geeky arcane lore. But Weiss makes it clear that such fan collecting overlaps in significant ways with more respectable scholarly activities: research, sorting, cataloguing, interpreting and reinterpreting. It makes perfect sense, therefore, that the obsessive Adam Pennyman once began but never finished an undergraduate thesis on symbolism in the obscure sadomasochistic Chinese novella, *Leng Tch'e*. Fandom and pedantry are just two phases of the same obsessive collecting and interpreting behaviors. Adam is an almost Talmudic scholar of games, collecting every possible fact about their platform, manufacturer, processor, screen resolution, and top scores, as well as thematic and symbolic readings of them. He is compelled to discover and reveal latent rather than manifest meanings. In one *Catalogue* entry he interprets "the Pac-Man's insatiable hunger" for Power Pills in its mazes allegorically: "we are reminded of Marx's 'need of a constantly expanding market' that 'chases the bourgeoisie over the entire surface of the globe' (*Communist Manifesto*) with the 'vocation to approach, by quantitative increase, as near as possible to absolute wealth' (*Capital*)." These Marxist "metaphors" Pennyman first sees as "obvious," as "lurking just beneath the surface of the game" (6–7), but then, he abruptly decides, perhaps they are too obvious, too close to the surface to count as legitimate interpretations.

> These kinds of interpretations belie the poverty of imagination that has become all too typical of practitioners of the interpretive arts. If Pac-Man and the games that followed in its wake mean anything to us, if they are central switching stations through which thousands of our most important memories are routed, it is our duty to dig deeper. (7)

The imagined need to "dig deeper" into these artifacts of the entertainment culture is arguably Pennyman's downfall, as he pursues ever-more-profound metaphysical readings, traces of presence, driven like Thomas Pynchon's Oedipa Maas (in *The Crying of Lot 49*) to uncover conspiratorial intentions behind every flash of light on the screen or random programming glitch. His ultimate goal is transcendence in the space of pure desire, in the hidden realm "beneath the glass" of the garishly painted console. Eventually, the games literally "speak to him" with messages from other "levels" of existence.

As we quickly learn, Adam Pennyman is the classic unreliable narrator, who like his predecessors in Conrad or Nabokov, for example, is morally reprehensible (he treats human relationships as video games) and becomes increasingly unhinged as he delves deeper into his lore, running further away from his social failures. In the end, he may or may not actually travel to Osaka, Japan (there are multiple alternative endings) to attempt to complete Stage 3 of his favorite cult game, the fictional *Lucky Wander Boy*, in the office of its creator-auteur, Araka Itachi, a quest begun with an encounter at a gamers' convention with Tetsu Bush, a Japanese-American otaku-type (whom Adam reads as a samurai). An otaku is a culturally-specific instance of the fan phenomenon, something more specific than just "geek" but (very) roughly translatable into English as "fanboy." The word itself refers to the home, so may suggest someone who stays inside, and it connotes overly obsessive fandom, especially of manga (comics) and anime (animated films), as well as of games and game-related merchandise. The image of the otaku is loaded with special allure for some of their American fan equivalents, often based on a vague sense of the otaku's greater authenticity (since many desirable collectible objects are Japanese), and also because the very act of knowing about, of collecting otaku lore, is itself for an American an instance of global transactions in "multicultural capital," a competitive otaku-like behavior.[17] This is in keeping with William Gibson's characterization of the otaku as "the passionate obsessive, the information age's embodiment of the connoisseur, more concerned with the accumulation of data than of objects. . . ."[18] We might question Gibson's use of the term "connoisseur," here, remembering Walter Benjamin's discussion, since material objects in all their concrete, sensual realities and the aura thereby created, not merely knowledge of or data about them, have traditionally been the focus of connoisseurship, but his underlying point is sound: true collectors collect "data" or lore as much as they collect objects. The aura surrounding a desirable collectible is arguably, especially in today's culture, made up of information, history, knowledge, like the tag cloud of keyword labels produced by a community of users in a social-software environment and attached to a digital object online.

This focus on the accumulation of data, or specialized knowledge, is crucial for understanding game culture. It's what the large conventions like the one where Adam Pennyman meets Tetsu Bush are all about. In effect, knowledge of otaku knowledge becomes for Adam a kind of second-order collection. The legend of Nintendo, for example, is a driving force in Adam's personal mythology, in all its historical and cultural specificity, and he is clearly deeply interested in what he imagines as the company's pre-existing status among Japanese fans, making his a mythology of a mythology, an act of collecting what an imagined culture of specialized others has already deemed eminently collectible. This phenomenon is, of course, the basis of much actual commerce, from the electronics and games districts of Japanese cities (Tokyo's Akihabara being the most famous) to the place of Japanese games, manga, and anime in the global marketplace.[19] The best-known mainstream example in the West (besides perhaps *Hello Kitty*) is *Pokémon*, a game that was cannily marketed to a global audience as it was expanded into a whole universe of cultural objects and lore, driven by the quintessential collector's motto: "gotta catch 'em all!"[20] This global exchange is an integral part of game history, as Chris Kohler shows in his knowledge-filled account of Japanese games in America, *Power Up*. *Katamari Damacy* has been from the start a self-consciously transcultural product, a very knowing and late entry into the Japanese and American game culture that treats Nintendo, especially, and a pantheon of auteur game designers as romantic signifiers of a certain kind of rarefied geek/otaku transcultural experience. A recent example is the forthcoming *Dragon Quest Monsters Battle Road* for the Japanese arcade market, in which players first collect physical cards with monsters on them, like the *Pokémon* or *Yu-gi-oh* cards with which Americans are familiar, then load them into the arcade console slot to make them appear in the game.[21]

In fact, Japanese arcades are built around collecting of various kinds, and the things lying around the maps of *Katamari Damacy* resemble nothing so much as the collectible objects found in Japanese arcade prize machines, especially the capsule vending machines (*gashapon*) and skill-crane claws or "UFO catchers." As Chris Kohler points out, the name *gashapon* (or *gachapon*) is onomatopoeia; it derives from the sound made by the machines as you crank them: "gasha-gasha"—and the plopping sound of the capsule ("pon") as it drops into place. These are something like gumball machines in America but much more varied and with higher-quality prizes inside. The *gashapon* machines often fill whole floors of aracades and might specialize in, say, anime figurines; and "a few games—Capcom's fighting games like *Street Fighter*, Nintendo's *Mario* games, and the like—tend to inspire sets of *gashapon* as well" (200). The mechanism is different, but it's hard not to notice the basic resemblance between these machines and *Katamari Damacy*—how rolling (capsules, katamaris) in order to capture assorted prizes is central to both. With skill-crane machines or UFO catchers, collectors are even more directly targeted, and skill is involved in the act of collecting. The analogy to *Katamari Damacy* becomes even clearer when we realize that the prizes available in the Japanese machines are often sorted by category and there are series to be collected; a slip of paper inside the capsule often depicts the entire set to which the object belongs (Kohler, 201). These paper inserts are the data records in which the objects are literally wrapped. And the floors full of the machines are like physical versions of the levels of *Katamari Damacy*, littered with objects waiting to be captured and sorted. (The difference is that in the game they are randomly sorted and relatively un-described until they enter the player's Cool Collection.) In Japanese arcades, machines for collecting objects of various kinds stand alongside video games themselves, are just another coexisting form of game. Using a controller to move a UFO catcher crane into place in order to grab a box with a figurine or plush animal or a bagged snack-food item is a kind of visceral, haptic-feedback gameplay not far from using analog thumbsticks to roll a digital ball of stuff—and collecting is in both cases the motive and the essence of the gameplay, the fun.

This context of Japanese arcade machines, within which it is possible to understand collecting in *Katamari Damacy*, like the sometimes un-Western representations of nubile sexuality that are hinted at in the "Virgo" level and elsewhere, and like the somewhat more familiar aesthetic of *kawaisa* or "cuteness" of many of the objects themselves, are all attractive to the cult audience for the game in the West but are also likely to be misunderstood or mistranslated even by those who value their "foreignness." Just to name one example: *Katamari Damacy*'s apparently weird or surreal mixture of live animals, snacks, and toys and other objects is in fact perfectly normal inside the Japanese arcade, where UFO catchers may grab a plush toy, a plastic game-based figurine, a bag of chips, or—as one website reported complete with posted picture—a live lobster![22] It's hard not to see this as the inspiration for the crabs waving their claws around from within the katamari on the Cancer level of *Katamari Damacy*.

Weiss's *Lucky Wander Boy* is, among other things, a satire on the inevitable dislocations, decontextualizations and absurd mistranslations that result from this kind of global market in collectible lore—collecting culture and the culture of collecting—as American fans of Japanese-made games model their geek obsessions on stereotypes of the otaku, in effect making them one more thing to collect. Along the way, however, the novel also satirizes "the interpretive arts" in general as implicitly another form of obsessive collecting. Pennyman's Marxist reading of Namco's *Pac-Man* is, of course, a parody, and it would be too easy to simply apply it to *Katamari Damacy*—another game by Namco (now Namco Bandai), which appeared one year after Weiss's novel was published. Clearly the Prince *can* be read or interpreted as a sort of enslaved consumer, one who is compelled to labor to gather things so quickly that they are necessarily decontextualized, alienated from their use value and instantly—in a simple act of steamroller-like violence—conglomerated into a ball of fetishized commodities ready to be exchanged for status with the King and for the cosmic currency (and false consciousness) of the glittering stars. And so on. But to say all of that is to miss what is most compelling about playing the game, the joyful irony or ironic joy with which fans (and I include myself) play it. The game's finale is an apparently post-ironic celebration of global peace in which the credits roll against the backdrop of space as you roll up all the countries of the world. The Prince is no mere consumer or (as McKenzie Wark has it) Sisyphean slave-laborer; he is more like a fantasy of a royal otaku with cosmic effect (and, yes, father issues). He is a parodic version of the ultimate geek gamer, alienated, perhaps, suspicious of power, but gaming on in the midst of the jumble and noise of the mixed analog and digital arcade, the world full of things, ironically recognized as potential fetish objects but collected with a shrug and converted to meanings at the will of the player, in the end, the gamer, who controls the database and knows that the King is a buffoon.

Adam Pennyman's complaint about the limits of interpretation unwittingly reveals the serious interpretive possibilities in a case like *Katamari Damacy*, though of course they remain just out of the limited reach of his own obsessed point of view. He talks about the need to "dig deeper," for greater *depth* in interpretation, arguing at one point about his beloved games that it is "important that someone begin to peel back the layers of meaning beneath their colorful surfaces" (37), but it's significant that Adam actually justifies the importance of games using a metaphor of aggregate *surface* effects—the packet switching that is the heart of the Internet itself. He sees games as the "central switching stations through which . . . our most important memories are routed," as nodes in a network of transactional meanings and overlapping discourse fields. Those meanings take the form of collective histories ("*our most important memories*") in the arena of culture. The network *is* the aggregate of all the routes of transactional meaning-making, across cultures, subcultures, and levels of culture, the movement of countless "packets" of meaning, broken up, exchanged, and reunited, and replied to, over and over again, passing along the complex surface that is the sum of its parts—whether of the silicon-wafer or, scaling up, of fiber-optics and cables sheathing the globe. Indeed, elsewhere Weiss has Adam observe that "video games can traverse the entire range of imagined experience, and resonate effectively with the wider world of which they are a part" (17).

The important *meanings* of *Katamari Damacy* are right there on the surface, where the ever-rolling constructivist gameplay takes place, and the surface meaning of *Katamari Damacy* is all about collecting and sharing collections. This is not an allegory but an expression of a widespread mode of interaction with culture. It's not really even a metaphor—or anyway it's a procedural metaphor in which the tenor and vehicle are so closely connected they are almost identical; it's what you *do*, the gameplay itself. Just to play is to collect and, at the same time, is to perform collecting in a self-conscious arena of cartoonlike representation, is thus to parody collecting in today's culture, procedurally as much as semiotically. You perform the parody as play. The game itself is a node in the larger cultural network through which the meanings of collecting are defined, routed, and connected—often in unpredictable or whimsical ways, just like in the game. This kind of collecting is inherently an activity that points outside itself, outside the game itself, to "resonate effectively with the wider world," because it only truly has meaning in the context of a fanbase or other kind of community of like-minded collectors with stuff and knowledge to share and display.

At one point in *Lucky Wander Boy*, Adam Pennyman's rejected lover Clio (whose name invokes the muse of history), not only accuses him of being a "selfish monstrosity," she suggests he is not even a true geek, "because a *real* geek endeavor" such as actually completing the *Catalogue* "would involve thousands of hours of diligent geek labor," the kind of disciplined commitment Adam cannot make (232). In other words, Clio suggests, true geek appreciation is like a hacker's version of scholarly labor, a matter of collecting and sorting historical and material facts over "thousands of hours" (hours dedicated being the unit of measure for serious gameplay, as well), the sort of "labor" that is not Sisyphean because it is motivated by love (or obsession), fueled its own process rather than through enforcement by power or serious goals, whether hermeneutic depth interpretation or material acquisition. Geek collecting is ultimately knowledge collecting, a constructive process of multiple combinations and not a predetermined unitary product. In this it bears a remarkable resemblance to scholarship, including textual studies, book history, and scholarly editing.

## Unpacking Walter Benjamin's text

And this brings me back to texts, and to Walter Benjamin, who said in the *Arcades Project*: "Collecting is a primal phenomenon of study: the student collects knowledge" (210). He also noted suggestively at one point an alternative to the Freudian version of fetishistic collecting: "But compare collecting done by children!" (208). The tension between fetishistic commodified collecting and childlike or punk collecting, appropriative recombination, between connoisseurship and *gashapon*, is the cultural space from which a game like *Katamari Damacy* emerges, which rolls up everything in sight into its own great ball of anarchy; and it parallels the contradiction at the heart of the *Arcades Project* itself, not only in its content but also in its textual form and textual history.

Benjamin's unfinished magnum opus is itself, famously, nothing but a massive collection of quotations, observations, and descriptions, a kind of catalogue rather than a traditional argument.[23] Theodor Adorno's critique of the work centered on its unmediated, undialectical, near-"vulgar" materialism— that is, it was not rigorously Marxist enough in its theory—and it often seems that Benjamin could not stop himself from simply amassing and juxtaposing magically resonant objects from the culture, then rolling them up in his own "magic circles," and the spirits of surrealism and dada permeate the montage-like study in cultural history. Working in the Bibliothèque Nationale in Paris from 1927 to 1940, he collected copious notes on a kaleidoscopic array of topics centered on the cultural history of nineteenth-century Paris, organizing the manuscript into 36 lettered and numbered "Convolutes" (Adorno gave the fragments this name, taking it from the German *Konvolut* or "bundle"), linked by keywords. "Notes" does not do justice to the array of kinds of writing in the bundles, which included quotations from other works, epigraphs, as well as his own bits of commentary, readings of literary texts, observations on material culture, and descriptions of concrete historical objects and events. Concreteness in pursuit of the material substrata of modern history was Benjamin's stated goal. The manuscript fragments survived by being carried out of Nazi-occupied territory—when Benjamin did not. He committed suicide during what he thought was a thwarted attempt to cross the border into Spain. Edited and published posthumously, the *Arcades Project* is a book that never really existed for its author in a finished book-state.[24] A famous photo of Benjamin working in the library shows him writing in front of a cabinet of card-file drawers—the library catalogue that was the source of his own catalogue-like project. He once wrote that a scholarly work is meant to be "read like a catalogue," and asked: "when shall we actually write books like catalogues?" Elsewhere in the same work he asserts that "Everything that matters is to be found in the card box of the researcher who wrote it, and the scholar studying it assimilates it into his own card index."[25] Like a database, the project consists of discrete records at a level of granularity that presumably allowed the author to exercise his imaginative combinatorics, to act as a lifetime collector of fragments. But not only the author and not only in his lifetime. The *Arcades Project* is a book literally collected by readers, beginning with Adorno but reaching forward through a whole chain of modern textual-studies laborers.

In this, the eBay era, collecting stuff is a mundane global pastime. The cumulative effect of surfing the crest of those millions of auctioned fetish-objects often feels like rolling an ever-growing katamari across the surface of the culture and its material products. That's surely one reason playing *Katamari Damacy* comes so naturally to so many, compared to other console games: nothing is more fundamentally ludic than rolling a ball—unless, nowadays, it's gobbling up lots of cool stuff. As if to refute poor Adam Pennyman in *Lucky Wander Boy*, this game is all about surfaces rather than depths, literally about what sticks to the surface of your katamari as you roll it around, a strange *flâneur* on a mission. The King of All Cosmos can be read as a challenge to interpretation, a caricature of psychoanalytic interpretive impulses and the entertainments that bait them. At any rate, he is no serious threat to the fun.

The cutscenes that conclude levels in which you fail to meet the minimum size are hilariously exaggerated scenes of paternal verbal castration, with the "tiny" or "silly" Prince (your avatar) humiliated by the gigantic and oddly playboy-like, sexualized and capricious King. He is so literally larger than life he becomes goofy, Rabelaisian, a monstrous rockstar gamemaster exercising his whims. (In the second game in the series, we learn more than we really want to know about the King's own troubled childhood and his relationship with *his* father, the Emperor.) It's all too strange to take seriously, and players generally don't—even, in my experience, fairly young players. You can play with the back-story in mind but you have to acknowledge its arbitrariness; it's in the end a caricature of psychologically "deep" game back-stories, and it ends with the King's voice trailing off so you can get back to the ludic surface of the game, where the true punk fun is.

The crazy cosmic royal family romance is played out against the parallel story of a bourgeois human family of four, the Hoshino family, who begin by watching the game's events on TV, then travel to meet with their father, an astronaut. His mission has been canceled because the moon is missing, but they are all rolled up in a giant katamari and thus are united, intact, on the moon. One of them, the little boy, makes an appearance in the 2005 sequel, *We Love Katamari*, as a fan. In this sequel Takahashi playfully honored the fans by putting them into the game, even giving their avatars voices and some directorial control over the gameplay. They appear in the game as a metafictional group— or a paratexual group, really, derived from actual fan communications— cheering for the game and the King and expressing their desires to be more like him or their admiration for his beard (for example). The King even refers to them as his "fanbase." But they also show up in more individualized form, such as the boy from the first game, making requests of the King and thus of you (the Prince, or, if you like, one of his cousins) for specific kinds of katamari missions to be conducted on a variety of levels, underwater, in the snow, out in the woods (with the katamari as a fire), catching fireflies, and so on. This is like moving the first game's Internet message boards and fan forums inside the second game (rolling them up?), giving the fans, through their in-game avatars, a collective dramatic role in the game.

Besides paying tribute to real fans and their intentions for the gameplay design, this paratextual gesture also reminds us that *Katamari Damacy* is a game predicated on generating such fandom, on getting fans to collect *Katamari Damacy* itself (and its surrounding lore), making the game a kind of cool collectible or "otaku-bait." Takahasi clearly understands the collective and collecting tendencies of game-fan culture and—what is even more significant— the potentially constructive results of such otaku obsessiveness when it comes to an emerging game franchise. *Katamari Damacy* insists that such collecting can be more than mere consumerism, that it can also be fun. This kind of fun can be meaning-making while appearing to be childishly destructive, just as, playing the Prince, your rolling ball of destruction can actually put constellations of mythic meaning back into the night sky. Fan collecting is a self-generating and self-rewarding phenomenon that fans pursue defiantly, in the face of the devaluations of the high/low cultural divide and even of moral disapprobation, for the pleasures of making ephemeral connections, meanings at the surface level of everyday material existence, like punks making fashion out of the trash of culture. The work of Walter Benjamin anticipates this kind of pleasure as one side of a dialectical problem, the tension between depth and surface meanings in collecting culture, the attachment to the aura of objects *and* the fascination of their decontextualization in the marketplace. Benjamin remained deeply troubled by that tension, and mostly we have come to accept it as a given, so comparing his arcades with our own video game arcades may help us to understand key historical differences, differences that matter. It may also help us to appreciate the powerful appeal of cultural expressions such as *Katamari Damacy*, which so brilliantly and with such cartoonish wit embody the energies of fandom, its community-based drive to collect. Earth really is full of things. To a certain kind of game fan, this suggests a possibility space for punk-rock fun.

In May, 2006, it was as if the cartoon fans from *We Love Katamari* crossed back over the threshold into the real world, as some actual fans of the game paid it the ultimate geek compliment: they engaged in the otaku-like practice, common in Japan, of "cosplay" ("costume play"), dressing as the characters out in public. This was only one instance of many such cosplay tributes documented on the Internet; in this case, the purpose was also to play a live version of the game. Looking like the Prince and the King and the Queen and the cousins, they rolled a giant-sized cardboard katamari, decorated with site-specific objects along the way, in the San Francisco Bay to Breakers footrace. Significantly, their costumes and katamari were made, like all katamaris, from found objects, carpet padding and refrigerator boxes,and so on. Photosets of their performance were posted and widely reported on blogs.

Cosplay like this is of a piece with the kind of otaku-baiting reception that the game itself had seemed to call for, to have generated from within its structures from the very start. *Katamari Damacy* produced its own otaku-like fanbase because it so deftly represented the fundamental cultural element of that fanbase in potential. Like textual scholars, fans are experts at making meanings out of what they collect, navigators of the material conditions, surviving objects, and chance discoveries that determine the combinatorics by which meaningful "texts"—or whole constellations of texts—can be made and remade over and over again.

*Figure 2.1   Katamari Damacy* cosplay during Bay to Breakers race, 2006. Photograph by Kathryn Hill, used by permission of Kathryn Hill.

*Katamari Damacy* is a cult hit, unusual in many ways. In the next chapter we'll look at another example, a more mainstream video game about the cosmos and a threat to the stars, an FPS (first-person shooter) in which you move around collecting ammo and weapons and vehicles—and kills. Otherwise, it has little else in common with the world of the Prince and his katamaris. *Halo* is designed to induce sublime paranoia rather than punk playfulness. It's sublimely cinematic rather than cartoonlike. It's all about shooting aliens rather than collecting earthly stuff. But there are some shared conventions, nonetheless, between these two games—and, significantly, when it comes to their modes of production and reception, the construction of their meanings in social contexts. Though in a different way from *Katamari Damacy*, the *Halo* games (and especially *Halo 2*) were also created and marketed by tapping into the constructive energies of the existing and potential fanbase, treating players as creators of the universe within which the game multiplies its possible meanings.

# Chapter 3

# The *Halo* universe

What constitutes the "universe" of a video game? Technically, the term usually refers to the story and back-story and imaginary settings, even across different works in a consistently imagined franchise. But who gets to decide on its exact boundaries? You might think it's the "authors" of the game, the development and design team, including especially those initial designers often known as the creators; or perhaps it's the specialist writers in charge of the game's story, or the novelists who license paperback fiction telling the back-story; or the scriptwriters and directors for film adaptations. In practice, the universe of any successful game (by which I mean any game with fans) is more than its scripted story: it's the amorphous and always shifting, contested space within which the game is given meaning, and this space includes broader paratextual events as well as actual formal gameplay. By convention, fans may debate the details of the story, but they usually look to a game's creators for rulings on what counts as "story canon." Some development teams create and keep what they call a "story bible" or set of storyboards, at least, which contains the larger story arc of a trilogy of games, for example, including the necessary facts about the gameworld(s): timelines, histories, multiple alien races, genealogies or family trees, locations in planetary space. Nevertheless, almost any successful game exists in a system of many worlds, only some of which are strictly story-worlds but all of which, I would argue, add to the sum total of the game's universe. Some are created by fans, some by hired comic-book artists or writers or filmmakers, and some set in motion by marketers, and not always in perfect concert with the intentions of the official creators of the game. When you think about it, the very term canon implies its opposite, implies a need for policing the universe. If there is official story canon, then there is likely to be unofficial apocrypha, sectarian dispute, Gnostic reinterpretation—and at the outer reaches, fan fiction and slash fiction, mashups and parodies—all of which may be imagined as numerous other small planets or satellites or artificial worlds orbiting along in the collectively cobbled-together universe that contains but is not entirely coextensive with that smaller subset of orderly authorial stories and characters, designs of maps and objects, not to mention the rules and formal constraints on potential gameplay events that are sometimes naively referred to as "the game itself."

Consider Microsoft and Bungie Studio's blockbuster hit *Halo*, which debuted in 2001 and as I write this exists as two science-fiction FPS (first-person shooter) games for PC (and Mac) as well as Xbox and Xbox Live, with a third game on the way for Xbox 360, and a fourth game planned outside the main trilogy, an RTS (real-time strategy)game called *Halo Wars*. In addition, there are special editions of the games, including, for example, one custom edition that allows players to add their own mods from a special editing kit, and a special booklet with a more detailed back-story. Console versions have been ported to PC (and the series began as a Mac and PC game recreated for Xbox), with separate companies hired to do the porting (the results can be seen in the multiple logos in the opening credits). There is a series of novels narrating the canonical story, there are official graphic novels and at least one book of artwork for the games, and there may or may not be a film. Outside the official circle of what the game creators, Bungie Studios, and their parent company, Microsoft, recognize as canon there are many, many objects and discourses circling in erratic and expanding orbits. Consider the by now well-known animated "machinima" films, *Warthog Jump* and *Red vs. Blue*, for example, made inside the gameworld using the *Halo* game engine with voiceovers. Or, an even more pertinent example, the fan-created 2-D side-scroller game, *Halo Zero*, with sprites who move against backgrounds. Clearly non-canonical (it fills in a part of the story of the battle taking place on the planet Reach, a prequel to the first official *Halo* game), it was nevertheless an extremely popular free download after it was released in December 2005.[1] The list could go on and on. At the very least we have to say that the borders of the *Halo* universe are always being re-negotiated by its creators and its fans.

At the center of the universe, however, there are the video games themselves, starting with the first, *Halo: Combat Evolved* (2001), set amidst an interstellar war in the year 2552. Someone unfamiliar with the game, watching the screen, would notice brightly colored shiny carapaces of armored fighters (of various species) scrambling over wreckage or driving fast or flying through sublime and eerie science-fiction landscapes, and (of course) shooting at one another with exotic weapons, with the indicators of the HUD (heads-up display) on the screen and the first-person gun looming in the player's immediate foreground. But, even leaving aside any question of story (who are these fighters? where are they? what are they fighting for?), the colorful combat scenario would only be part of a larger story, and the story would only be one part of the complex array of possibilities surrounding and incorporating those armor-clad fighters (and the trajectories of their crossfire), which is what makes *Halo* both popular and a lasting franchise. But how should we talk about what Gerard Genette might refer to as the paratext of a massive hit such as *Halo*, that cloud of extra media objects swirling around the game, without just using it as an excuse to avoid talking about the game itself, the action on the screen? That's precisely the interesting problem that game studies should address, it seems to me. What *is* the specific nature of the relationship between the formal game and its expanding universe, as defined by both the game's creators and its fans? That's surely what's involved in the reception of the game. That's where we begin to get at the *meaning* of a game like *Halo*, and it is the focus of this chapter.

## The continuity of Cortana

First, a little of the *Halo* story, by way of a bit of marketing, the trailer for *Halo 3*. Early in 2007 it appeared in traditional media outlets, and from there was posted and linked to from official and unofficial websites, transcribed and discussed and dissected on multiple wikis. (At the time I am writing this, the third game has not yet been released.) The trailer opens with a piano chord, then fades in to an image of a ravaged Earth landscape as the music builds. A degraded, skippy video image flashes across the screen, a stylized female figure speaking in an electronically distorted voice, which fans of the game will recognize as the AI (artificial intelligence) construct, Cortana. "I have defied gods and demons," she burbles, as the transmission is interrupted. Then, "I am your shield; I am your sword—" and the cybernetic supersoldier, the Master Chief, appears in his battered metallic green armor with reflective visor, swinging a large gun into position. Then Cortana again: "I know you, your past, your future," and the scene speeds up, airships fly by in a huge lightning storm, the music builds, and the camera pulls back to reveal the Master Chief standing alone on a giant cliff like an epic hero, or like the Romantic figure in a sublime painting by Casper David Friedrich. A flash shoots up out of a strange giant object down in the desert and in the blackout that follows Cortana intones "This . . . is the way the world ends" as the *Halo 3* logo appears. That last is a line from T. S. Eliot's "The Hollow Men" ("Not with a bang but a whimper"), and in context it could mean "this is the way the trilogy concludes," but the point of the clip is as much visual as intertextual: Cortana and Master Chief are superimposed again. Only now (as we know from the previous game) they are physically separated; she is being held by the Gravemind. The third game, the trailer suggests, will be about reconnecting them.

The close relationship between the two has been at the heart of the *Halo* core story from the start. She's a shipboard AI who enters the fray, manifest in

*Figure 3.1   Halo: Combat Evolved* screenshot: the AI Cortana, cybernetic supersoldier
Master Chief, and human Captain Keyes on the bridge of the *Pillar of Autumn*.

a purple holographic projection of a diminutive manga-style female. He's an oversized, genetically engineered cybernetic supersoldier, a weapon-wielding avatar. Their combination is a sort of dual personification of the underlying structure of *Halo* and other games of this type. The first mission in campaign mode of the first game, *Halo: Combat Evolved*, really begins when she is pulled from the ship's controls and slotted on a cartridge into the back of the neck of his armor. The first real single-player mission of the *Halo* series is for you (playing as Master Chief) to get Cortana safely into a lifeboat and off the starship, the *Pillar of Autumn* (which is under attack by Covenant forces), and fly down to the surface of Halo, a giant artificial world in the shape of a ring, a little like a massive space station orbiting a gas giant. If the enemy aliens capture her, the captain warns, "they'll learn everything" and Earth will be endangered. After she joins Master Chief (you) in a cutscene on the bridge, the two characters engage in some comic dialogue and then your mission begins with the motto: "AI Constructs and Cyborgs First!"

As the dedicated *Halo* wiki suggests, Cortana may have been inspired by the fairy Morgana in the legend of the hero Charlemagne (hence "I am your shield;

I am your sword") (http://halowiki.net). In the larger back-story of *Halo*, as told in novels such as Eric Nylund's *Halo: The Fall of Reach* (2001), she was created out of the cloned brain of the troubled scientist behind the UNSC (United Nations Space Command's) SPARTAN-II program, the origin of Master Chief and others like him, Dr. Catherine Halsey. Halsey served as a kind of surrogate mother-figure to the young Master Chief as he was being formed, and her AI "avatar" (in another, more literal sense than in most game situations), Cortana, is therefore a complex and ambiguous character in relation to the Master Chief, one who may even be headed for "rampancy," a kind of rogue leap into AI autonomy and insanity. She fights alongside Master Chief in the first two games, ultimately helping to destroy the Halo ring-world before it destroys all sentient life in the galaxy, and outwitting another AI, the mysterious rogue 343 Guilty Spark. *Halo 2* ends with a cliffhanger, revealing that Cortana has been separated from Master Chief, detained by the Gravemind creature, which is hosting the parasitic lifeform known as The Flood.

Notice that my explanation has had recourse to a dedicated wiki, the series of novels, and the trailer for the third game, not to mention actual gameplay. Only some portion of that story, probably only uncertain fragments of Cortana's role, can be gathered from the gameplay itself, and then only by an

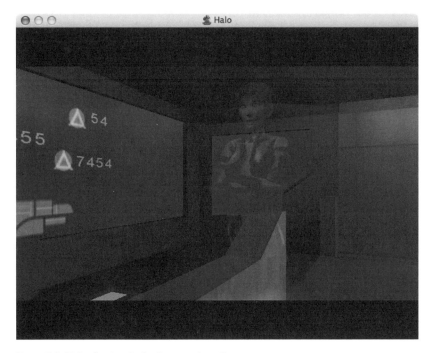

*Figure 3.2  Halo: Combat Evolved screenshot: Cortana.*

assiduous player who played both games through to the end and has stayed with the franchise for years. Even then, he or she would not be able to discern the complete story of Cortana and Master Chief from the sometimes ambiguously depicted situations of gameplay and cutscenes alone. This participant-observer's account of the role of the story in gameplay describes many players' typical experience: "Trying to follow the story of *Halo 2* amidst all the action is akin to trying to read *Moby Dick* while sticking your head out of a car driving 75 miles per hour." You have to try to understand the rules, make sense of the gameworld, and test various strategies for achieving your goals, all while playing (navigating, shooting, and being shot at). The "grand theme" of the "narrative," according to this player, is "washed away" as you become absorbed in the "interactive trial and error," the looped routines of gameplay.[2]

In a moment I'll turn to that actual gameplay, the "interactive trial and error" (not to mention the increasingly common social interaction) that makes up most sessions of actually holding the controller (or mouse) and playing *Halo*. But first, I want to stick with the story and its "grand themes[s]" for a bit, because I think it *does* matter to gameplay, even if any individual player, like the one quoted above, is more or less unconscious of some part (or most) of the story while playing. Player and fan intelligence is by its nature modular and distributed, at its best when it is collective. A notion of the ideal collective audience for a game franchise such as *Halo* is built into, self-reflexively present in, the game and its expanding universe. The dual personification of the Master Chief and Cortana figures the essence of the game: the improvised interplay (and tension) between action and intelligence.

NPCs (programmed non-player characters) that serve as companion or helper figures like Cortana are common in action RPGs (role-playing games). Midna in *The Legend of Zelda: Twilight Princess*, for example, is another small "onboard" helper with special knowledge of the story and maps who provides tips and encouragement. Midna literally rides on Link's (the player avtar's) back when he is in wolf form and in turn resembles the 1-inch tall artist, Issun, in another game with a wolf avatar, Capcom's *Okami* (and Issun is later revealed to be the primary narrator of the game). Both are clearly descendants of Navi in a previous *Zelda* game, *The Ocarina of Time*, whose name suggests "navigator" and who looks like a blue fairy (not unlike some manifestations of Cortana). It's possible (though perhaps not all that helpful in the end) to expand the type into other forms of story to include, very loosely, *Peter Pan*'s Tinkerbell, for example, or the animal-form "daemons" of Phillip Pullman's *His Dark Materials* series of novels. Cortana, however, is explicitly an artificial intelligence, a kind of diegetic, in-game helper, and she is thus implicitly a metaphorical figure, a personification of both the authorial intelligence behind the gameworld and the literal AI programming code that runs the NPCs and other features of the environment in *Halo*. Cortana is an important reminder of that something else—the supplemental intelligence, broadly defined—that makes interesting (by adding meaning to) the combat maneuvers of anyone who plays as the Master Chief, or another soldier, or member of an alien species.

Compare the conventional role of the HUD, which, like the helper NPC, also conveys to the player helpful or necessary information about the game in progress. Some combination of icons and numbers on the screen, showing health and ammunition levels and so on, is conventional across a wide variety of games; in *Halo*, as in some other first-person games, the fictional device of a helmet-mounted display allows the information to be at once outside the fictional gameworld and inside it, part of the user interface that is also diegetic, in the narrative, because it is shown on the inside of the visor of your character (Master Chief, for example), who sees the same display that you, the player, see. Arrows appear to point to advancing enemies, who also show up as dots on the radar, crosshairs help you aim, levels of ammunition and health are indicated, you see the status of your defensive shield. In *Halo 2* the health status bar is removed, but most of the rest of the display remains constant. In a boon to makers of machinima films, picking up a certain skull in *Halo 2* makes the HUD invisible during campaign mode, so a director can get cleaner screens for filming. Some see the traditional display, a kind of screen between player and gameworld, as a distraction hampering immersion or the suspension of disbelief, but it seems to me it is an essential part of the particular kind of engagement (not immersion) a gamer experiences, as opposed to a theatergoer, for example, a reminder that gameplay is in the foreground, literally and figuratively, of his or her experience.

The *Halo* HUD, because it is fictionally part of the Master Chief's armor and part of his point of view, while also providing the player with information on the ongoing gameplay, refuses to be placed entirely inside or entirely outside the fictional gameworld. The same is true for a helper-NPC such as Cortana. Though she might seem more firmly embedded in the fiction of the gameworld, because she's written into its primary story arc, so is the helmet of the MJOLNIR armor written into the sort of the SPARTAN-II project. Cortana, too, is pretty transparently "artificial" in her role as the AI conveyer of special "intelligence" about the game. She offers intelligence in the military or espionage sense of the term, mission-critical semi-secret data and point of view. Cortana's presence onboard your player-character, her voice inside your head, is the internalized voice of the game itself, as it were, reporting things detected before you can sense them, recommending action, warning and reminding you, speaking from knowledge of a larger slice of the game's universe than you can know during any given instance of gameplay. As she says in the *Halo 3* trailer, she really is your shield and your sword.

Many of the portentous recitations in that trailer, including the T. S. Eliot line, are self-quotations of the very earliest appearance of Cortana, as the unknown writer of email "letters" sent out in 1999 to fans of an earlier game by Bungie, *Marathon*, posted to a prominent fansite.[3] (The Eliot line was deliberately changed in the letters to "this is *not* the way. . . .") It's now known that a Bungie employee wrote the letters under the name of Cortana in order to create a sense of mysterious anticipation, to generate buzz about the as-yet-to-be-released *Halo*. He responded in character to challenges from some fans, quoted William Blake, and made oblique references to alien invasion: "The fear of not being the only sentient species in the universe was forgotten in the giddy excitement of a new era for humanity. No one was prepared for their arrival." Bungie has since cautioned that the letters were written before *Halo* was finished and that their content should not be taken as canon. But by returning to and quoting from them for announcing *Halo 3*, they have apparently connected the earliest thread of Cortana's story with the final installment in the main trilogy, at least suggesting that the Cortana character, and the whole idea of the AI as a threshold character, is central to *Halo*, whether considered as a saga or as a franchise.

## "This medium will metastasize"

The Cortana Letters were in effect an early version of viral marketing, were on their way to being an example of what have come to be called ARGs (alternate reality games), like *The Lost Experience* discussed in Chapter 1. Like a virus, such campaigns use an existing networked community—usually an existing fanbase, whether for a TV show like *Lost* or, in this case, for the game *Marathon*—to spread a message generating interest in a new product. The basic idea of viral marketing—to exploit the social energies in existing communities of interest, was also behind the fad for flash mobs in the early 2000s, when groups of spontaneously assembled people (one might as well call them players) showed up in a public place at the same time, a mall or city square or the atrium of a skyscraper, in response to networked communication via cellphones, web pages, and e-mail. Sometimes there was a topical or political occasion for the mob, but in most cases the gathering itself, a kind of acting out of artificial life and species-evolution games, *was* the event, and the media event was the halo of interest and documentation surrounding the mob meeting. The Cortana Letters attempted to generate some of the same kind of attention and spontaneous excitement, but they took the form of a textual mystery to be solved, a back-story to the back-story, a game played on the web. Admittedly, this remained in crude form: the textual fragments never really resolved into more than a handful of themes (among them, alien invasion and the complications of an AI becoming sentient) that foreshadowed the story of *Halo: Combat Evolved*.

The next time around, the game development company Bungie had been for some time fully ensconced in the headquarters of their new parent company, Microsoft, and the viral marketing campaign for the sequel to *Halo* was raised to an entirely new level. In the summer of 2004 theatrical trailers for the then forthcoming *Halo 2* concluded with a logo for Microsoft's Xbox including, running below it in a smaller font, an URL (xbox.com) that, just for a second, flickered, warped, and morphed into another address: ilovebees.com. For alert viewers who noticed it flickering on the screen (or saw it reproduced by fans soon after on the web), the second URL was a mysterious first clue, hidden in plain sight. It led to what looked like an amateur-designed small-business website ("Margaret's Honey"). This site turned out to contain the fictional beginnings of a cross-platform or transmedia game that at first refused to give away the fact that it *was* a game. This was an ARG for marketing *Halo 2* in advance and called *I Love Bees*, a sprawling game deliberately designed to bleed over into the real world.[4] To many alert viewers the game would have revealed itself to be a viral marketing campaign for the video game (its initial clue did after all appear in the Xbox trailer for the game), but it remained effective at generating attention, including press about itself. A game on this scale had first been used successfully in *The Beast*, an ARG created as part of a 2001 advertising campaign for, interestingly enough, Steven Spielberg's movie, *A.I. I Love Bees* was the product of the same innovative advertising and gaming group behind *The Beast*, 42 Entertainment, though no one knew that for sure at the time. As all successful viruses do, *I Love Bees* quickly took on a life of its own and spread throughout its host, the web and the social networks behind it, as its fictional website spawned wikis and blogs and specialized groups of players following the unfolding story of a mysteriously menaced webmaster, Dana, for her aunt's honey business site.

The website soon began to erode, defaced by what looked like a hacker attack using a computer virus, but by decoding what was there and comparing hints posted on other sites (including Dana's own blog), players could gradually discover clues, including eventually over 200 GPS coordinates for real-world locations. Over time, the players collectively determined that these were locations of payphones all over the U.S. There, on set dates, they could take phone calls at these locations, speaking live with fictional player-characters delivering what were in effect individual fragments of a distributed drama, sometimes winding up with their pictures on the web, but at any rate finding themselves inside the game in a vivid way. Legendary examples included a fan's taking a call from a public telephone booth in Florida during a raging hurricane, and a group of players holding up an "I love bees" sign, an image that

*Figure 3.3  I Love Bees Web page (www.ilovebees.com).*

made it into mainstream news reports, during a campaign event of the fall 2004 presidential election. Completed phone calls caused new MP3 audio tracks to be posted on the game's website, like the disordered and distributed fragments of a lost radio play. (Orson Welles's 1938 radio adaptation of H. G. Wells's 1898 science-fiction classic *The War of The Worlds*, which was also about an alien invasion and also worked by crossing fiction with reality, is an ancestor of *I Love Bees*.) Pieced together through the editorial work of the fan/player community, the fragments added up to a coherent six-hour audio drama, a story running in parallel as it were with the back-story of *Halo 2*. It involved alien invasions and an AI named Melissa, who was created from the cloned brain of Yasmine Zaman, a member of another iteration of the same SPAR-TAN-II program that created cyborg supersoldier Master Chief and his AI companion, Cortana. Like Cortana, Melissa was a shipboard AI; she was herself corrupted by another viral program, then was blown apart in an explosion that sent the fragmented pieces of her intelligence, including the viral addition, like multiple personalities, traveling through time, coming to rest on—of all places—the Margaret's Honey website server, from which platform the AI began to broadcast cryptic messages. Melissa's fragmented parts played different characters in different voices in the ARG materials. The story was attached by several tentacles to the main back-story of the *Halo* games but focused in part on Earth in the twenty-first-century present (there was also a plotline that takes place in the future) and was self-consciously about the problem of frag-mented bits of meaning that needed to be reassembled in order to reveal an overarching narrative meaning. Which is, of course, how the ARG itself was to be played.

The fictional story of *I Love Bees* was distributed across and in a real sense took place on actual networks, on websites, including the fan-created ones, and out in the phone booths and public locations via GPS coordinates. The game-universe of *I Love Bees* was the real world, re-imagined in an act of collective make-believe to incorporate—and thus make more real—the co-extensive fictional universe of *Halo*. The ARG extended the universe of *Halo*, demonstrated that it was infinitely extensible, in a way that neither the narrative alone nor the gameplay alone ever could have accomplished. The effort required of its players resembled nothing so much as the collaborative, distributed labor of putting together a scholarly edition, discovering, assembling, and sorting the relationship of disparate texts, annotating, interpreting, making them into a coherent, meaningful whole, a model of the work in question. Or perhaps the collective effort of playing a cooperative-mode game.

The endgame of the ARG closed the circuit and reconnected it to the video game. It rewarded the successful players of *I Love Bees* (and some additional gamers) with the opportunity for what it mysteriously called "combat training" at one of four real-world locations. This turned out to be a chance to be among the first to play a pre-release version of *Halo 2*, but also to come together in one place as a community. All of this happened before the video game itself even appeared on the market on November 9, 2004, when fans lined up overnight in great numbers to purchase their copies, helping to drive sales to a record $125 million (reportedly nearly twice the box office take for the hit film *Lord of the Rings: Return of the King*).[5]

A phenomenon such as *I Love Bees* might seem at first to derive from the kind of deliberately oblique or ironic strategy of marketing seen everywhere in the tech-boom years of the late 1990s, in which ads avoided direct reference to the product and instead produced a series of affective associations, involving participants in the company's demographic targeting while offering them the illusion that they were maintaining a cool resistance to the product tie-in. Even once the connection was made, oblique ads gave the consumer enough ironic distance to make participating (and buying) seem reasonably cool. These ads still usually appeared in print or TV or other traditional media, though some experimented with the web. In most cases, however, they were still following the traditional top-down broadcast model, targeting a particular kind of consumer with emotionally manipulative content. In recent years, a different model of marketing has emerged by taking careful note of how fan culture already works. Henry Jenkins has cited TV shows such as *Survivor* and *American Idol*, linked closely to the fan communities they foster and to whom they advertise, as examples of this new model, harnessing the energy of what

Pierre Lévy calls "collective intelligence" towards the "mutual production and reciprocal exchange of knowledge."[6] In this model, fans form communities that in effect collectively co-produce what they also consume as entertainment, along the way accepting various linked forms of marketing as part of the deal. According to the lead designer behind the ARG, Jane McGonigal, even the plot-points of the story of *I Love Bees*, not to mention numerous smaller details, were altered on the fly in response to gameplay moves on the part of the player community, a true circuit in Lévy's and Jenkins' sense, and one created by canny designers and writers with a sense of how to stage a flash-mob-like happening, and an experienced-based sense of how to serve as hidden "puppetmasters" for a massively multiplayer real-world game.

Viral marketing has from the start been like a game, with obscured object-ives that must be uncovered, hidden rules that must be figured out, artificial obstacles to overcome, and social cooperation or team play encouraged. But more recent campaigns, culminating in *I Love Bees*, have deliberately modeled themselves not just on fan culture but more specifically on game-fan culture and its collective modes of play, rule-discerning, problem solving, knowledge-making and world-building, the structures and skills that game fans already have for creating and sustaining and extending a make-believe paratextual universe around a chosen media object. Actually, this effect is less paratextual in Genette's more limited, literal sense, and more a way of allowing the very idea of the paratext, the threshold as a grid of different possible receptions, to take over the primary functions of the text itself.

Paratextual fan culture is the subject of William Gibson's 2003 novel, *Pattern Recognition*, which some players of *I Love Bees* immediately recognized as an influence on the ARG. On the fictional Dana's blog (written by Jane McGonigal; http://ilovebees.blogspot.com, August 2004), one user, "Sorcerer" (if there ever was such a user), posted this winking comment early on in the game: "Anyone here ever read William Gibson's 'Pattern Recognition'? Seems like someone has." Gibson's protagonist, Cayce Powell, is a gifted marketer who works as a "cool hunter," a consultant on elite corporate logos and ad cam-paigns. She makes the most of her tendency to apophenia—obsessive pattern recognition—in order to read the trends in popular culture. She is also in her private life a member of a worldwide online fan community, people who "follow the footage" of fragments of serially released video clips from a mysterious underground film. Cayce ironically encounters, with a certain dis-orienting cognitive dissonance, a viral marketing campaign invading her beloved subculture of "footageheads." Presumably 42 Entertainment would have been very interested in Gibson's explorations of the ambiguous relationships between fan culture, art, and commerce that constitute viral marketing. Moreover, Gibson is also the author of the influential original cyberpunk novel,

*Neuromancer* (1984), in which two parts of an emergent AI reunite in order to evolve into self-consciousness and infect the global network ("the matrix"). The hero is pursued by the AI through a series of mysteriously ringing phone booths, an uncanny image of communication networks haunted by an artificial presence that shows up again in different forms in the later films, *Lawnmower Man* (1992) and *The Matrix* (1999). This image, ultimately descended from *Neuromancer*, seems a likely influence on the use of phone booths in the *I Love Bees* ARG, and the original cyberpunk novel is a likely influence on the story of *Halo* as a whole, which has its own version of fragmented and "rampant" AIs working with and against human agents.

At one key point during *I Love Bees*, the AI Melissa sent out an ominous-sounding message from the Margaret's Honey website: "This medium will metastasize." Though it had meaning inside the story, this was also clearly a self-reflexive or metatextual manifesto on behalf of *I Love Bees* itself and ARGs in general (this campaign is not just viral but rampant). *I Love Bees* and *Halo 2* represent a kind of media packaging designed from the first to extend itself everywhere throughout the existing host-body, throughout the larger media universe. 42 Entertainment's own mission statement says that they aim "to carve the client's world into the cultural landscape so that, like Middle Earth or Hogwarts, it becomes a priority destination for the audience's imagination."[7] They do this by creating "communities passionately committed to spending not just their money but their time and creative energy in the worlds we represent." But of course also their money. The company seems to be serious about simultaneously trying to provide with its marketing the kind of entertainment associated with gaming. *I Love Bees* jumped the species boundary of marketing, as it were, just as it was designed to do, when some players found themselves immersed in playing the game for its own sake. Then that outcome became part of the lore that contributed to the campaign. All viral marketing campaigns aim to exploit existing networks in order to create "buzz"—one can imagine these bees being "hatched" as a pun on the familiar marketing term; and even, perhaps, "you can catch more bees with honey . . .?" The first move on the part of the puppetmasters was to mail actual jars of honey to members of the game-fan (and especially ARG-fan) community, jars that contained letters that spelled out *I Love Bees*. Meanwhile the pre-game was afoot.

Jane McGonigal has referred to the "distributed fiction" of *I Love Bees*, which she tellingly characterizes as "a kind of investigative playground, in which players could collect, assemble, and interpret thousands of different story pieces related to the *Halo* universe" (7). The players act as detectives or editors, reconstructing fragments into meaningful texts, thus collaborating to write the "bridge" between *Halo: Combat Evolved* and *Halo 2*. Note that it's the production of this bridge, rather than the consumption of it, that's distributed and collective. She has also described the designers' deliberate use—in the game and in thinking about the game—of the cyberpunk metaphor of the "hivemind" (again, bees) to describe the desired collective effect. Along with the announcement that "This medium will metastasize," a counter appeared on the website to mark the days until an ominous-sounding event: "Countdown to Wide Awake and Physical." Clearly the ARG arose from a rich, suggestive stew of thinking about the meaning of AI in the *Halo* story and in gameplay, starting with Cortana and other in-game AI characters, but perhaps leading to specula-tion on CI (collective intelligence), in a way another kind of "artificial" intelli-gence because it *is* an artifice, is collective and is deliberately fostered and constructed, the cooperative social group producing together a gamelike cap-ability for search and analysis, for uncovering and sifting through "intelligence" in several senses, that is more than the sum of its distributed parts. Fan culture always works in this way: as a collaboratively embodied knowledge base, a massively multiplayer network for making new stories—and new or extended universes—through acts of collective make-believe. And as McGonigal points out, Bungie/Microsoft's assumption in 2004 was that games were moving increasingly to networked collaborative modes of play. This imperative shaped the emphasis in *I Love Bees* on collaboration and community building (9–10). In the end, like any successful ARG, *I Love Bees* exceeded its creators' intentions and became more than mere training for cooperative play on Xbox Live, though it was that as well. The thematic content—beginning with a multi-personality AI spreading virally—as well as procedural design of *I Love Bees*—the CI of ad hoc cooperative groups—corresponds to the desired essential character of the *Halo* games as they were designed and marketed, especially with the advent of *Halo 2*, as based in a networked and collective, loyal fanbase, a multiplayer community inhabiting and helping to perpetuate the *Halo* universe.

## "*Space Invaders* in a tube"

What does all of this—the ARG and the extended back-story—have to do with holding the controls, whether the WASD keys (the navigation keys of PC computer gaming) and mouse or the multi-button and thumbstick controller, and playing *Halo*? For some players, as my accounts below will confirm, it would seem to mean next to nothing—at least nothing of which they're consciously aware. However, the fact that mere action-based, story-innocent gameplay seems to be fairly widespread doesn't diminish the importance of the universe-building going on behind the scenes or at the margins of any given casual night of shooting at aliens (or at your friends who are playing as aliens). As Henry Jenkins has said in a discussion of the virtual world *Second Life*, we need to be careful about assuming that cultural significance correlates directly with statistical numbers of people involved.[8] Even if, as seems a safe bet, no single player of *Halo* exists who has mastered knowledge of the whole *Halo* universe, or is even interested in vast reaches of it, even if many or most players know only an outline of the back-story and keep it in the back of their mind during gameplay, that does not mean the *Halo* universe doesn't matter to the meaning of the game. To be sure, for some players the detailed story of the fight against the Covenant (and the threat behind the Covenant, the parasitic Flood) is merely a pretext for play, like the premise of an improvisational drama. Actual gameplay takes off from there and sometimes doesn't think twice about the story once it has begun. On the other hand, for some few fans, every novel and epitextual media artifact related to the game matters and must be experienced. Like the individual bees in the concept of the hivemind, each contributes something to the collective intelligence of the whole fanbase and its collective constructions of the game universe. The meaning of *Halo* lies in the complex picture of the range of possibilities represented across the whole spectrum of *possible* engagements by players.

The *Halo* series began as a single-player FPS (originally for the Mac), and it remains essentially an FPS. The point of view begins with and inevitably returns to the first-person combination camera-gun, as Rune Klevjer has explained it (though the camera switches to third-person shots for vehicle-driving and during most cutscenes); in this way it retains a close family resemblance to earlier shooters such as *Wolfenstein-3-D* or *Doom*.[9] In *Doom* you play as a space marine—not unlike the Master Chief or the UNSC Marines of *Halo*—as the last surviving human hero fighting non-human enemies, in this case demons and zombies, on Mars and its moons. In *Halo* the enemy is the multi-species coalition of aliens, a civilization known as the Covenant, made up of Prophets, Grunts, Jackals, Hunters, and Elites, and so on. Weapons can come from both sides of the battle, allowing for a more diverse and task-specific arsenal.

Even the very earliest arcade-style shooting games can be included in the broad generic family to which *Halo* belongs. What some consider the first real computer video game, as it came to be understood, complete with multiplayer mode, a CRT (cathode ray tube) graphical display, and keyboard or peripheral controller, was *Spacewar*, developed by 23-year-old MIT student Steve Russell (with Alan Kotok, Peter Samson, and Dan Edwards) on the PDP-1 mini-computer in 1961. In a scenario directly inspired by science fiction novels, two players maneuver two spaceships on the screen, shooting at one another. Though the first version was, technically speaking, third person (you control your own rocket, but the combat is viewed from a distant point in space), a later version experimented with a true first-person point of view. Clearly this

*Figure 3.4  Halo: Combat Evolved* screenshot: first-person gun.

early third-person shooter paved the way for the FPS proper. The rockets are drawn on the screen against a 2-D backdrop of stars. (In a 1972 interview, Russell revealed that having the stars was necessary in order to create a better sense of range and motion, an early example of the importance of physical/ fictional setting and background imagery even in a simple shooting game.[10]) A kind of black hole or gravity well at the center of the screen pulls the ships toward it as they fire torpedoes (little lines of light) at each other; firing your thrusters at just the right time in order to use the gravity to swing an arc around your opponent is part of the game, as is entering hyperspace (jumping to another entry-point on the screen) and cruder back-and-forth evasive actions. In this ancestor of most video-game shooters, the trigger key is already all-important.[11]

The developers of *Halo* are aware of their own place in gaming history, and one of them once joked that their game could be seen as "*Space Invaders* in a tube."[12] The joke contains a double-edged insight: on the one hand, *Halo* is first and finally about shooting aliens; on the other hand, even the 1978 2-D arcade shooter, *Space Invaders*, designed by Tomohiro Nishikado for the company Taiko, is more interesting than that would suggest. Interestingly, Nishikado later said that he considered tanks or airplanes as targets for his shooter, and considered human enemies, but that he "felt it would be immoral to shoot humans, even if they were bad guys."[13] Inspired by H. G. Wells's *The War of the Worlds* and the popularity of *Star Wars*, he decided to target an invading alien horde. Wells was the source for the squid-like or spider-like design of the different alien species, who "march" back and forth and down across the screen in waves while you shoot at them from behind "degradable" barrier arches with your laser canon, sliding back and forth along the bottom of the screen to fire or evade missiles and bombs dropped by the aliens. Besides picking off aliens from their descending ranks, you can shoot through the cleared lines at the occasional bonus-point spaceship passing "overhead." The heartbeat-rhythm synthesizer music keeps pace with the marching aliens, who speed up as the game progresses, increasing tension and requiring new levels of shooting skill.

Game theorists Jesper Juul and Ian Bogost have commented on the role of even this very simple back-story in *Space Invaders* (keep shooting in order save humankind from an alien invasion).[14] Even in an FPS, and even when a player is only half-conscious of them, such story elements serve as what psychologists studying altered states of consciousness call "set" and "setting," the contexts that partly determine the mood and feel of the gameplay experience. At the very least, the story "lend[s] flavor" to the gameplay, as *Halo* Project Lead Jason Jones has said, working along with music and other cues to enhance the player's sense of immersion in the gameworld.[15] They may also increase replay value, since any given player may learn a little more about the game's universe over time, thus altering his or her perceptions of the context of gameplay. Or the story may be more important between gameplay sessions, or as a way of

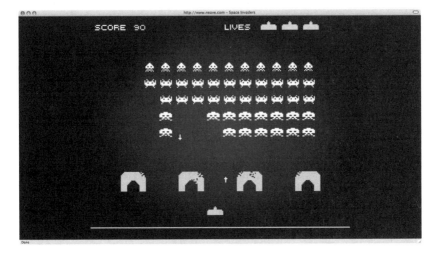

*Figure 3.5* *Space Invaders* screenshot (online emulator).

holding together a diverse community of gamers with different styles of play and different levels of commitment. Actual play sessions mostly involve more immediate tactical decisions about territorial control, evasion, targeting, and shooting.

In the sixth chapter of *GAM3R 7H3ORY*, McKenzie Wark discusses "targeting," using as an example the experimental cult game by Sega, *Rez* (2001; interestingly enough, the same year *Halo* was published), precisely, one imagines, because of its differences from mainstream shooters such as *Doom*, *Quake*, *GoldenEye 007*, *Half-Life*, *Counter-Strike*, *Resistance*, or *Halo*, its more extremely abstract and psychedelic, unrealistic mode of representation.[16] These features allow Wark to bracket-off questions of mimesis—of what it means to simulate violence and war—though these questions arguably return to his chapter under the sign of the "alien" or other. In *Rez*, an on-rails shooter, your "missiles seem more balletic than ballistic." You fly or swim along and press the trigger to lock on and "target" things that swoop by, but the experience is more like a "nightclub" than a "war" (126–7). Targeting is a way of extending one's presence in gamespace, which is why a similar effect can be achieved with a targeting grappling hook (see Nintendo's *Zelda*) or a targeting virtual ink brush, for example (see Capcom's *Okami*). Wark argues that targeting is a way to first extend and then to cut off the connection—a way to carve out one's identity vis-à-vis the alterity of the "enemy" and the gamespace in general. The goal of any shooter, Wark writes, is "the overcoming of death through the targeting of the other" (138). But even that highly abstract goal is usually pursued against the "backdrop" of a back-story. You'd think the story would be least necessary in a shooter, but stories persist in FPS games and have a reason for being, even when the player ignores them. They frame the action, establish the enemy, excuse the shooting, among other functions (141). With this summary I agree. Even a dim awareness of the existence of an extensive back-story subtly alters the "feel" of an alien landscape in *Halo*, lending it an intuitve sense of depth, of a world beyond what's in front of you on the screen.

This role of targeting in context was vividly illustrated by Wark himself during a kind of book-tour interview on the online video show *This Spartan Life* (episode 4.3).[17] The show, filmed inside *Halo* as machinima using the game engine, is itself an example of the explosion of mods and appropriative extensions of the *Halo* universe. Probably the best-known examples are the machinima videos, *Warthog Jump* (in which military vehicles are blown sky high in interesting ways) and *Red vs. Blue*, a comedy series made inside the game-world using recorded voiceover dialogue to match the actions of game avatars. The episode of *This Spartan Life* is a strange and often funny mixture of talk-show book-tour interview and game demo, using two cameras in a professional way, as the host and Wark move around live in *Halo* maps discussing Wark's book and game theory concepts, including the idea of targeting in *Rez*. Significantly, given his theory of the dynamic of alterity in shooters, Wark chooses to appear as a Covenant Elite. As they walk and talk (or their colorful avatars do), vehicles fly by with whooshing sounds, other players occasionally pass in the background, sometimes pausing to take and return fire, grenades explode. When the discussion turns to the concept of targeting, we see the camera-gun of the interviewer lock-on to Wark's avatar. And at one juncture in a vast cave the host uses his gunfire to point out a ledge high above them near a sunlit opening he has never been able to reach, as if to reinforce Wark's theory of abstract targeting in gamespace. The interview concludes with Wark reading from the book, his avatar standing on a high balcony before a live audience of gamers, who (of course) break into noisy combat in the cave beneath him as he reads. Vehicles fly by, firing missiles at soldiers who are running past firing guns. The segment ends, comically, but also appropriately in terms of Wark's theory of targeting, when Wark himself is shot: "Ow!" he cries, and falls to the floor of his balcony, his reading evidently concluded.

This show and Wark's theoretical and theatrical appearance on it may be a paratextual phenomenon related to *Halo*, but it's not really *playing Halo*, is it? Those gamers in Wark's audience are arguably playing the game, running and jumping and diving for cover, shooting or flying by in vehicles, when they engage in combat while he reads. What is the difference between that and any other instance of gameplay in which they might engage? The host jokes at one point about how he and his crew are *not* playing the game inside which the show takes place, but when you think about it, why not regard the actions of Wark and his host as they move around the map, exploring, shooting, even talking to one another, as yet another instance of gameplay, if a rather eccentric one? On any given night, many Xbox Live sessions contain even more radically unstructured (if less talky and academic) exchanges, instances of such relatively limited-objective gameplay, one-on-one death matches, for example. Even in games based on actions as direct as targeting and shooting, in practice the lines between text and paratext, gameplay and story, between extending the *Halo* universe and playing *Halo*, are not as clear as some formalist accounts might lead one to believe.

## "Countdown to wide awake and physical"

In earlier times, children's games of "war" involved multiplayer action of a physical sort, collective make-believe in which "Bang—you're dead!" was a performative linguistic act based on the temporary social contract that is the magic circle of such games. Or one could play with loud and smoking cap guns or with plastic water pistols. In more recent times, laser tag took up similar conventions, more technologically mediated. In video games today, there are single-player FPS games galore, and basic targeting is everywhere on Flash- or Java-based online casual games, often in nostalgic and/or ironic imitation of arcade classics. Though graphics and programming may grow more sophisticated, the history of gaming conventions is not progressive in any simple way. *Halo*, at least as most players encounter it these days, is a social experience, usually fundamentally more like laser tag than, say, Nintendo's *Duck Hunt* (1984). At this point in the history of the game, "playing *Halo*" almost always means playing with other people—matching wits and reflexes with other players. Often they are physically present in the same room with one another (which was all that was possible in the first game).

Even when playing *Halo 2*, the physical proximity of two- or four-player cooperative or competitive play is the norm for one avid player I interviewed, John (not his real name). He definitely considers himself a fan of *Halo* but plays it mostly with his college roommate and their guests. They sit on the couch with two or four wireless controllers and a split-screen layout, playing regularly and keeping track of their competitive standings, but mostly in straightforward competitive head-to-head death-matches (the winner has the most kills) or, less often, online in team games of capture the flag, one team defending a location while the other moves in and tries to take it. John's roommate is an even more dedicated player: his nickname is "Halo Dave," and everyone knows he holds first place in their circle of players. Others may play in larger system-link LAN (local area network) parties, in rooms with multiple large-screen TVs, but for John and his friends the cost of such a setup is too great. He says he's interested in what he knows of the back-story of *Halo*, and he knows the basic canonical plot arc in its entirety. John's a fan of science fiction in general and a more serious, dedicated fan of MMORPGs (massively multi-player online role-playing games), especially *World of Warcraft*, in part because he values a complex game universe and finds it easier to sustain in the MMOR-PG's persistent world, where you play with the same guild and meet the same people week after week. In *Halo*, by contrast, "people come and go" and so the fictional gameworld (and by implication the back-story that helps to create it) seems to matter less. It seems significant that John's engagements with different versions and experiences of *Halo* on different platforms are determined in large part by the material conditions under which he can play (which is also the case with "Jacob," whose interview I discuss below). His friend's large-screen TV, his roommate's console, lapsed subscriptions to Xbox Live, the absence of the infrastructure to allow for system-link LAN parties, all determine what part of the *Halo* universe is available (and perhaps interesting) to him, and these have further effects based on the different processors and different sound cards of the different systems. John prefers PC games for other reasons, too, but it may also be the case that the barrier to entry is lower with the PC he already owns and the broadband connection that comes with his dorm room.

Another serious gamer I interviewed via email, whom I'll call Jacob, uses the online version of the game on Xbox Live primarily as a convenient way to stay in touch with out-of-state friends from college days. They log on separately from their distant locations and spend the first ten minutes in the pre-game room chatting about comic books and movies, then play relatively casually for a while, a not-uncommon appropriative middle ground, not a mod but a modified form of gameplay. But—interestingly enough—as far as Jacob is concerned, this counts as "playing *Halo*." He says he cares a good deal about well-developed back-stories in most games but doesn't take *Halo*'s story very seriously, and doesn't seem to know much about it beyond the idea of an alien invasion. Jacob says he "despises" what he perceives as the mostly adolescent (and, he says, trash-talking and often gay-bashing) chat on many of the *Halo*-themed message boards. Again, though even more strikingly than with the case of John as described above, Jacob's gameplay is determined by financial considerations that in turn determine his platform. As he put it: "When I play H2, it's always online. The hardware requirements—and sheer logistics—of setting up LAN play is prohibitive for me and my friends."

A third player I interviewed, whom I'll call Cole, is a more dedicated, serious fan, someone who admits to collecting "an embarrassing amount of stuff," including action figures (he focuses on the alien Grunts), T-shirts from Bungie.net and *Halo 3*, and the first *Halo* graphic novel. He even made his own silk-screened hoodies printed with his *Halo* clan's logo. He was aware of *I Love Bees* and thought it was "an amazing concept," but didn't delve into it very deeply himself. For a long time, his own homepage was set to Bungie.net. Mostly Cole plays on Xbox Live, using the game to stay in touch with his brothers who live elsewhere. But when he can, he enjoys LAN play, for instance at an annual party sponsored locally by the gaming website for older players, *2 Old 2 Play* (http://2o2p.com). He also appreciates the level of discussion at that site, because like Jacob he finds the majority of what goes on around *Halo* out on the boards "rather juvenile." When asked about the role of the *Halo* back-story, the whole universe, when it comes to his gameplay, Cole replies:

> I think that the effort Bungie puts into deepening and detailing the *Halo* universe really makes a difference. I don't know that it affects the mechanics of my gameplay, but it certainly adds entertainment value. There are plenty of generic shooters out there, but not many with an entire universe and history attached.

All of the gamers I talked to, despite their different styles and circumstances, are clearly drawn to the multiplayer modes of *Halo*. From the release of *Halo 2*, the game has been marketed as being all about social play. Its developers bragged from the start that it "redefines the social experience of online gaming" and its release was very closely tied to Xbox Live, treated as a "system-seller" that would cause people to buy the console and subscribe to the service. Subscriptions to the online service roughly doubled, it was reported by Microsoft, from about one million to about two million, after the introduction of the game in late 2004. Bungie has on its staff a "Community Manager," as any large game company is likely to have nowadays. It would seem that *I Love Bees* thematized its client's goals even more explicitly than has been appreciated. The ARG's creation of a metastasizing community of "loyals," of dedicated fans ready to play not only one game but also to help construct the universe in which the game is situated, mirrored the simultaneous push by Microsoft during 2003–2004 to redefine "the social experience of online gaming," to build a community of loyal subscribers to Xbox Live, ready to inhabit the *Halo* universe. To do that, they knew (and clearly 42 Entertainment knew) that they would have to create a universe of many possible thresholds bridging from the game to the players' worlds, with plenty of opportunities to blend elements of the back-story with action gameplay and with the emergent events, improvisations, and surprises that can still be created most reliably by human social interaction. The game design seems to have aimed at combining multiple opportunities to configure social gameplay with procedures for having players interact with multiple AI-driven NPCs. The thematic obsession of *I Love Bees* with various forms of artificial intelligence was no accident but a reflection of the formal goals of the design team for *Halo 2*.

In a Powerpoint presentation given at the Game Developers Conference in March, 2002, *Halo* developers Chris Butcher and Jaime Griesemer discussed specifically their use of AI in the first game and while working on *Halo 2*.[18] AI is a complex theoretical and applied field in computer science. Game AI is more like an artisanal craft, with something more of a hacker ethos. As the developers make clear, the goal in a game such as *Halo* is not to create truly intelligent programmed objects but only to create the *illusion* of intelligence in the NPCs, and they reveal some of the tricks for doing this. For example, the different species or "races" of alien enemies are type-characters whose basic behaviors are determined by their profiles: Grunts are always comical and cowardly, running way and making excited noises when fired on, whereas Elites are always tough and aggressive. What follows from this, for example, is that when you kill an Elite, Grunts will run away in distress at the loss of their braver leader, creating a scenario among the NPCs that feels like the display of different kinds of intelligence. The basic goal for the alien AIs is to have them react during combat in ways that foster this sense that one is interacting with smart opponents, so that they duck when fired upon, dive for cover, approach you cautiously (or not), and so on, depending on the variables in any given situation, such as distance from the player's character, whether there is clear line of sight, what level of difficulty has been set by the player (Easy, Normal, Heroic, or Legendary),and so on. Butcher and Griesemer point out that, paradoxically, an AI can be too intelligent to work in the heat of actual gameplay. They deliberately avoided making the NPCs "psychic," for example, allowing them only to know what their senses would tell them in a given setting. Their behavior should not be too complex; they learned that too much in the way of hidden states (or inner motives) can make it difficult for a player to "read" the AI as intelligent, making it appear merely opaque and confusing. Random behavior is not the goal, but some degree of unpredictability is, by which the developers mean "not repetitive" behavior. The idea is to make a virtue of necessity, to make the human player, rather than the NPC, the truly unpredictable element in the equation.

The developers' model for how to achieve a sense of emergent behavior on the part of the AI draws upon the real intelligence of the human player, who is inevitably going to react in different and unpredictable ways each time he or she plays. They say they exploit this relationship to create a "cascade effect":

> Unpredictable player
> puts the AI in unpredictable situations
> which causes unpredictable reactions
> and this leads to a unique experience.
> This causes a feedback loop because the unique experience leads to more
> unpredictable Player reactions and starts the cascade all over again.

As they say, this kind of feedback loop "allows small changes in the situation to be amplified by the AI to yield large changes in behavior", using many small predictable effects "that combine and cascade" to provide the player with a sense of "fluid and deep gameplay".

The developers opportunistically use the combination of AIs and the designed features of the gameworld to produce an experience that is more than the sum of its parts. The world of *Halo* is simulated with enough complexity, they argue, with enough lavish images, dynamic animations, detailed maps, features such as destructible buildings and vehicles that really do get shot up and wrecked, and in-game elements from the story, that any given AI doesn't have to behave in overly complex ways to *seem* intelligent in such a context. The sense of being immersed in a complex and intelligent, meaningful environment is produced by the *distributed complexity* of designed world + AI behaviors + player actions. This can be seen as exploiting a form of distributed intelligence, part artificial and part human. At the beginning of the second mission in the first game, the lifeboat has crashed on the surface of the Halo world and you find yourself standing amidst dead marines (by now you know to pick up their weapons and ammo). The landscape is sublime, with the rising arc of the ringworld you are on soaring up into the alien sky overhead (you can look almost straight up at it as animated comets shoot overhead), and nearby, mountains, rocks, a high waterfall (whose sound shifts around ambiently as you move). Almost immediately, however, before you have too much time to admire the view, Cortana reminds you to (literally) head for the hills, since incoming Covenant ships have been detected. Your HUD reveals enemy on the radar as you spot a log-shaped narrow bridge and take off, looking for cover just as the ships begin swooping in, looking for *you*. Or not. It all depends on you. If you don't listen to Cortana and just stand around too long admiring the view, or make the category error of thinking you are in a *Myst*-like environment to be explored at will, you will be shot down fairly quickly by the Covenant forces, die on the wrong side of the river, and have to start the level over in order to try again to evade the enemy.

This scenario, combining the player's human intelligence with the fictional AI's, pitting both against the AI-driven enemy forces, is just one of countless instances of the basic principle of distributed intelligence that runs throughout *Halo* and outward into the *Halo* universe. That universe now includes *I Love Bees*, with its fostering of CI through hivemind gaming aimed at reconstructing a story about an AI (Melissa) attempting to assemble its own distributed intelligence into something "wide awake and physical," something real in the world. This successful resonance between the ARG's CI, the game's in-game AI, and the company's drive to create distributed intelligence in the form of a community of users for Xbox Live, is surely one reason Bungie has now openly "embraced" *I Love Bees* as official story canon.[19] This is how a game universe begins: not with a *fiat* (let there be *Halo*) but with a cascade of distributed and cooperative constructions. Just as any individual AI-driven NPC enemy may know only a few things (be afraid; run for cover; stick together in cluster) while the game universe as a whole knows many things, so any individual player of *Halo* may know only a limited portion of the game's universe, but himself or herself makes up, in large or small ways, a portion of that universe, the overall ongoing reception history of the game. Starting with *Halo 2*, the ideal player of *Halo* has been a social player in precisely this sense. Even a relatively casual player may, in the context of many social interactions, come to have a sense, if only in the back of his or her mind, that there are depths of meaning, multiple possibilities, just beyond the interstellar horizon of any particular battle.

## The social text and the game universe

When D. F. McKenzie argued that textual studies scholars were shifting their attention away from questions of the authority of texts, of which particular verbal readings their authors intended, and toward questions of texts' patterns of dissemination and reception, of how they were produced and received by readers, how they made their way through the world, he anticipated the inclusion of other forms of media.[20] So we can now understand that "a video game" can be substituted for "a book" in his claim that "a book is never simply a remarkable object" (4). Like books, games are never merely remarkable objects. Nor are they merely formal structures. They are, as Espen Aarseth has argued, simulations, systems of rules-based possible acts, abstract structures consisting of the vectors of people's engagements with the games' possibilities, acts of gameplay.[21] Those acts, however, are always performed in cultural contexts of one kind or another, including the blend of make-believe and actual contexts that constitutes the game's universe. Contextualized gameplay acts *are* the meaning(s) of video games. Every text is a social text in this sense, and in this sense, so is every game. McKenzie and others have shown that it was necessary to break the hermetic seal of the text, to interpret across the boundary dividing the formal aesthetic object from the social world into which it is received. Similarly, game theorist Ian Bogost has decried the "functionalist separatism" of much of game studies today, which he calls "essentialist and doctrinaire" (52, 53). There is little to gain by walling off game studies from the humanities in general, Bogost insists. He calls instead for a procedural criticism that is the "practical marriage of literary theory and computation," a potentially more "useful framework for the interrogation of artifacts that straddle these fields" (ix). Instead of just looking at the formal structures of games, he suggests, we should "turn to what they do—how they inform, change, or otherwise participate in human activity . . ." (53).

Meanwhile, textual-studies theorist Jerome McGann has called for using digital simulations to represent the social text as McKenzie described it, not the verbal object but the dynamic social acts that make up the text's reception, what it does in the world.[22] The idea is for textual scholars to build models not of textual objects, whether rare manuscripts or the first editions of poems, but of complex reception histories, of what they have done and are doing in the world. "[Y]ou will not want to build a model of one made thing, you will try to design a system that can simulate all the realized and realizable documentary possibilities—the possibilities that are known and recorded as well as those that have yet to be (re)constructed" (parag. 37). You would build a simulation, a virtual machine for recreating and creating textual history—for playing out the possibilities.

Think of it this way: there are many models in many scales of Shakespeare's Globe theatre, where many of his plays were performed in his lifetime, whether made from cardboard on in a 3-D drawing program or as a large building on the river Thames. Recently, Edward Castranova has begun to develop an experimental Shakespeare-centered MMORPG, "Arden," which will model a construct—Shakespeare's "world"—*World-of-Warcraft* style, but with the plays serving as "the back-story, the lore, the culture."[23] But any traditional book-based edition of *King Lear*, say, scholarly or popular, is another kind of model, a different kind from these physical replicas and themed virtual worlds. It is a textual model of the work, and the paratextual apparatus—the notes and encoded lists and collations of variants, stemmatic diagrams relating documents to one another—testifies to the constructive editorial acts that went into building it and serves as a set of cues for its ongoing reception. The apparatus of an edition is thus a kind of virtual grid of possibilities for extending the work's life in the world. A digital-era textual model (or edition) of *King Lear*, according to McKenzie's and McGann's theories, might want to extend this simulation function, implicit in all editions, to model the socially-embedded production and reception history of specific texts, including ephemeral "performances" of those texts, by critics and readers as well as actors and directors. The result would *not* be a multimedia archive of textual objects, however remarkable, but a simulation machine that would map any number of possible meaning-making acts, vectors of meaning radiating outward from the work known as "*King Lear*," including responses to versions, physical books, responses to adaptations in film and other media, critical and popular interpretations by scholars and "groundlings" (those in the cheap seats at the Globe) and fans. A model or a map of the physical Globe theatre might be included in such a system, but it would only be represented for the purposes of enabling historically-informed interpretive performances. Such a system would map what game designer Will Wright calls the "possibility space" surrounding the work known as *King Lear*.[24] It would amount to something like a map of the *King Lear universe*, to use the fan-culture term, an open-ended field representing any number of possible moves or (re)interpretations in response to the work.

Such a model sounds like a gamespace, and it's no accident that McGann has in recent years begun to call for serious gameplay as a mode of humanities scholarship. His interest in modeling the social text as a critical-discourse field has led to the experiment of *Ivanhoe*, a gamelike space for dynamic digital simulations of the ongoing reception histories of literary works.[25] It's a way of visualizing on a pie chart the critical "moves" a group of players make in interpreting or rewriting a selected literary text (one early version was played with Sir Walter Scott's *Ivanhoe*). It's also a kind of RPG: players must play in character, whether a character chosen from the text in question, or the author, or a later critic, or book dealer, or historical figure, or someone purely made up. The relation of the character to the text and its whole semiotic field of versions and competing interpretations is what you, as the player, have to establish. That relationship is what matters and what makes gameplay interesting. A dynamically updated graphic tool represents the moves of multiple players. As innovative as *Ivanhoe* is within the humanities, conceptually speaking, this form of modeling—mapping the actual and possible moves of avatar characters in relation to each other, in a shared digital space that visualizes the results of actual moves as a set of feedback loops—is of course what video games already do, and at a much more sophisticated level, just in terms of their computational power and the power of their visualizations.

During development for *Halo 3*, Bungie observed, recorded, and analyzed gameplay patterns of hundreds of players in a laboratory setting, including mapping where they were at every stage of the game and what happened to them there, especially where they died. These maps reveal players actually exploring the game's possibilities (and reveal glitches in making that feasible).[26] As with the complex verbal texts we study, we need to understand games such as *Halo* as existing at the center of a kind of spreading possibility space, a multidimensional virtual grid running off in many directions, the imagined vectors of any number of possible moves, performances, or instances of gameplay, all of which are contained, in potential, within the "code" of the object itself, whether or not any particular state of the game or sector of the grid is activated at any particular time. The whole possibility space, then, would be a

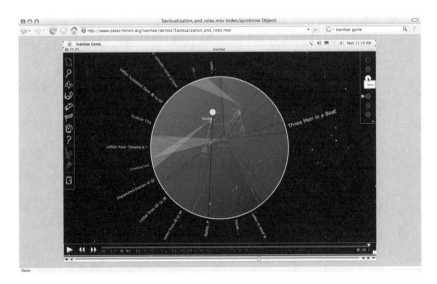

*Figure 3.6  The Ivanhoe Game* (www.patacriticism.org/ivanhoe/).

model of the game's own reception history waiting to happen. Such a grid of realized and realizable possibilities seems to me the most accurate way to imagine what we mean when we speak of the *Halo* universe.

McGann and a number of other textual-studies scholars have been experimenting with using gamelike environments to study the interpretive universe surrounding texts; the implication is that the social text is like a game. I simply want to suggest that the converse is also true: games are examples of the social text, and they can and should be studied in the same way *Ivanhoe* can be. Games are *already* complex digital models of engagements with their own possibilities. This is why I have been arguing that truly studying *Halo*, for instance, has to include more than the formal features of "the game itself"—that anyway, those features, when properly understood, are thresholds to the possibilities represented by vectors of the expanding *Halo* universe, including the artificial and real intelligence driving the engagements of players and NPCs and fans and scholars of various disciplines who might be playing in and studying that universe, helping in their own ways to construct its meanings. Understood in this light, video games are social texts with a vengeance.

# Chapter 4

# The game behind *Façade*

The opening cutscene takes place in the dark. You hear an audio track against a blacked-out screen, a phone message from Trip inviting you over to his and Grace's place. After a brief title screen showing the two of them and the interior of their apartment, and another blackout, you find yourself (via a cursor-hand from the first-person point of view, reminiscent of *Myst*, say) in the hallway outside, facing their front door, behind which you overhear the couple arguing—either about getting rid of something or about where to find wine glasses (it varies in replay). Your first action is to move forward (using the arrow key) and knock on the door (with your mouse). In response, the now-whispered argument turns to a dispute over the time of your arrival, but after a few seconds (maybe you knock again), Trip opens the door and a graphic novel-style animated NPC (non-player character) standing in the 3-D apartment greets you by the name you'd selected before starting to play *Façade*, the award-winning 2005 experimental interactive drama by Michael Mateas and Andrew Stern.[1]

But is *Façade* a game? It has certainly been reviewed and discussed as if it were, and it *feels* like a game, despite the fact that its creators have usually been careful to refer to it as a "research experiment" and a "one-act interactive drama," and that its home website is "interactivestory.net." What does it matter? I think asking the question is helpful precisely because of what *Façade*, which exists at the border of games and interactive drama, can teach us about games and their relations to other, different forms of expression. Among other things, it's a vivid reminder of the importance in almost all video games of bounded improvisation.

## The game/not-game game

Testing boundaries was clearly part of the creators' intentions for *Façade*. As a research project it's a self-conscious experiment in exploring the genres and

*Figure 4.1* Screenshot from *Façade*: Welcome.

forms to which it *might* belong. But I also think that *Façade* simply can't escape from the determining conditions of its own production and reception in the present moment, circumstances in which an audience for such a form is mostly a *gameplay*ing audience. This is an especially interesting dilemma because interactive drama, the ideal of "*Hamlet* on the holodeck," as Janet Murray famously articulated it—and according to many who have been critical of it—supposedly wants to be something more than a game, to leave games behind in pursuit of more properly literary qualities. If, as Markku Eskelinen argues, you mostly configure or give shape to the literary text in order to interpret it, but you only interpret along the way in order to be able to configure a game,[2] then Murray's ideal form, cyberdrama, with its emphasis on immersion in the story and emotional catharsis, is clearly more literary than gamelike. She describes the *Star Trek* holodeck experience of her title as looking "more like a nineteenth-century novel than an arcade shoot-'em-up," and she praises the particular novelistic program under discussion as "making the holodeck form itself seem worthy of adult attention" (16). The implication is that mere gameplay might not be worthy of adult attention, that true cyberdrama would be more sophisticated than games because it would be more like a novel, more immersive and sophisticated in the nineteenth-century sense. Elsewhere, Murray seems to dismiss the content of many video games as consisting of "more varied finger-twitching challenges against more persuasively rendered opponents"

(51). It's not surprising that ludologists have reacted against this comparison and the implied value judgments they see reflected in her terminology. In a response to another piece by Murray, "From Game-Story to Cyberdrama," Espen Aarseth sardonically questions whether "the problematic, largely unplayable story-game hybrid will dominate the future of digital entertainment," and suggests instead that in the future, "euphemisms such as 'story-puzzles' and 'interactors' will no longer be necessary. Games will be games and gamers will be gamers."[3] His point is that storytelling or drama already have forms to which they are well suited, so why expect them to take the form of games? By the same token, why force gamelike environments to do things better done in a book or on stage?

Partly, this exchange was another phase in the ludology vs. literature or game vs. story debates I've already discussed above. And it's partly a matter of semantics. Pretty clearly Murray is interested in many different forms of media including games, and she understands the appeal of games as well as more conventionally literary forms of interaction. The creators of *Façade* are even more obviously aware of the importance of games and are working from experience in the world of game development. But *Façade* was, I think, powerfully influenced by the theories expressed in *Hamlet on the Holodeck*—which was after all written to explore a particular ideal (interactive drama or "cyberdrama")—and so I think it's worth revisiting some of the assumptions implied in those theories.[4]

For example, it's interesting in this context that one of Murray's "harbingers of the holodeck" is a real-life holodeck, one of several such experimental immersive 3-D virtual reality environments using a giant screen to allow a human player standing in front of it to interact with artificial-intelligence agents such as an animated dog. She tells us, however, that when the giant screen at MIT is not being used for these cyberdramatic interactions, graduate students use it for—what else?—playing giant-sized VR *Doom*, "by projecting its cavelike landscape on the screen and standing in front of it holding a plastic gun." She had the opportunity to try it for herself, she says, but on the day she took up the gun it was malfunctioning: "but the fluid navigation through the enormous three-dimensional spaces was rapturous in itself" (62).

This anecdote can be read as a parable of the conflict over games and cyberdrama: hacker-gamers in their off hours take back the platform, recapture it from humanities researchers trying to go beyond "mere" games into more "adult" forms of interactive media, and they allow the giant screen do what it "wants to do" (to use engineering parlance)—be a game. It's almost too good to be true that the gun wouldn't fire for Murray, thus prompting her to turn even the quintessential shooter *Doom* into a "rapturous" and immersive VR experience. Now, elsewhere in the book Murray famously describes her own ambivalent attraction to playing the arcade old-West shooter, *Mad Dog McCree* (54). She's by no means against the pleasures and interesting features of games. In more recent presentations she has rightly argued that a more universal kind of fictive world building or make believe underlies games as well as drama.[5] But *Hamlet on the Holodeck*, at least, which has been widely influential, seems at times to imply a kind of evolutionary story in which future media escape from the conventions of mere gaming as it exists today. The book's arguments about cyberdrama clearly informed the conception of *Façade*, just as the controversy around the book continues to affect its reception. The Parable of The Giant-Screen *Doom* reveals a basic assumption still shared by many more besides Murray (and whether or not she would still share it)—that true interactive drama, when it is finally achieved, will have to go beyond many of the most gamelike features of today's games.

Even the creators of *Façade* sometimes sound in their earlier comments as if they share the basic evolutionary assumption. Andrew Stern, for example, has suggested that the user interface for interactive drama should be less transparent than for other kinds of games, because you want the "humanistic NPC's" to behave in emotionally realistic ways.

> The thing is, people are messy. They're complicated, mysterious, nuanced, moody, fickle, often surprising and unpredictable when under pressure. They change their minds, they sometimes act illogically and irrationally. . . . If the NPCs are to act like fascinating people, in order to serve the performance of interesting drama, at best they're going to be unpredictable, surprising, at times confounding, even frustrating in response. Compelling characters are not transparent. You can't control them, and that's the point. That's why they're interesting to interact with.[6]

Is it true that NPCs are "interesting to interact with" only if they behave in opaque—and thus emotionally realistic—ways? I'd suggest that it depends on what you mean by "interesting," that there are different kinds of engagement in games, for example, many of which are not dependent on psychological realism in the traditional sense. In fact there are other kinds of engagement in the history of the drama, some of which might be considered closer to the kind of interest provided by many video games.

Whatever its creators may have intended, as an actual media object *Façade* challenges the assumptions that privilege emotional realism is the inevitable future of all interactive drama. It does this just by being what it is: an interesting, experimental, highly impure form of cultural expression mixing dramatic with ludic conventions. *Façade* is a hybrid form, one that is pragmatically and heuristically, just as a matter of course in the current media climate (it can't help it), both interactive drama and game. It emerges out of video game conventions and player expectations, even though *Façade* seems to have been a deliberate attempt to realize an early version of Murray's ideal (even Stern's earlier work on the virtual *Petz* cited Murray's cyberdrama as a theoretical goal). Like *Hamlet, Façade* is a play. Instead of a holodeck, you play it on a PC (or now a Mac), relying on the clunky but familiar interface of the keyboard and mouse. You type what you say, though Grace and Trip speak aloud to you through recorded bits of dialogue, and you use arrow keys to move around in the apartment. It certainly *feels* like playing a game, even though it may aspire to be something else, something more.

Mateas and Stern have said explicitly that their target audience is the "non-gamer," the "adult movie-and-theater-going public" interested in good stories about people's emotional lives.[7] And yet they've found that those non-gamers have trouble with the simplest features of the interface, are not familiar with using the arrow keys to navigate, for example, because they "aren't used to interacting in gameworlds, aren't used to the conventions of gaming." In other words, if their ideal audience is movie-going non-gamers, for the most part their actual audience, at least right now, is more likely to be made up of gamers. Indeed, *Façade* has been shown at the annual Game Developers Conference, for example, where hard-core gamers played it and were "confused . . . because it doesn't fit prior genres." Mateas reports:

> I remember when *Façade* was an IGF finalist at GDC 2004, one guy walked up, watched someone play for about ten seconds, and said "What the hell is this?" It was just so outside his expectations about what you do in a game, that he didn't even know how to think about the experience. I really liked the comment; it showed that we've been successful at pushing game-like interaction into new territory. If the experience felt familiar and comfortable to gamers, we wouldn't have been pushing hard enough. Our real audience right now is probably the frustrated gamer, someone who's familiar with the conventions of gaming, but is tired of the current game genres, who is hungry for deeper interaction with characters and for real story progression. But we of course want to grow our audience beyond the frustrated gamer—we want to create a new interactive drama audience. (Harger)

Meanwhile, most of those who play *Façade* will approach it with game-based expectations. The tension between those expectations and the self-definition of *Façade* (as more than a game, as interactive drama) makes up the real horizon of expectations within which the reception of *Façade* has so far taken place. This is an interesting fact of media history that provides a unique opportunity: *Façade* exists at the jagged edge of the category "game"—and that genre-position is precisely what makes it such a compelling experiment.

More recently, Mateas and Stern have admitted that they have given up their earlier attempts to differentiate *Façade* from games. In a 2007 interview they say simply that they are "creating interactive experiences that offer the agency of games but the character richness and structure usually associated with stories."

> Normally you get one or the other in inverse relationship to each other— think low-agency design approaches to story like cut-scenes. Since we totally agree with most game designers about the primacy of agency as a design goal, it's OK to call what we do games. "Game" is an elastic term that keeps expanding anyway.[8]

In a sense, the creators of *Façade* are just giving in to the vernacular collective understanding of the nature of their creation. You might be tempted to dismiss *The New York Times* when it refers to *Façade* in the most recognizable terms, as "the future of video games,"[9] but even Ernest Adams, a game designer who worked on the *Madden NFL Football* franchise, opened his June 28, 2005 review with this excited pronouncement that a "new video game" had just been released, that it was "one of the most important games ever created, possibly the most important game of the last ten years. More important than *The Sims*; more important than *Grand Theft Auto*; far more important than *Half-Life*." To his audience of developers he insisted, "you must play this game."[10] Maybe Adams and all the other reporters and game-reviewers who keep referring to *Façade* as a "computer game" or a "video game" are not making a category error after all. Maybe they're responding to something intuitively obvious when it comes to the "family resemblance" of *Façade* to existing computer games, a resemblance it can't quite hide even while it defines itself against it.

Adams puts the key difference most succinctly: *Façade* isn't technically a game because of its structure. It doesn't define a clear goal for the player, a way to win or lose, how to play better or worse games. You can of course try to save the marriage, but that's an odd sort of game objective. This is in the same review that explicitly refers to it as "a new video game" and, in the passage quoted above, tells game designers that they "must play this game." Adams can't help seeing it as a game of sorts, despite the fact that the rules are more social than ludic (the setting is after all a social occasion, a dinner party), and that the goals are defined in narrative and dramatic terms. For Mateas and Stern, *Façade* and video games both aim to provide a high degree of *agency* for their players. Agency is one of the key features of electronic narrative according to Janet Murray, which she defines as "exerting power over enticing and plastic materials" (153), and which seems to be more or less what other game theorists mean by the "configurative" quality of games. But in the case of *Façade*, agency or configuration is a more precisely theatrical way of exerting power over the materials and form of the performance in which you find yourself engaged.

Another report on *Façade*, a TV story on San Francisco's Channel 5 (November 17, 2006), highlighted the connection to games and, simultaneously, to drama.[11] In the demo and interview for that story, Mateas and Stern themselves describe *Façade* with extremely interesting—and potentially contradictory—analogies to the different parent media. On the one hand, Stern compares it directly to an FPS (first-person-shooter) video game, only "instead of firing bullets, what you're doing as you type is you're sort of firing off flirtations or disagreements or provocations." On the other hand, he immediately moves on to a different comparison, that of improvisational theater: "Playing *Façade* is a little bit like being on a stage with two really smart improv actors that are trying to make a dramatically interesting drama happen." Well, which is it? Do you "fire" off typed speech in a gamelike competitive battle against Grace and Trip? Or do you collaborate with them to "make a drama happen?" In some ways you do both, and sometimes the difference isn't clear-cut. This is one key way in which *Façade* reminds us of how gamelike theater has always been.

## Theater games

When Andrew Stern says of his own experiment that "Playing *Façade* is a little bit like being on a stage with two really smart improv actors that are trying to make a dramatically interesting drama happen," he's engaging in a bit of wishful thinking when it comes to how "smart" those actors are. After all, Grace and Trip are flat comic-book-style drawings, NPCs brought to life by voice-over acting and driven by several layers of custom-created AI (artificial intelligence) programming: the ABL (a behavior language), a separate natural language engine that processes sentences you type, a parser that translates that typed text into a series of "discourse acts," and a "drama manager," a program that collects input and attempts to shape it into a general "tension arc" according to the classical Aristotelean plot structure—rising to a crisis, then falling to a denouement.[12] Sometimes the two NPC actors pick up on your keyword, along with where you're standing in their apartment, what's been said so far, and whether you've developed an early affinity for one or the other of them, and they are able to respond in a "dramatically interesting" way: "Ed, you sure are paying Grace a lot of compliments tonight." Other times, they just can't seem to pull it off. You'll type a question or response and one of them may arch an eyebrow quizzically, say something like, "—you're such a kidder, ha ha . . ." or "H-mmm . . ." Or they'll just change the subject.[13]

When the collaborative drama fails and the exchange breaks down altogether, it's reminiscent of conversations with an *Eliza*-style programmed "chatterbot" in an old MUD multi-user domain dimension or dungeon) or MOO (MUD object oriented), the distant primitive ancestor of Trip and Grace, in which the computerized bot would "improvise" something from its default repertoire such as "Do you have any hobbies?" In response, the human player could choose to go with what the bot had "offered" or not, making chat with bots a disjointed and sometimes surreal experience. Such primitive artificial agents could only come close to appearing to pass the Turing test when they were set inside a highly structured, artificial discourse situation: playing a Rogerian therapist, for example, or a bartender, or someone you encountered in a singles bar. In effect, such situations were theatrical scenarios that limited your own human improvisations, supplying a premise and setting, then applying rules or discursive parameters within which the bot's crude AI could compete with you dramatically, could make a real-feeling conversation take place. Chatting with a bot in an early MUD was a lot like being onstage (or better yet, in an experimental theater workshop) with another not-so-smart actor and attempting

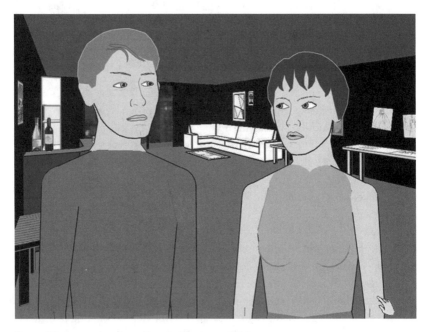

*Figure 4.2* Screenshot from *Façade*: Grace and Trip.

to improvise a believable scene. As Janet Murray says, *Eliza*'s dialogues always amounted to "a kind of collaboratively written comedy skit" (73). She goes on to cite *Eliza* as evidence that the computer is a "compelling medium for storytelling," but what *Eliza* actually reveals is the more specific point: that computer-based dramatic dialogue and more traditional stage performances have in common the use of procedural interactions requiring improvisation.

Procedural interactions are, of course, not unique to computers; they're also what happens on the rules-based improv stage. Improv involves a kind of "computation," in the form of randomizing or premise-generating devices, cards or slips of paper submitted from the audience, a bag of props, all are in one sense like the many-sided dice of a session of *Dungeons & Dragons*. The drama only happens insofar as players are able to make interesting moves in relation to such constraints, to negotiate the dynamically modified labyrinth of evolving possibilities created by layered premises, constraints, and other players' moves.

One of the manipulable objects in Grace and Trip's apartment is a Magic Eight Ball toy sitting on the bar. Like other objects in *Façade*, it's a prop that can become the excuse for an improvised exchange. In some sessions, Trip picks it up and carries it around and everyone can discuss the Eight Ball. (We even learn in a bit of the Freudian back-story that it was given to Trip by his mother!) But it's also a kind of Easter egg, a toy left in the environment for the player to discover. You can pick it up and play a kind of simple mini-game with it, seeing answers to your questions, just as you can with a physical Eight Ball toy. Mateas and Stern likely provided in this object a metatheatrical commentary on the difference between their goals for their more complex artificial-intelligence conversationalists and the dumb Eight Ball that can only return "Yes" or No" answers (or teasing variations thereon) in purely random, forking-path fashion. On numerous occasions in various sessions of *Façade*, one of the NPCs will ask you to respond to a question with a simple "yes or no?" But these are the least interesting prompts in the game, moments not unlike being given a multiple-choice menu of textual responses in a conventional video game and being constrained to click on one of them. At its most interesting moments, *Façade* affords instead the chance to improvise and the possibility of experiencing relatively unexpected, emergent-seeming outcomes produced by the interaction of your improvised moves and the game's AI. The whole experience depends on the quality of your improvisational interactions with the two artificial characters. Aristotle said that drama consists of characters in action, but, with the exception of a few emoticon-like gestural verbs (clickable hugging and kissing, for example) or walking around, sipping a drink, or picking up an object, the meaningful actions of *Façade* are all discourse acts. The game of *Façade* is all about how well or poorly your own discourse-acts successfully interface with those of Grace and Trip, which is to say, with how you interact with what lies behind them—the game's overarching procedural intelligence, its programming and what that allows to emerge during gameplay.

As a player of *Façade*, your actions involve acting; you play the game by playing along with the program in order to make a play. The linguistic ambiguities that allow for this wordplay around the words "play" and "act" are not trivial: they're reminders of the deeply resonant cultural contexts shared by drama and games. *Sims* creator Will Wright has said that "It's almost like 'play' is a word that was designed not to be precise . . . . to cast an umbrella over activities that we do not want to be overly specific about, and leave a certain amount of creative latitude to its interpretation."[14] The point is that the word "play," highly indeterminate, cross-platform, both noun and verb, may have emerged over time to signify certain cultural practices that are themselves socially imprecise, are important because they are counter-factual, imaginative, simulation-based transformations and explorations of possible situations, scenes, characters, complex systems. There's a reason the term "play" covers both ludic *and* dramatic activities. As Wright said earlier in the same talk, a dramatic actor can be seen as "an elaborate simulation" of certain human possibilities. And, I would add, this is as true of NPC simulations as it is of human actors.

The dramatic situation of *Façade*—having drinks in the home of a volatile couple whose marriage is itself on the rocks—is directly indebted to Edward Albee's 1962 play, *Who's Afraid of Virginia Woolf?*, as Mateas and Stern have repeatedly acknowledged.[15] It's not just the theme and situation: from the start Albee's play is all about "games," as anyone who has read it or seen it performed will recall. The first act is titled "Fun and Games" and the whole play is structured by dark social games that the husband, George, refers to with sardonic titles such as "Humiliate the Host," "Hump the Hostess," "Get the Guests," and so on. At one point he remarks, "We must know other games, college-type types like us;" at another point he pulls out a fake shotgun and uses it as a theatrical prop (of course it *is* literally a theatrical prop), pointing it as his wife Martha, shooting a parasol out of its barrel. The plot can be seen as a series of improvisations played out by George and Martha in ugly competition with one another over the subject of their apparently imaginary son and their dominance of the poor guests, but it can also be seen as a cooperative effort on their part to make a drama happen. The guests, Nick and Honey, are foils against which this improv exercise gets played out; or you can see them as secondary "players" who must figure out how to respond to the offerings of their hosts. They are baffled by the marital secrets George and Martha are toying with (very much like the way the player feels when interacting with Grace and Trip).

Emil Roy argues that *Virginia Woolf*'s dominant mode is "gamelike," with the "crucial central game" being all about telling the difference between illusion and reality, a game that takes place inside Huizinga's ludic "magic circle."[16] He points out that George's speech revealing the made-up death of the fictional son is in effect a "brilliant improvisation" in response to Martha's having introduced the topic in the first place, in violation of their private rule (92). Albee was well prepared to draw upon improvisational stage business: as Linda Ben-Zvi reminds us, his grandfather was a major innovator and marketer of vaudeville, a dominant form of popular entertainment in America until the coming of the "talkies."[17] Though Albee worked to distance himself from this family background, he later said such popular stage entertainments were his "first experience with Theatre of the Absurd" (179), and Ben-Zvi points to the use off "Gags and bits without narrative continuity" the "surprise turns" and "word games" and sight-gags that find their way into the structure of Albee's drama (178). In *Who's Afraid of Virginia Woolf?*, the verbal games, the sight-gag of the shotgun with the clown-like parasol, the battling repartee and (in this case dark and violent) punch lines, are reminiscent of vaudeville—and are clearly gamelike: competitive *and* dramatically cooperative.

Historically, game playing and play-acting have always overlapped: both are ludic rituals and (later) entertainments inside a magic circle of stage or game, acts of make-believe with social consequences. But rather than speculate about the supposed rituals of so-called primitive culture, as some game theorists are wont to do, I prefer in this case to focus on the vernacular and intuitively obvious cases of more recent culture, such as vaudeville and *Who's Afraid of Virginia Woolf?*, in which theater in its modern forms is self-consciously like a game, determined by rules and constraints as much as by a script. This is never clearer than in the case of improvisational forms of theater, which go back to the Italian *commedia dell'arte* and street performers, the *improvisatori*, and the antics of the *commedia*-derived characters of the popular eighteenth- and nineteenth-century British pantomime, for example, and extend to certain forms of music-hall performance and vaudeville in the early twentieth century but were formalized—and explicitly in terms of games—as improv. Mateas and Stern have repeatedly connected *Façade* with improv theater, even mentioning in their documentation some of the conventional terms of the form, to "make an offer," for example, which means to set out a premise for another actor to take up and build on, to "accept," augment, take off on. Janet Murray speculates that cyberdrama may eventually come to be taken as "an essentially collaborative art form," involving "amateur improvisers" (278). But my point is that improvisation is central not only to the ideal of cyberdrama and to *Façade* as an attempt to embody that ideal but to all games, to one degree or another. Making improvisational moves is something games already share with theater, especially (but not exclusively) the tradition explicitly known as improv.

Viola Spolin is probably the best-known theorist of improvisational theater as a method of training actors and as a form of expression in its own right. From the 1940s she established a workshop system that eventually led (though her son, Paul Sills) to the creation of the famous Second City troupe in Chicago and influenced improv companies around the world. Her method, as documented in her book, *Improvisation for the Theater*,[18] consists of a series of games—scenarios including sets of rules within which actors act, perform their characters and dialogue in dynamic reciprocal feedback loops. Games offer a model for improvising acts, making moves, within a system of constraints. The improv process of making an offer and accepting the offer, playing the "yes, and . . ." or "yes, but . . ." games, or (less often) "blocking" the offer, is transparently like making moves and countermoves in a game. Either another player or the game itself (through an artificially intelligent NPC or in another way) makes an offer that you, the player, respond to, by accepting and augmenting or accepting and altering the course of gameplay, or, more rarely, by refusing and looking for an end-run around the gameplay, a hack or cheat.[19] Like improv, games are inherently social, though this is not always fully acknowledged by critics of video games. They are played within the magic circle of a temporary social contract. Spolin makes it clear she has actors play games because "Any game worth playing is highly social and has a problem that needs solving within it" (30). She recognizes that value of games as training exercises for more gameplay, the fact that they "develop personal techniques and skills necessary for the game itself, through playing" (25). Improv training has historically involved actual ball games or games of tug of war. But the best-known theater games are like brief scenarios in which two or more actors interact with one another bounded by a limiting premise or set of parameters (the rules).

This sounds a good deal like *Façade*, and it's no accident that the *Improv Encyclopedia*, a compendium of improv games used for workshops and classes for decades, includes, for example, the Guest Game, in which one player enters a room full of suspicious-acting players who reveal some secret, known to everyone but the new player, by the end of the scene. This is the essence of most sessions of *Façade*, which end with the player's learning that Grace blames Trip for her failing to pursue a career as an artist, for example. This description of an opening for what's called the Guest Game from the *Encyclopedia* is very close to the opening scenario for *Façade*: "For example, a player might ring a doorbell at a house, ready to pick up his date. . . ." A recent TV game show, *Thank God You're Here!*, makes use of this same improv exercise. The guest actor, like the player of *Façade*, must improvise in response to whatever scenario he or she finds on the other side of the door, but the other actors always begin with the catch-phrase. A celebrity judge (with a buzzer) and an audience (with laughter and applause) view and rank the performances, implicitly based on how much the guest is able to make out of whatever situation he or she is given. Another game in the *Improv Encyclopedia* is the *Rashomon* Game, named after the classic Kurosawa film, in which you replay a single scene from multiple points of view. *Façade* is deliberately designed to be replayed many times in order to tease out different complex dramatic outcomes that result from changes in your interactions, thus revealing points of view associated more with Trip or with Grace or some combination thereof. Of course in this it resembles many replayable and thus variable video games as well. Or consider the *Improv Encyclopedia*'s Party Game, with hosts and a guest who comes through the door and must interact with everyone, basically the scenario behind Mateas's and Stern's new project now in development, a commercial interactive drama using more AI characters and a more polished interface, more actions beyond mere dialogue, and called *The Party*.

*Façade* illuminates connections between games and theater but can also help us to understand the theatrical elements of video games. My interest here is not in the future of computerized entertainment in general but in existing video games, what Rune Klevjer has called "the typical textual practice," the "impure" forms of actual gameplay that involve *both* interpretation and configuration, ludic engagement combined with responses to narrative elements, forms of popular culture, and external cultural contexts ("In Defense of Cutscenes"). As Jesper Juul puts it, games are in effect "half real"—the "real" half being the rules-based actions of the player (you really *do* something); the other half consisting not of the unreal so much as of the imaginative, of make-believe or cultural representations of one form or another. Playing video games involves combining elements of both kinds, ludic and cultural, in an always impure mixture, depending on the game and on the contexts in which it is played.[20] Playing video games is always a cultural activity, never merely a mathematical or strictly logical one. It takes place in the world of constantly reconstructed meanings. Video gameplay requires the player to put together dynamic combinations of logical decisions, moves, impulse reactions, interpretive and configurative responses to both structures of play and cultural representations, all in a series of feedback loops, stops and replays. In this sense, video games always require improvisation. You have to make something out of whatever you are given, "on the fly," in cooperative or competitive response to programmed bounds or constraints (including fictive premises). In this way every video game shares something fundamental with the traditions of theater. Which takes us back to Stern's dual analogies to FPSs and improv theatre: games are like improv because improv is already like a game. Both are based on competing against the constraints of the rules-system (and other actors, human or artificial, representing that system) and, at the same time, cooperating with that system (and other players) in order to make something interesting happen, something meaningful, whether that something is primarily a game or a drama.

You have to cooperate with your fellow actors in any improv exercise in order to pull off a dramatically interesting scene. But it's also true that improv techniques lend themselves to head-to-head competition, at various scales. There has been an Improv Olympics, for example, and a similar practice known as "Theatresports," and many versions of the short-form competitions like those seen on the popular television shows, *Thank God You're Here!* and *Whose Line is it Anyway?* Judges may assign points, or the competition may be about which actor is able to make the other break character, or get up and leave an imaginary bus stop, or utter a particular word. More broadly, improv often takes the form of a kind of competition between the audience and the actors, in which audience members call out premises (or submit them on paper) and the actors have to perform the given scenario "cold." In Chicago, the Neo-Futurist company has for twenty years performed *Too Much Light Makes the Baby Go Blind*, a shifting menu of very short plays—thirty in an hour—combined using audience input to form improvised collages. It's no accident, then, that Stern and Mateas hired two voice actors to play Grace and Trip who are key performers from the Neo-Futurists, Andy Bayiates and Chloe Johnston, both of whom have written for and performed in *Too Much Light*. Just as the audience participates in making improv happen, so the player of *Façade* is simultaneously like an audience member and one of the actors in an improv production, coming up with premises to make meaningful what is otherwise disjointed dialogue, making and accepting or rejecting offers, guessing at hidden motives. The outcome is in the same sense improvised—which is not to say made up from nothing, but instead constructed, performed as a series of responses to inputs within the constraints of a set of rules. Like a game, theatrical improv is both cooperative (play along, agree to the rules, stay inside the magic circle, collaborate in the make-believe) and competitive (try to achieve dominance of some sort, complete the task first, remain standing, make something meaningful out of what you are given, against the odds). It makes sense, actually, that Stern should describe *Façade* in terms of both a competitive FPS (you "fire" discourse acts) and the cooperative effort to "make a drama happen." Both possibilities are already afforded by the long-established conventions of improvisational theater.

## The theater of games

Some of what happens in improve theater games is improvised and some is scripted or rules-bound (if only the basic situation or conventional cues). Without the rules and premises, without the boundaries, the improvisations would not be interesting; without the improvisation there would be no moves, and thus no game. Similarly, *Façade* consists of "natural" speech acts by the human player (and to a limited degree other acts, such as looking at or picking up objects and moving around the apartment); and "artificial" speech acts (and other acts) by the two NPCs, acts driven by (1) AI and the procedures of the game's program; and (2) interactions between the player's input and the AI. The makers of *Façade* see not only the human player but also the NPCs Grace and Trip as essentially improvisational. Andrew Stern said in one interview that "an AI that can understand the gist of what the player is saying—for example, the player's tone, attitude, and topic being addressed—can be very effective for driving the reactions of improvisational NPCs in a rich, flexible, and robust interactive story world. This requires careful design and engineering of the NPCs and story world. . . ."[21] In this way, *Façade* points to something fundamental about almost all video games—that they depend on improvised, collaborative, and dialectical interactions between various forms of natural and artificial intelligence. Players make moves and the game AI (including NPCs) makes moves—not in the limited ludological sense of the term but including all kinds of procedural rules *and* forms of diegetic artifice meant to create events within the gameworld. Gamers experience this dialectic of natural and artificial intelligences most vividly in their interactions with NPCs, where they play along in order to make something interesting happen (primarily to advance in the game). Helper characters such as Cortana in *Halo* or Navi in *Zelda* make this relationship clear, but it happens every time an NPC enemy sneaks up on your flank and fires at you, or a villager gives you directions, or a shopkeeper sells you needed inventory items, or day turns into night. There is something fundamentally theatrical, improvisational, about every instance of such interaction between human intelligence and the intelligence of the game.

The most blatant form of such interaction, where the invisible barrier between natural and artificial intelligence is most visible (often awkwardly so), in the cutscene. Though hard-core gamers tend to skip through them and radical ludologists tend to dismiss them as mere window dressing, Rune Klevjer (2002) has defended cutscenes as integral to computer gameplay. He argues that game theory has suffered from a "confusion of 'game' as a discursive mode and 'computer game' as an actual cultural product." Cutscenes are obviously important features of actually existing, "typical" (rather than structurally ideal or formally abstracted) video games. Indeed, as Klevjer suggests, they are where the fictional or "intertextual" elements of cultural expression—characters, stories, symbolic motifs—that make up the game-world make themselves explicit. In actual gameplay, Klevjer says, games are "at once" both "configurative and interpretive" and the "most accentuated expression of such an impure duality is found in the oscillation between cutscenes and play in typical story-based action games." This is exactly right: cutscenes are revealing in the very awkwardness of their mediating roles. Nowadays, video games are more often than not "rhetorical-ludological bastards" hybrid and impure forms (to use Klevjer's term), not because they are straining to be something else, something purer, but "because we want them to be" mixed, impure, because (as Klevjer shows) what is most interesting about them often takes place in their admixtures.

Formally and structurally, cutscenes can do important work, if they sometimes do it clumsily. They are almost never merely cinematic for their own sake, as Klevjer points out. They provide narrative exposition, reward effort, establish back-story, character, motivation, or the mood of a particular map or series of challenges. But in structural terms, they also provide useful gameplay information, brief training in skills or weapons, say, and they almost always, at the very least, alter the rhythm of gameplay, offering breaks between missions or levels but also, for example, serving as a "catapult" for missions to come—"building up suspense and creating a situation, only to drop the player directly into fast and demanding action-gameplay" (Klevjer, 2002). In many cutscenes the gameplay is more or less halted while the scene runs. The player loses all or partial control of the avatar and/or camera. In traditional arcade-era and early home-console games, the cutscenes' graphics and production values would differ markedly from the game's, since cinematic animation replaced playable avatars and NPCs run by the game engine. But in many recent games this clean duality has been challenged in many ways. Some games, such as *Katamari Damacy* or *Super Paper Mario*, parody by way of exaggeration the boring, "skippable" nature of many mechanical cutscenes. Others, such as *Resident Evil* 4, for example, or *God of War* 2, keep the player engaged by running the cutscenes with the game engine and even remaining partly configurative, requiring the player to push a button at key moments during the scene and within a set time limit. Other games (*Half Life*, for example) allow you to look around or explore the environment while the scene is running. But even the most cinematic, scripted cutscenes offer interesting parallels to *Façade*.

Consider the acclaimed *Kingdom Hearts* games, a kind of gameworld mash-up combining the Disney universe with that of Square Enix's *Final Fantasy* games. Conceptually, this is a deliberate genetic experiment crossing cinematic characters and stories—the Disney catalog, from *Bambi* to *Pirates of the Caribbean*—with a coherent set of RPG (role-playing game) characters, stories, and gameplay conventions, as well as a new set of all of these features, created just for the games. The result is surprisingly successful and engaging. The cutscenes in *Kingdom Hearts*, however, must work to both tap into the player's knowledge of the original films and differentiate themselves in order to fit into the game. So, in the first game, as the avatar Sora, you may find yourself standing with a party consisting of Goofy and Donald Duck, during a cutscene involving, say, the Genie from *Aladdin*. The voice actor even repeats some of the famous lines (originally performed by Robin Williams) from the feature film, but while taking you on a journey from one part of the gameworld to another and preparing you for the next battle. The cutscenes in *Kingdom Hearts* mostly work, I would suggest, because they are openly, brazenly, "rhetorical-ludological bastards" in this way. They are little transitional movies about characters from actual movies that make a virtue of their necessary impurity. Players move in and out of cutscenes with the pleasure of improvising a new role in a well-known "scene" from a beloved film, even if mostly in their heads, while they hold the controller and wait for the scene to end. That the scene plays out very differently from what would be in the Disney film—with references to gameworld features such as the enemy Heartless, for example, or by referring to a vast conspiracy to trap all the Disney princesses, or just because you're aware of your playable character's place in the scene—is part of the recontexualizing pleasure of the game.

A cutscene involving cartoon Disney characters in *Kingdom Hearts* often feels like one of those films in which worlds collide: where a live-action character is mixed with animated characters and settings. (In this case, the live-action character is you, though of course you are playing as an animated avatar.) The most famous examples are probably Disney's own *Who Framed Roger Rabbit* (1988), moments in Warner Brothers cartoons, and the scene in *Anchors Aweigh* (1945) in which the animated mouse from *Tom and Jerry* cartoons does a dance number with Gene Kelly (playing a sailor). In *Hamlet on the Holodeck*, Janet Murray cites some of these examples, including one of the earliest such combinations of live-action and animation, *Gertie the Dinosaur* by Winsor McCay (105–6). The famous cartoonist McCay created a line-drawn animated film of a dinosaur coming out of her cave and doing some tricks, and then he performed with the film on the vaudeville circuit, standing onstage in front of the screen and interacting with the animated Gertie, timing his actions so that he gave her commands to which she seemed to respond, like a circus animal-trainer act. At the end of the performance, McCay slipped behind the screen and was replaced with an animated version of himself, a cartoon avatar, and Gertie picked him up and carried him into the background. Murray cites this as an example of the allure of immersion, and of a new medium allowing for the experimentation at the boundary of what is represented and the real world (103). In the digital era, Murray says, we have now "been invited into the mouth of the dinosaur" (106).

For Murray the ultimate goal is to "define the boundary," the "digital equivalent of the theater's fourth wall," in order to lose ourselves in the represented illusion, "to surrender to the enticements of the virtual environment" (103).

But Gertie can also illustrate something else, a very different kind of "enticement": the constitutive theatrical pleasure of constructing and deconstructing theatrical pleasures, including constructing that very boundary, as show, as a performance, like the mechanics involved in gathering audience premises, sometimes shouted out, during an improv performance. You could say that in fact most interactive media does *not* invite us all the way into the mouth of the dinosaur, to be fused with the animation and immersed in the illusion, but instead invites us on to the stage, like McCay, to stand in front of the projected image, to "play along" in order to make the interactive drama happen. A one-hundred percent realistic dinosaur mouth, into the illusion of which we are enticed, would arguably not provide that specifically theatrical kind of pleasure at all (though it might indeed be more overwhelmingly "immersive"). McCay's act was a blatantly mixed-media stage performance. Its success was exploited by the release of a longer film with a framing narrative, meant just to be watched, but the original vaudeville act was live—or rather half-live—and its dramatic effect was achieved via the interesting and sometimes awkward interaction between human and animated characters (including McCay's own animated avatar). This was no more a totally immersive or realistic cinematic experience than was the Lumière brothers' famous 1895 film of an arriving train, which, despite the popular legend, no one was likely to have actually mistaken for a real locomotive. Only historical condescension allows us to assume that a *fin-de-siècle* audience would have been that naïve. Surely part of the thrill would have been *knowing* that one was reacting viscerally to an image on a screen despite knowing it was only an image, not the simple-minded reaction of one who cannot tell the difference or has become totally immersed in or surrendered to the virtual railway station. I imagine that the audience's double awareness, of the somewhat clumsy fusion of the train made of light and the real bodies in their chairs, would have been fascinating in its own right, not just as a weak prototype of some future medium that would be more and more realistic, its illusions more and more immersive.

McCay's interactions with Gertie involved creating an illusion of interaction, scripting the cartoonist's encounter with an AI of sorts (Gertie as an animated character). What McCay was performing in the stage version of

*Gertie the Dinosaur* was less like the virtual reality immersion of the holodeck and more like giving a Turing test to *Eliza*, or "playing along" with a good dramatic cutscene—or a session of *Façade*. The vaudeville act, like many forms of vaudeville, was partly improvisational in its appearance and effect, even when scripted, and was surprisingly gamelike; McCay tossed a pumpkin to Gertie, for example, and generally played at playing with her. In all of these cases—McCay's vaudeville show, video game cutscene, *Façade*—a human "player" must improvise (and/or script ahead of time) ways to play along with animated artificial actors. The "boundary" in question, between human and artificial actors in a gamelike setting, is not something one seeks to dissolve; on the contrary, it's the primary source of interest and pleasure. It is in effect part of the magic circle of this particular form of play, perhaps best figured in this case as a series of spotlights one steps into and out of while making interesting moves.

The point is that there is a whole history of theatrical conventions that are gamelike, especially, again, if we look at the broad popular tradition that includes the Italian *commedia dell-arte*, the British pantomime, American vaudeville, and modern drama including improv. When video games do something theatrical—from "cinematic" cutscenes to *Façade* as a whole—they are no more strange than a mixed-media vaudeville act or a typical improv performance at *The Second City*. They are theatrical in the gamelike way that certain forms of theater have always been gamelike. By the same token, interactive drama in the future (like *Façade* now) may continue to "want to be" like a game rather than like, say, a totally immersive holonovel. In fact, when you look closely, the *Star Trek* holodeck itself, as the TV series' writers imagined it, is less like conventional immersive theater than like hybrid video games, both those that existed in the 1980s and those that have come after.

The totally immersive fiction, or holonovel, such as the *Jane Eyre*-like story played out by Captain Janeway and cited by Murray, is only one kind of entertainment and simulation available in the holodeck, as viewers of the show may recall. The holodeck was introduced with the 1987 advent of the series, *Star Trek: The Next Generation*, in a scene in which Commander Riker enters the sliding doors (which disappear behind him) and finds himself in a VR forest.[22] Matter is manipulated and synthesized to make tangible objects, not merely realistic images, inside the room. At one point Data, who is demonstrating the system to Riker, throws a rock against the back wall (which pixelates briefly under the impact) to reveal the outer boundary of the illusion. Besides this "woodland pattern," there are thousands of other simulation programs (or "patterns"), he says. Over the course of this and the subsequent series these include simulations of the bridges of earlier starships, for example, and an eighteenth-century seagoing ship named *The Enterprise*. But the holodeck is explicitly intended for the entertainment of the crew, as well. Holoprograms (as they come to be called) don't include *Hamlet* but do include *Prospero's Island* (based on *The Tempest*), other earthlike environments like the woods (a beach for example), a jazz club, erotic simulations, and puzzles. In fact a whole category of holoprograms is made up of sports and games, including a poker game in which one can play against famous scientists of the past. Even the holoprograms that are like immersive novels are also like video games in key ways. In one episode, Worf and his son Alexander play a holoprogram, called *Deadwood* and set in the "Ancient West," that is clearly a kind of FPS.[23] They are gunslingers in Western town under siege and at one point Alexander pauses the shooting to complain that that the difficulty level is too easy. If it's not set higher, he says, then the program won't be any fun. The computer is told to set the level higher and restart the program. At another point in the simulation, Worf, playing the role of Sheriff, beats a villain during a saloon fight and quips like a gamer: "I'm beginning to see the appeal of this program!" Lt. Commander Data is plugged into the ship's computer at the time and a glitch causes multiple rogue copies of him to appear in the simulation in the role of a series of cloned enemies. The episode opened with Alexander sprawled on the floor playing with his computer, and it's clear that the western shoot-'em-up, however immersive and dramatic, is primarily a futuristic form of video game.

If Murray seems to imply that digital media are evolving toward the ideal of a fully immersive kind of interactive drama, more like *Hamlet* than *Mario*, the fictional platform she chooses as the harbinger of that ideal, the *Star Trek* holodeck, was actually created under the assumption of the continued relevance of the video game as a form. From the perspective of the late 1980s and 1990s, when it was created, the holodeck images a future in which programs vary widely but are assumed to consist of an eclectic mixture of gameplay, narrative, and dramatic performance. Total sensory immersion is not assumed, even in the twenty-fourth-century virtual reality that the show's writers imagine. The example I've just cited, the Western FPS in which Alexander resets the difficulty level and restarts the program, reveals just how much holodeck players can (and should) remain in control of the programs they are playing, adjusting, configuring, shutting them off when necessary. At least that's the idea. In that episode, Worf at first finds it impossible to stop the infected program he is playing. This is such a common plot device on the show that fans refer to "holodeck-malfunction episodes" as a genre type. When the player is not in control of the holodeck, when glitches happen causing the boundary between reality and illusion to become confused or to break down altogether, it's cause for serious alarm, not rapturous celebration. In one episode crew members are trapped in the illusion by way of a neural interface so that they believe they are really members of the French Resistance during World War II.[24] The enemies who have taken over the ship use their unwitting immersion in the story against them, hunting them with bullets that have real effects. Indeed, the *danger* of total immersion in the holodeck is arguably the point of the episode that Murray cites in *Hamlet on the Holodeck*, "The Persistence of Vision:" playing in the holonovel must not be confused with running the starship. Being able to play along and still halt a kiss or reset the difficulty of a shooting scene, head out of the automatic sliding doors and back on to the decks of the *Enterprise-D*, is part of the everyday, typical holodeck experience. Normal holodeck play always involves knowing where the door and the controls are, a basic awareness on the part of players—which never dissolves altogether during play—of the spacious grid-mapped room in which one is playing and the embedded devices that synthesize images and objects, the treadmills that give one the illusion of movement. Like a game, the holodeck is a possibility space within which the player makes moves, performs roles, improvises in response to various stimuli, both representational and structural. Ultimately it's a platform for playing along with highly sophisticated AI, acting out various gamelike scenarios in order to make something happen. In this sense the holodeck is an apt metaphor for *Façade*'s aspirations. But, despite all its imagined sophistication, the holodeck never stops being essentially a futuristic video game platform.

Holodeck programs allow for multiplayer scenarios, such as when Worf and Alexander shoot at bad guys together in *Deadwood*. *Façade* is, however, a single-player game, and so far I've been discussing the basic interaction between human player and NPC. But what about playing live with other interactors, possibly with many other interactors? Nowadays the most literally theatrical games, the ones where people act out roles in cooperation or competition with one another, live, are the MMORPGs (massively multiplayer online role-playing games). If you want interactive drama right now, actual cooperative or competitive interactive role-playing, visit *World of Warcraft*'s Azeroth, along with some of the game's over eight million players. It's not *Hamlet*, but it takes place in a persistent fictional world in which players adopt fantasy roles and identities. Despite the genre label of RPG, many players not accessing the explicitly role-playing levels see themselves as playing *as* themselves, not playing fictional roles. They speak in their own voices, for example, and pay attention to gameplay—raids and quests and player level and the economy—rather than story per se. Nevertheless, in a reminder of how theatrical mainstream gaming has become, the software environment, fictional gameworld, and character-avatar system of *World of Warcraft* ensure that to some degree even these non-role-players are always playing *en masque*, as a Dwarf, say, even if they are choosing not to play in character. And they still inevitably encounter and interact with AI-controlled NPCs via "scripted events"—a term with programming roots that also reminds us of the theatrical nature of such in-game encounters. In this way video gameplay in an MMORPG is theatrical and improvisational even when explicit role-playing is not the focus and when one is playing more or less in single-player mode. The point is that we needn't look for full, cathartic VR immersion, traditional narrative, or dramatic illusion in which the player gets lost, in order to find theatrical interaction in video games. Modern, impure forms of drama such as improv, with its gamelike exercises and self-conscious social contract, provide a useful model for this drama.

Self-consciousness about role-playing and a divided attention to the "half-real" nature of the theatrical experience are crucial features of today's video games. But we should not forget that, historically, these features too were built into modern stage drama from the early twentieth century, for example, the Epic Theatre of Bertolt Brecht.[25] The Marxist playwright and dramatic theorist promoted for political reasons the "alienation effect" of a theatre that called its audience's attention to the artifice they were witnessing. Textual labels and signs carried onstage, direct address to the audience, broadly theatrical gestures, are among the techniques Brecht proposed for productively "alienating" the audience from the illusions of the play, *preventing* them from suspending disbelief and provoking in the audience a critical response to what was being represented. Game theorist Gonzala Frasca has argued for a politically active "video games of the oppressed," modeled on Augusto Boal's Theatre of the Oppressed, which is in turn based on the Brechtian tradition.[26] Frasca recognizes that a socially engaged and activist gameplay might need to find inspiration outside the Aristotelean model, might want to resist immersion, might want to call attention to the apparatus of representation in order to encourage critical thinking about representation itself. Frasca mostly imagines thematic representations of ideological and social conflicts in games: for example, a simulation that represents dysfunctional family relations, "video games as tools for education and sociopolitical awareness" (90). But as Stuart Moulthrop observes, "the immersiveness of games differs crucially from that of narratives, and much may depend on the difference."[27]

I would argue that typical video games, not experimental art projects or political interventions, are *non*-immersive in important ways—just in terms of their formal structures and conventions of interface—and at least a large number of players seem to want them that way. *Grand Theft Auto San Andreas*, for example, is potentially more effective than other forms of discourse at exploring social constructions of race and media identities (such as "gangster") because it is a game in which you *play* these constructions, configure them rather than just talk about them, and because it engages these constructions *as* constructions, roles and moves under the control of the control-pad buttons of the PS2, the player's moves in response to the game's AI and highly-charged urban maps.[28] Brecht's theatre, created in part in response to the Frankfurt school's debates, was based on the idea that normalized *formal* innovations, and the collective experience of formal effects for what they are, are the prerequisite for a truly critical and revolutionary theater. The aware audience should ideally not lose themselves in the illusion but should as a matter of course engage the drama, as Brecht imagined it: smoking, discussing, and pushing back against what is represented onstage *as* representation. There's a perfectly reasonable argument to be made for more explicitly political and engaged experiments in video game form, but this needn't necessarily take the form of explicitly political content.[29] Instead, one could argue that a politically critical game could work by foregrounding what games do best, offering the improvisational experience of configuring *and* interpreting various dramatic, narrative, culturally representative materials via gameplay moves.

Stuart Moulthrop rightly suggests we define "configuration" more socially, not just in terms of the in-game experience but also as it relates to the material and social conditions of the game's production and reception—and then perhaps the "conditions of other rule systems such as work and citizenship . . ." (66). Although he concludes that it therefore "may be very important to insist upon the difference between play and interpretation, the better to resist immersion," I would suggest that it might be more effective to insist upon the complex interrelationship of play and interpretation, to be precise about how they are related in specific works in different genres and different media. You can configure to interpret (in literature), or interpret in order to continue configuring (in games). But in practice you usually interpret and configure in interlocked loops of attention in both forms of cultural expression. As narrative theorist Karl Kroeber has argued, there is no reason to see even traditional narrative (or, I would add, Renaissance drama such as Shakespeare's) as unitary, self-identical, strictly authorially created, or passively immersive—quite the contrary. All "[n]arrative discourse is capable of endlessly reconfiguring itself. . . ." Retelling stories with numerous variations is the norm in preliterate cultures, for example, and in preliterate societies private acts of make-believe are not easily separable from the public sphere. The norm over the long duration of human history is "reconstructive feedback between individual and community," giving make-believe "social viability." Even today we are aware that "the meaning of stories is changed by the changing ways they are 'received'—that is, reimagined—over time."[30]

Configuration perhaps plays a more material role in games, however, because you actually re-structure not just the narrative events but also the material and diegetic elements of the gameworld and its objects and settings as you go, rather than just reinterpreting the meanings of a text. But that does not mean that literature is not also configurative in a different, less physical sense—and especially if we consider not isolated verbal texts but unstable and changing textual histories of books and documents as part of larger histories of reception, the performance of literary works. Every new printed edition literally, physically allows the editor to reconfigure a text, of course, but it's also true that every act of engaging and receiving a literary work restructures or reconfigures not only the individual verbal texts in question but also the field of possibilities associated with the work, what we think of when we think of *Hamlet*, say. The same verbal configuration means something different—*is* different—when its publication venue or social context changes the way it's interpreted. Viewed in its entirety, the reception of any complex text involves some form of configuration as well as interpretation, strictly considered, even if the level of *material* configuration, the user actually altering the object's form, is proportionately less significant than in the experience of games.

*Façade* is a work that foregrounds the player's acts of configuration and reconfiguration through acting, as you improvise your way through the drama from minute to minute. Every move changes the possibilities for every next move. A series of discourse-moves made in the opening of the game may ultimately cause Trip to walk out on Grace at the end (or cause them to reconcile); the NPC who more often receives your attention more often bonds with your character in ways that affect the rest of the game; picking up an object prompts the NPCs to discuss it; refusing to "speak" leads to awkward attempts by the NPC AI to read your intentions and, not infrequently, breaks the game altogether. Your agency is a real part of the make-believe of the game and the outcomes of the drama.[31] This is why it seems to me that, for all its flaws, *Façade* affords more interesting opportunities for critical consideration of ideological conditions of marriage, social class, production and alienation, than some more explicitly thematic game we might imagine. It's not a "serious game," it's a game about taking social games seriously. It's about configurative make-believe, coming up with improvised moves in response to social and material conditions, fictive and contextual, inside the gameworld and out of it, in the player's real world, replaying and reinterpreting what is given. Although its creators always discuss openly the limitations and failures of *Façade* as they move ahead with development of their new "interactive drama game," *The Party*, I would argue that *Façade*'s relatively limited software interface, those textual dialogues that cross the screen as you type, the cursor-hand and keyword prompts ("comfort" or "flirt"), the comic-book look of the images, even the stuttering of the AI as it attempts (and often fails) to play along with you—all paradoxically, if fully appreciated, make it a *more* effective theatrical experiment in the Brechtian or improv sense (if a less polished work of dramatic art): a non-immersive, self-conscious, reconfigurative, profoundly improvisational experience. Every time Trip or Grace fails to get the point of what you have said (or typed), the drama breaks down and you are faced with the fact of the difficult collaborative game in which you are involved, and faced with a new kind of obstacle to try to overcome. You find yourself playing something like the "Interact with the AI" game.

## Textual history as cultural improvisation

Part of what I've been arguing is that "*Hamlet* on the holodeck" would be much more gamelike than either Janet Murray or her critics have emphasized, first, because the imaginary holodeck is actually a futuristic game platform, so it serves as a useful reminder of the cultural significance and robustness of games, the importance of the game model for defining foreseeable interactive forms of expression and entertainment. So even a more advanced form of interactive drama would likely remain gamelike in crucial respects, as the experiment of *Façade* in fact demonstrates. *Façade* is a drama that is also a game, as its creators have recently begun to acknowledge in their terminology, referring to *The Party*, the successor to *Façade*, as "an interactive drama/comedy game."[32] Even existing mainstream video games are already in many ways dramatic or theatrical, in terms of character, improvisational moves, and interactions between players (via playable characters or avatars) and NPCs or other players, often *en masque*. From the other side, the theater contains a rich tradition of games and gamelike conventions: you perform or play (and sometimes improvise) roles made up of actions as well as words, moves within set parameters and in cooperation or competition with other players, as well as the system of the play itself. This is a way of acknowledging that a drama is never merely a unitary verbal text that gets voiced, but is instead a composite form of art made up of texts as scripts for always changing performances, acts of collective make-believe, which in turn *produce* texts: transcripts, revisions and documentation, as well as commentary, criticism, and scholarship. Each performance becomes part of the reception history of the work by reconfiguring it *and thus* reinterpreting it. Actors speak of interpreting their lines—and they interpret them by acting them out. Moreover, most performances are to one degree or another improvisations, making something out of what is afforded, the offerings or "moves" made by the text or script, by other players, directors, and sometimes audiences, as well as by the material conditions of any particular staging, theater, lighting, sets, and so on.

The relationship between text and performance in Shakespeare, for example, is historically complicated, but most scholars now agree that the "platform" of the Elizabethan theater was at its core collaborative, inherently social, and endlessly reconfigurative. So what about *Hamlet* not as mere text but as a work for the stage? *Hamlet*, it turns out, is the Shakespeare play that contains the most explicit passage in his corpus on this complex relationship, which goes to the heart of the nature of the social text in the world of Elizabethan drama. In Act 3, scene 2, the Prince directs a traveling theatrical troupe in how to perform without too much gesturing: "do not saw the air / too much with your hand, thus, but use all gently" (ll. 4–5), and offers this bit of practical advice to the actors: "suit the action to the word, the / word to the action" (ll. 18–19). This is of course a reference to decorum, the fitness of the right gesture to the right speech and so on, a typical Renaissance rhetorical concern. For Shakespeare's audiences the scene would have addressed a perhaps more mundane version of the tendency for words and actions to diverge, the productive tension between texts and performances. The common tendency at this late date in the history of "bardolotry" is to read the lines as a frustrated expression of the genius author's superior intentions for "his" text; but of course Shakespeare was an actor, a player, and a stakeholder in the theater, as well as an author, and the lines can be read backwards, too, as a humorous acknowledgment of the player's co-creative power on the Elizabethan stage, even when it might annoy authors. Either way, the scene reminds us that two things—what was written and what was performed, the word and the action—were combined in order to make a play happen. Hamlet, perhaps speaking for Shakespeare, seems particularly concerned about the improvisational freedom enjoyed by those actors who specialized in the parts of clowns or fools: "let those that play / your clowns speak no more than is set down for them," he says, instead of improvising stage business to get laughs and maybe distracting the audience from "some necessary question of the play" (ll. 39–40; 43). Presumably, comic actors, such as the popular William Kempe, took even more license than other actors when it came to configuring the play around their own performances. One leading comedian from a slightly earlier era, Richard Tarleton, was famous for a repeated "gag" in which he would poke his head out of the "tiring house" or dressing room door during the performance, looking out at the audience and making them laugh.[33] This kind of response from an audience playing along with the actor may well have been common. Shakespeare's audience was usually not concealed behind the "fourth wall" of a darkened and hushed theater, but included many who were standing around the stage, often outdoors, as at the Globe, close to the stage, and some who were sometimes actually seated on the edge of the stage, so it's likely that a fairly high degree of audience interaction with the plays was the norm.

The "platform" of the theater, including the physical staging, the actual "boards" of the stage, and resulting audience expectations, provides the context in which another strangely metatheatrical scene in *Hamlet* must be understood. In Act I scene 5, Hamlet has taken his friends out to see the ghost of his father, and asks them to swear an oath when the Ghost, the actor hidden beneath a trapdoor in the wooden stage, in the "cellarage," cries out, "Swear!" "Come on, you hear this fellow in the cellarage," Hamlet says, seeming to wink at the audience like one of the comic actors he will later criticize, responding to the Ghost as if he were not in Purgatory or Hell, which is what the cellarage space conventionally represented, but literally under the boards of the stage. Then the Ghost seems to move around, causing Hamlet to follow from above, taking his friends with him. When the Ghost calls out again "Swear by his sword," Hamlet retorts, "Well said, old mole. Cans't work I'th'earth so fast? / A worthy pioneer!" When we connect this scene with the directing scene discussed above, it seems like an instance of Shakespeare's indulging in the very kind of playing to the audience he has Hamlet criticize. Indeed, most critics have understood this scene as a bit of comic relief, a moment when Shakespeare has his actor play to the crowd for laughs about the artificiality of the stage itself as the voice comes first from one spot and then from another, a momentary break in the dramatic illusion or feeling of immersion. But the Elizabethan theater was apparently not about creating a total sensory illusion anyway, as far as we can tell, and we may be tempted to read too much *difference*, too much of the exceptional, into this scene. Perhaps the point is that it indicates a fairly common kind of mixed experience on the part of playgoers and players who must cooperate in order to make believe together that the space under the stage is hell, say, and that an actor is a ghost. It's worth remembering, as we consider the tensions between the author and the actor, that Shakespeare may even have himself played the part of the Ghost.

Stephen Orgel has noted the connection between the two scenes and has argued that "the jokes about the voice in the 'cellarage' and all the rushing about the stage to avoid the 'old mole' beneath will look to an audience without access to the script like a particularly disruptive kind of comic improvisation."[34] For Orgel, this reveals an integral feature of the theater of Shakespeare's time, "the tension between text and performance" (253). A given work, "*Hamlet*," for example, not only in his lifetime but increasingly in the centuries that followed, "included broad areas of possibility and difference, and was not at all limited to the text of 'the true original copies' " (as the Folio edition says), and "the text of a play was thought of as distinctly, essentially, by nature, unfixed; always open to revision" (267). Orgel implies that scholars ought to be "less exclusively concerned with establishing texts and more concerned with the nature of plays" (253).

In fact, Orgel is one of a group of scholars, including Gary Taylor and Stanley Wells, among others, who have helped to establish a new paradigm in Shakespearean textual studies that is more interested in the fundamentally unstable and reconfigurative nature of performance history than in establishing behind the surviving verbal texts the author's true, unitary intentions.[35] When modern Shakespearean textual studies was first established by W. W. Greg, A. W. Pollard, and R. B. McKerrow early in the twentieth century, the goal was to sift out through careful study and stemmatic mapping of textual relationships as much as possible of the contamination introduced by scribes and printers and actors and others in order to get back to an authoritative text, an ideal text now lost (and probably never materially realized even by Shakespeare himself in his own manuscripts). Some quarto editions of plays were thought of as "good" and some as "bad," just in terms of their distance from the posited lost original.

More recently, as part of the changes in textual studies theory I have associated in earlier chapters with Jerome McGann and D. F. McKenzie, the dominant emphasis has shifted to a recognition that even Shakespeare's intentions for any given work were likely multiple and changing, that there were probably multiple versions of each play, and a given work was always under revision for various occasions, different troupes of actors, and in difference playhouses, as part of what McGann has called "the entire developing process of a literary work's historical transmission."[36] As Orgel summarizes the now widely (though not universally) accepted view, actors improvised variations in their performance depending on the particular audience for whom they were performing.

> —the play before the king was not the same as the play at the Globe, and neither of them was the text that came from the author's pen. . . . Our printed texts are not what Shakespeare's actors spoke. (252)

The most direct evidence of this that Orgel adduces is the fact that a play such as *Hamlet* is much longer than almost any performance would have been; cuts would have been necessary and were probably taken for granted. But one can also look at the title page to the first printed edition of *Hamlet*, the Quarto of 1603, for a suggestive reminder of the tension between any one single text and the more multifarious space of possibility that added up to the performance and reception history of "*Hamlet*," how *Hamlet* happened: "The Tragicall Historie of HAMLET | Prince of Denmarke | By William Shakespeare. | As it hath beene diverse times acted by his Highnesse servants in the Citie of London: as also in the two Universities of Cambridge and Oxford, and else-where. . . ." As Hamlet says elsewhere in that capacious and multifarious work, "The play's the thing."

Video games, especially experimental games like *Façade*, are useful reminders of how all texts are pretexts for one sort of performance or another of cultural works. All performances involve improvised responses or moves made within a possibility space bounded by given constraints and affordances, and these moves make meanings. A quarto of *Hamlet*, like any text, is a snapshot of the larger dynamic reception history of the whole work and its field of possibilities.

Compare Shakespeare's texts to the actual verbal texts made available in *Façade*, the "stageplays" generated automatically after the fact of individual sessions. Though they look like scripts for performances, they are actually post-scripts, transcripts capturing as textual snapshots the performances that have already taken place, records of instances of gameplay by the human player and Grace and Trip, complete with non-verbal discourse acts and basic stage directions. The following is a portion of a stageplay from a game I played showing one of several possible endings (in this case I'm playing as Adam):

*Trip:*   No, Grace, this isn't about you, or me, it's about us . . .
*Trip:*   Our marriage. I see that now.
*Grace:*   Us . . .? Our—our marriage . . .? Hey, no, wait!
*Adam:*   But wait . . .
*Trip:*   And no, . . . Adam, enough of that already . . .
*Trip:*   Adam, I'm sorry. You really helped us though, so, thanks.
*Adam:*   You can work it out.
*Grace:*   Trip!
          (Trip closes the front door.)
          (Trip opens the front door.)
*Grace:*   Trip!!
*Grace:*   Oh my God . . .
*Grace:*   I should have told him that . . .
*Grace:*   I could have told him that . . .

When I played this iteration of the game I was not entirely sure why Grace almost repeated her final line (was that a glitch or a dramatic emphasis?), but I did know that I felt engaged in the process of making something interestingly dramatic happen, rather than immersed in an illusion, when Trip cut me off and dismissed my final attempt to intervene in the breakup.[37] And that was just one session of the game. A whole folder full of stageplays is produced by anyone who plays *Façade* over a period of time, so that the multiplicity of open-ended possibilities when it comes to meaning-making acts is vividly demonstrated by the growing collection of text files on your hard drive. These texts are not *Façade*, just as the 1603 Quarto is not *Hamlet*. They are only part of the game, the other more important part of which is played out in repeated and replayable, meaningfully different, acts of performed reception history. Player moves, always more or less improvised, make the meanings. The gameplay's the thing.

# Chapter 5

# The Wii platform

Nothing in recent years has generated more general public interest when it comes to how people play video games than the release of Nintendo's Wii console in November 2006. During development it was codenamed "Revolution," and its reception as a gaming platform has been shaped by high expectations, set well before it was released, that it would offer something new in the gameplay experience. At the same time, the marketing has stressed simplicity, accessibility and a revolutionary *return* to the kind of simple fun long associated with Nintendo as a brand. These high expectations have all been focused on the controller for the system, the "Wiimote": a plain white rectangular wand, shaped like a TV-remote control or a cellphone, a wireless device that maps analog movements by the player—swinging a tennis racquet or a sword or putting spin on a bowling ball—to digital movements in the game. But the overall effect of the Wii platform has involved much more than this innovative controller and other hardware. It has involved more than the software, too, whether the system software or the games that have been adapted or created for the system (so far, mostly the former). The effect of the Wii has been based on the successful production of a charged atmosphere surrounding the platform—a cultural aura—to the extent that, it has become increasingly clear, the platform *is* the cultural aura, or at least is inseparable from it. This chapter looks at the Wii as a culturally defined platform, examining some of the mediating connections between its hardware and its software at the crossroads of the culture, the place of the Wii's reception.

What does a platform mean? This chapter was inspired in part by the announcement of a new book series recently launched at MIT press, edited by prominent game theorists Ian Bogost and Nick Montfort, called *Platform Studies*. The resonance of that series title is no accident, since the aims of *Platform Studies* are in keeping with the general aims of a materialist textual studies. The books in this series, we are told, will "explain how the technical make-up of the Atari VCS/Atari 2600 (and other platforms) has influenced the development of games, art, literature, music, and other expression." Most important, the editors understand the shifting, amorphous nature of the object of their study:

> A platform is a perspective on parts of a computing system, not an inherent quality of some system or parts of it. To someone who is porting Linux to the Dreamcast, the Dreamcast is the platform. To someone developing the scripting language Lua on Linux, Linux is the platform. . . . It's true, therefore, that platforms do not exist in the way that a hard drive or a binary file does. They are, however, an essential way that computing systems are compartmentalized, abstracted, and managed by developers.

My purpose in what follows, using the Wii example (puns are par for the course when it comes to the Wii), is to extend this excellent definition of video game platform to include the cultural context, where platform is constructed as a "perspective," in part by its own reception and the reception of games played on it. Like D. F. McKenzie's social text, a video game platform is a dynamic field, the combined effect of a game system's hardware, software, and the whole system's complex life in the world.

## Book history and platform history

But first, a word about books. Textual studies has always been closely related to a broader academic field known as history of the book (or simply book history), the interdisciplinary study of the role of the book as a material object, and of print culture's relationship to cultural history in general. Books are a sophisticated form of technology for cultural expression and communication, but this goes beyond the codex format (as opposed to scrolls, for example, or carved runes, or tablets), the two-page opening with its conventions for printing and reading, and the formats by which gatherings of large folded sheets of paper are cut to size, gathered, and bound. For materials made since the fifteenth century, it has involved the technology of the printing press, including moveable type and later forms of typesetting, formes and frames for holding the type, and machines for pressing out its images onto paper. Book history includes as well the means of distributing the results, so it must examine the social "technologies" of institutions as well: copyright law, publishers, printers, sellers of books, libraries and monasteries and private collections of them, ways of getting them into the hands of readers or collectors, patronage, subscription, and (later) commercial marketing. Practices of reading complete the process, and this necessarily touches on the subjects of sociology or social history: class, degree of leisure, gender, religious affiliation, and level of education of potential readers for given books at specific historical moments and locations. As book historian Robert Darnton has said, this is less a linear trajectory and more a kind of "life cycle," a circulating system of production, distribution, reception, and more production.[1] This circuit as a whole is basically the same as McKenzie's and McGann's field of the "social text," the life cycle of texts in the world. In the past couple of decades, traditional book history, with its focus on print culture, has merged with theories of the social text (including a greater recognition of textual instability and a new emphasis on reception history) to make up the interdisciplinary practice I have been calling textual studies. At the heart of both traditions, book history and textual studies, is an emphasis on what might be called text technologies, the material methods by which texts of various kinds get made and distributed and received.

In this sense platform studies already is a form of textual studies, focused on objects that are not (primarily) verbal texts. By analogy, we can speak of the "platform" of eighteenth-century print culture as a social framework that included among its components the printing press, the bookseller-publisher (in various combinations of these two roles), and the reading practices of a multi-layered public. Formats of publication varied in their physical details, in terms of their material technologies of representation; and with these variations necessarily were produced differences of meaning. This idea of "meaning" is quite distinct from the semiotic, verbal meanings of the words in a given text, a poem, say.

Consider the British gift-book annuals of the 1820s to 1840s, what Jerome McGann has called "probably the most important venue for nineteenth-century poetry."[2] These collections were extremely popular; something like 100,000 copies of different annuals were sold in 1828; a single popular annual, *The Keepsake*, was selling over 15,000 copies every season by the 1830s.[3] Descendants (or replacements) of the traditional manuscript "commonplace books" young women in particular had kept in their own handwriting since the Renaissance, the annuals contained a miscellany of short fiction, essays, and poetry, but many were deliberately multimedia publications, containing reproductions of fine art along with literature, making them appropriate gifts and collectibles, lavishly produced and aimed at a mostly middle-class and female audience. The gift-books were something like collectible coffee-table books in our own time and they became a lucrative enterprise in part by their carefully timed release: they appeared at the end of the year, in November and December, with the date on the cover of the following year, so one would give one's beloved the *Keepsake* for 1829, say, for Christmas of 1828, ensuring that she would have the latest volume in the parlor all through the year to come. As Paula Feldman has said, "Savvy publishers" employed a "powerful psychological strategy" to sell them, linking gift-books to personal relationships and social reputation. Thus they became "some of the earliest practitioners of niche marketing in the history of the book trade."[4]

These books were not transparent content-delivery systems, in other words. They were self-consciously made physical objects to collect, "mementos of desire or intimacy" as well as status and taste (Feldman, 9–10), bound in silk or tooled leather with gilt-edge leaves and illustrations. These nineteenth-century gift-books, which existed in many competing series—*The Bijou, The Amulet, The Forget Me Not, The Literary Souvenir, The Keepsake*—were a new kind of format, a publishing platform. They were scorned by many in the literary establishment, including the Romantic poet Wordsworth, but were nevertheless the lucrative place to publish poetry in the 1820s and 1830s (including for Wordsworth). Their conventions can be traced to earlier forms, such as pocketbooks, almanacs, and manuscript commonplace books (Feldman, 10), but they were a new combination of verbal and visual media at the right moment for the right market, and they both enabled and constrained—gave form to—artistic expressions.

As a platform, the annuals were enabled by both old and new technologies. The conventions of special bindings and so on were gestures to long-established signs of worth in books, but their inclusion of so many images of works of art was made possible by the newly developed technology of steel-plate engraving, just coming into use during the 1820s. Steel plates allow for somewhat finer lines in their images, but their more significant feature in this context was their durability. Unlike copper plates, steel could stand the process of printing truly mass-produced books (Feldman, 13). As a direct result, the gift-book annuals "on an unprecedented scale, allowed ordinary people to own high quality reproductions of significant works of art" (7). *The Keepsake*, one of the most successful annuals, was founded by an engraver, who hired an editor. It was even possible to purchase the proofs of the plates separately as stand-alone works of art.[5] It was often the practice to start with an image, an engraved portrait or reproduction of a landscape by an important contemporary artist such as William Turner, and then commission a poet or story writer to write something in response to the image. This was a kind of publishing game encouraging interesting moves on the part of "content providers." Some, like Letitia Elizabeth Landon, wrote direct poetic addresses to the image itself ("Lady thy face is very beautiful . . ."). Others might spin off an imaginative tale only very loosely inspired by a landscape as a setting. But the expressive form itself, poem or story about an image, was shaped by the writers' moves in response to the determining constraints of the multimedia conventions of the new publishing platform, the gift-book annual. That platform came into being to reach an audience, part real and part projected by the publishers and marketers, who, in the event, responded to these conventions and demanded (or at least continued to buy) new, annual publications in this form. The conventions of the new platform were in turn made possible by a particular technology of image-reproduction, steel-plate engraving. Literal technology is only one part of a larger mosaic involving social and economic and cultural forces combined at a specific historical moment and resulting in new forms of expression.

## Wii technology

The example of annual gift-book publishing reminds us that many overlapping factors come into play to define any platform, including technologies of production and reproduction. We tend to think of each company's console in a given generation—Xbox 360, PlayStation 3, Wii—as a different platform because of the use of different proprietary technologies to achieve similar ends. If we were to pursue this analogy, we might say that the nineteenth-century gift-book annuals were less like the Wii and more like console gaming as a whole (in competition with online games, for example), less like a specific proprietary platform than like the overall platform of console games. The analogy is not a perfect fit, since our market for and definitions of platforms has radically multiplied in the past two centuries. Still, the point is that, just as steel-plate engraving helped to define the form (and ultimately, the meaning) of poetry in Britain in the 1820s and 1830s, so game console technologies help to define the form (and meaning) of video games inspired and constrained by those technologies. But different publishers make different uses of available technologies. The *Keepsake*, for example, founded by an engraver, was positioned to exploit the emergence of steel-plate engraving more extensively than other annuals, and so became known for its art. Similarly, the Wii has exploited certain emergent technologies in order to differentiate itself against other consoles, and in the process is helping to define the meaning of video games through its new platform.

The Wii is the fifth home console released by Nintendo, a Kyoto-based global giant with a long history, going back to the manufacture of traditional *hanafuda* playing cards in the nineteenth century, and a powerful reputation for innovation in game technology. The Wii (2006) followed immediately on the GameCube (2001–), Nintendo 64 (1996–2002), the 16-bit Super Nintendo Entertainment System or SNES (1990–2000), and the 8-bit NES (1983–1994). In addition, there have been two major Nintendo handheld systems, both extremely popular, the Game Boy (1989–) and DS (2004–).[6] The Wii is especially interesting because of the way it was designed and marketed against the prevailing assumptions driving console innovation: ever-increasing power and higher-definition, more realistic, graphics. The venerated video game designer and Nintendo executive, Shigeru Miyamoto, who started out as a staff artist designing toys and became the creator of the *Mario* and *Zelda* franchises, two of the most popular and highest rated game series ever, said about the Wii that "power isn't everything for a console. Too many powerful consoles can't coexist. It's like having only ferocious dinosaurs. They might fight and hasten their own extinction."[7] The analogy from evolutionary theory is telling; as a competitor, the Wii has so far succeeded against its competitors in this generation by taking a fresh approach to—or more like an end run around—its competition. This is allowing Nintendo to overcome a problem it had with the GameCube, "competing with its wealthier rivals on expensive technology-driven performance."[8] The Wii by contrast is dominating a hitherto uncrowded but extremely wide demographic niche in the game-market environment: the casual or first-time gamer, the older adult or female gamer, someone who just wants to have fun or to provide her [sic] family with fun. (Miyamoto has also said that the company asked itself, "What might convince moms to buy this for their kids?") The Wii is dominating this broadly popular niche. It's a big niche. Sales statistics throughout early 2007 showed the Wii far ahead of the competition. In April, for example, 360,000 Wiis were sold, as opposed to 174,000 Xbox 360s and 82,000 PS3s. (Although sales of discounted PS2s were next in line behind the Wii, at 194,000, Nintendo's handheld DS topped the chart with 471,000 units). During May 2007, Nintendo sold *five times* as many Wii's as Sony sold PS3s in Japan.[9] This success is partly due to Nintendo's marketing strategy and partly to the initial design decisions to make it small and stylish and inexpensive. The Wii has rejected sheer power and its affordances (such as realistic high-definition graphics, or the ability to play DVDs) in order to be smart and fast, the fittest rather than the most ferocious dinosaur, and thus to survive in a place—the niche to which it is uniquely adapted—set apart from the main competition between Microsoft and Sony.

In fact, the Wii's simple white box is both the symbolic representation and the literal embodiment of this targeted-adaptation model. It's smaller—roughly $6'' \times 8.5'' \times 1.7''$ as opposed to roughly $10'' \times 12'' \times 3''$ for the Xbox and PS3—what its marketing has referred to as the size of three DVD cases, and lighter—2.7 lbs as opposed to 10 or 11 lbs for the other two. Its modest 729 MHz processor (an IBM PowerPC "Broadway" chip) contrasts starkly with the 3.2 GHz processors of the two competitors. In terms of video, the Wii has an ATI ("Hollywood") 243 MHz GPU and 480p standard definition rather than the 1080p high-definition TV on the other platforms, the kind of graphics expected by hardcore players of highly cinematic games. Though different-colored models have been demonstrated, the first-released version came only in white and the slim console clearly resembled other minimalist design successes such as Apple's iPod or, for that matter, Nintendo's own extremely popular handheld DS. The developers strategically sacrificed power, probably in part to keep the box small and cool-running and help achieve this physical semiotic effect of "simplicity," but also, more importantly, to try keep the price below $250 (originally, Nintendo reportedly hoped to keep it to about $100). If the model is to be the fast and nimble smaller dinosaur exploiting its own niche while the behemoths beat each other up, the paradox behind the strategy is that the "niche" Nintendo aimed for (and seems to be reaching) is the vast territory of all non-gamers, actually much larger than the existing saturated space of the dedicated or hardcore gamer demographic—for the control of which Microsoft and Sony theoretically continue to compete.

The symbolic fetish-object at the center of Nintendo's comeback success is the wireless remote controller (the "Wiimote"), which has been repeatedly described according to company plan as "revolutionary." Although there's little in its technology that's entirely new, its combination of features in a console controller has never been marketed before, and especially not as part of a streamlined, deliberately simple and intuitive, user interface. Shaped like a slim TV remote with only a few buttons, the controller is designed to be used with one hand, though for some games you turn it sideways and use two hands and for others it gets connected by a 3-foot cable to a separate "nunchuck" controller with an analog stick and C- and Z-buttons, which allows for two-handed play in various configurations. Waving the controller around translates into actions on the screen, thanks to three very tiny accelerometers inside. These MEMS (micro electro-mechanical system) motion-sensing devices make use of a spring-mounted sliver of silicon the movements of which, both direction and acceleration, are measured by changes in voltage in surrounding plates. The accelerometers allow for measurements along three axes: up and down, side to side, and forward and back. The measurements are beamed to the console via a Bluetooth connection, where they're compared to a database of possible moves in a given game situation, so that if you swing your arm and twist your wrist, you roll and put spin on a virtual bowling ball on the screen. In addition, the Wiimote communicates via infrared with an LED (light-emitting diode) sensor bar mounted on top or in front of the TV screen, in order to register precisely where you are pointing. The controller also contains a small speaker and a motor for haptics, feedback effects of sound and vibration in your hand (though this last is not unique to the Wiimote controller). The button arrangement includes an A-button on the top and a B-button on the lower side that's curved like a trigger, so you can squeeze both with one hand, and a small cross-shaped D-pad. Because of the accelerometers, the controller can be used in any position, including vertically (as in swinging a golf club or baseball bat) or horizontally (held in two hands like handlebars for some driving and flying games), as well as pointing longwise at the screen.

The Wiimote's rectilinear form resembles the boxlike controller for Nintendo's classic Famicom system (or "Family Computer;" it was released as the NES or Nintendo Entertainment System in North America), which was no accident, since the Wii is meant to return Nintendo to the dominance it enjoyed in the late 1980s, and the NES is credited with helping to bring the whole industry back from the financial crash of 1983. Miyamoto has himself drawn the connection between the two systems and their controllers; the NES was intuitively simple, he says, unlike PC games that relied on the keyboard for input.[10] He characterizes the difference in terms of different "audiences" of potential players. The Wiimote and nunchuk (or *nunchaku*, a Japanese martial arts weapon), he argues, offers the best of both styles of play, appealing to both kinds of audiences—allowing for complex moves players have become used to but without as many overly complicated buttons to remember. Giving gamers access to something of the aura of 1980s Nintendo gaming is part of the company's strategy. The accessory most in demand after the nunchuk Miyamoto mentions (which is very nearly a necessity, given the number of games that require it), is probably the Classic Controller. It plugs into the base of the Wiimote, becoming a parasitic part of the controller, and is a stylized version of traditional two-handed controllers, with two analog thumbsticks and a D-pad, as well as a full array of conventional buttons. It's made of matching white plastic with the Wii logo centered at its top, but it allows one to play on the Wii earlier games available for download via the Virtual Console service, and the jacked-together hybrid controller is a material sign of the Wii's position between "retro" and "revolution."

In fact the Wiimote is a kind of material synecdoche, a part that stands for the whole, for the aura created by Nintendo's marketing strategy: a deliberate combination of relatively sophisticated human-computer-interface technology and retro-style intuitive simplicity, moving into the future of video games by returning to what Nintendo did best in its heyday in the 1980s. The Wiimote signifies simultaneously new and classic gameplay; it's a little goofy and a little cool in a way that fans understand. It's based on much more than simple-minded nostalgia. Instead, it works as a knowing citation of classic gaming, a claim that old Nintendo games were better than many of the current block-busters. In the end, the button combinations are not that much less complex than on any other system (especially once you add the nunchuk), and the movements do not map as precisely as in virtual-reality simulations (players quickly learn that you can just flick your wrist to hit a baseball; it's not necessary to take a hitter's stance and swing with two hands using the control-ler), but what is important to many new users is the relative sense of "freedom" conveyed by the controller as a symbolic object, which means in part relative freedom from long-established controls and the serious technical expertise with those controls possessed by hardcore gamers, and at a lower price. The difference, in other words, is as much cultural as technical. Jaded gamers may be enticed by the prospect of old-school fun, and a possibility space is created for the non-gamer or casual gamer, a space, as Nintendo's ads show repeatedly, for women, especially, or for anyone not in the stereotypic hardcore-gamer demographic, to stand or sit on the couch, to flail around in a silly way, and to see all of this as cool because it's not trying to be cool, because it's just "fun." Potential players seem to have responded in large numbers to the campaign or to the viral effects of it, the campaign's reverberations in the culture.

## Wii software

The Wiimote controller contains its own limited amount of memory, some of which can be used to save, store, and transport to other consoles the cute cartoon-style animated "Mii" avatars you create and customize. Nothing could be further from the serious form of cool expected from, say, the Xbox, and nothing is more representative of the spirit of the software that ships with the Wii. Miis are one of the key identifying features of the system. Once you make them they live in the console's memory but show up in many Wii games, either as playable characters or NPCs (for example, as team-members or cheering spectators in a sports game). On the Mii Plaza they can mingle online (in a Mii Parade) with your own and other people's Miis. The Plaza is accessible on a separate channel, one of several on the system, including news and weather and the Internet Channel, essentially a customized Opera web browser, and the Virtual Console, a kind of software store where you can download older games and, eventually, new games made for the Wii. The Mii Channel is a deliberately limited, lighthearted alternative to the live services and online communities attached to the other consoles, Xbox Live, or Sony's *Second Life*-like 3-D *Home* for the PlayStation. The brightly colored caricature-based Miis, which resemble Playmobil figures or exaggeratedly cartoon-like Sims, are graphic personifications of the strategically playful ethos of the Wii as a whole.

Game console technologies help to define the form (and meaning) of software, the video games inspired and constrained by those technologies. But the determining connections between hardware and software are often indirect and highly mediated. Many of the new game titles produced for the Wii at the time I am writing have been effectively ports or adaptations of older games, originally developed for the GameCube, for example. In these cases Wii-specific functions are added, but often without fundamentally altering the gameplay. The most direct connection between technology and form is evident in games where free-motion gestures affect gameplay, starting with the *Wii Sports* package that comes bundled with the system and has been especially popular with casual gamers—with tennis, golf, bowling, boxing, and baseball mini-games serving almost as demos of the system and its controller. These games provide the ludological base, as it were, for the Wii system as a whole. Not complicated sports simulations, they are graphically simple in a self-conscious way that calls attention to their simplicity; the Mii player characters and NPCs don't have arms, for example, but simply have tennis racquets or baseball bats protruding from the place near their polished-surface torsos where arms would be. And they're relentlessly cute, a kind of global version of Nintendo *kawaii*: large doll-like features, whimsical looking in bright colors, collectible and customizable as well as playable. The cooperation with the AI-driven characters is straightforward and intuitive: when you play doubles tennis with only two human players, for example, one Mii is designated as your main avatar, but you are also automatically given a cloned Mii as your partner (as is your human opponent). Playing at the net, he or she responds to your controller gestures in place of the main, baseline Mii in cases in which the ball comes within playable distance. Other Miis jump and cheer when the camera takes a shot of the stands. The later-released *Wii Play* continued the controller-and-Mii experiments; it contains *Table Tennis, Laser Hockey, Fishing, Billiards*, and other games, including *Shooting Range* and *Tanks*, and two extremely simple matching and manipulation games, apparently for children, specifically using the player's collection of Miis, *Find Mii* and *Pose Mii*. Completing one game unlocks the next, until all nine are available. It's telling, in terms of targeted audience, that the Japanese name for this package is *My First Wii*.

If the sports games seem like demos of the system, the same can also be said for *WarioWare: Smooth Moves*, which feels like it came straight from the R&D lab, still fresh and partly unfinished. It's a series of over two-hundred fast-paced timed micro-games that train you in various possible gestures (called "forms" in the game) using Wiimote: holding it on your nose like an elephant's trunk ("Elephant"), holding it on your head ("Mohawk"), balancing it like a tray ("Waiter"), setting it down on the actual floor or table and then snatching it up at just the right moment ("Discard"). Holding it in the standard way is ironically called simply "Remote Control." Besides testing the remote and training the user in pointing and waving as a game interface, *WarioWare* also applies its vivid graphics and the self-conscious irony already associated with the series to the Wiimote (which is mock-pretentiously called the "Form Baton" in the game). Planned Wii games include *Wii Music* (in which you conduct and orchestra with the Wiimote and play drums) and *Wii Health Pack* (an exercise game). These are all "party games," meant to be used in a casual social setting and for short bursts of gameplay. Other experiments with the Wiimote by third-party developers include games in different genres, for example, a new

*Harry Potter* game in which you use the controller as a magic wand, casting spells by waving it in different specific patterns.

Nintendo is clearly counting on developers to continue to come up with innovative ways to use the Wii. If one side of Nintendo's strategy is to go after the broad non-gamer and casual market through hardware design by making the Wii inexpensive and simple, then the other side involves changing the company's culture and courting third-party software developers as never before, seeking out creative games for the Wii made by Namco Bandai, for example, and Square Enix.[11] Already some developers are paying as much attention to Nintendo as to Sony in this regard, a significant change in the development environment since the GameCube. Moreover, Nintendo seems to be pushing the possibility of creative independent games being developed in Flash, say, and made available via the Virtual Console. But for now the less direct role played by the new platform's technology when it comes to deter-mining game design can best be illustrated with two of the longest lasting and most beloved franchises in the game canon, *Zelda* and *Mario*. Both were the creations of the legendary Shigeru Miyamoto, who is also behind the Wii. *The Legend of Zelda: Twilight Princess*, the latest action RPG (role-playing game) in the series, was released with the Wii in 2006. It was originally developed for the GameCube, however, and was only converted or updated for the Wii after the fact. GameCube and Wii versions came out almost simultaneously.

The new controller did determine some key changes in the Wii version. In general, weapons handling is different with the Wii, with some button-combinations being replaced by the pointing and waving afforded by the Wiimote to hack or slash with the sword (although the spin attack with the sword is activated by waving the nunchuk). Fishing also involves using the Wiimote like a rod. Locking onto a target with the Z-button still works in the old way: you see an arrow over an enemy as you approach, you Z-target it and the arrow changes color. But shooting at something, which you must do repeatedly in the game, whether with a slingshot or boomerang, bow and arrow or grappling hook, involves actually pointing at it with the Wiimote (though you can lock on with Z after spotlighting the target). The small speaker in the handheld control-ler is also used in interesting ways for feedback; when you fire an arrow, the whoosh sound travels from your hand to the console (and your target). Fans know that Link, the iconic hero and main player-character in all *Zelda* games, has always been left-handed—just like his creator, Shigeru Miyamoto. But because the sword in the Wii version is wielded by actually jabbing and slicing the air with the Wiimote, and most testers preferred to do that right-handed, the GameCube code was rewritten to not only make Link right-handed, but also to orient the whole gameworld, the well-known Kingdom of Hyrule and its environs, to his right-handedness. So all the maps and their orientations were flipped, with locations to the east becoming locations to the west, roads leading off to the left instead of the right, and so on.[12] So the GameCube and Wii versions of the *Twilight Princess* gameworlds are in effect mirror images of one another, the result of changes determined by the design of the new controller; and the resulting differences affect gameplay in subtle ways. Interestingly, some of the more committed fans posting online were disturbed by the change in what they saw as a fundamental characteristic of Link (despite the fact that there have been many quite different versions of Link in the course of the series). Others were bothered by the deviation caused by the mirroring from what the designers of the first GameCube version originally intended, even at the level of such details as which side an enemy approaches from and which eye is covered by a hat. The fact that fans knew about the change and had strong opinions about it is characteristic of gamer culture and a fundamental condition of the reception of games.

The *Zelda* games are among the most popular of all time, with an extremely dedicated fanbase. Miyamoto created the series and worked at the hands-on level of director on the games up through 1998 *Ocarina of Time* (for N64). After *Wii Sports, Twilight Princess* was probably the game most closely associated with the new system during its rollout in late 2006. Having a new *Zelda* game available for the launch of the new system was a first for Nintendo, and was both a crucial part of the marketing of the Wii to long-time fans of the series and a clever way to pull new purchasers of the new system into the *Zelda* universe for the first time.

The most famous game character of all time, however, is probably Miyamoto's little cartoon plumber, Mario. First conceived of as a carpenter called Jumpman, because his main action was to jump from platform to platform, Mario became a plumber and was first introduced in *Donkey Kong* (1981). He rapidly increased in popularity over the course of subsequent games, and quickly became Nintendo's company mascot. The Wii uses a running and jumping classic Mario icon as the graphical download-meter. Mario became a cultural icon with the platformer game *Super Mario Bros.* (1985), still the best-selling video game of all time. According to Chris Kohler, it sold 4,810,000 copies in Japan alone and probably over twenty million copies worldwide.[13] Until recently, every new Nintendo system came associated with the release of a new Mario game. *Super Mario Bros.* was released for the NES and was closely associated with the innovations of that system, and lent its own aura to the system in turn, in a kind of symbiotic development loop. For its time, the game was so extensive in its gameplay and graphics that Nintendo added a special additional processor chip to the game cartridge to assist the console (Kohler, 57). Kohler argues that *Super Mario Bros.* was a breakthrough in 1985 in terms of gameplay and narrative, the most complex and extended game to that point, and that it was the first game of its era to make reaching the story's conclusion the primary goal; though you were scored, the point was really to save the princess and see what happened in the conclusion (57). Side-scrolling screens extended the platform playing field along the horizontal axis, allowing gameplay to move through dozens of display screens in each level (58). Continuing to extend the dimensions of the gameworld, both literally and figuratively, became a hallmark of the Mario series.

In early 2007 Nintendo released *Super Paper Mario* for the Wii, a kind of conceptual sequel to the RPG *Paper Mario* for the Nintendo 64 (2000 in Japan; 2001 in America and Europe). The earlier game, developed by Intelligent Systems for Nintendo with consultation by Miyamoto, made use of a distinctive retro-style 2-D-looking paper-cutout characters in a gameworld, Star Haven (the story contains many star images). Gameplay involves obstacles, quests, puzzles, and battles. The sequel for the Wii, *Super Paper Mario*, is a brilliant variation on the original, and in fact blends elements from other Mario games as well (especially *Super Mario Brothers*). In terms of genre, it's a hybrid platformer RPG. Similar 2-D-looking characters run and jump and interact with blocks and turtle enemies (Koopas) and fight boss battles in dungeons in order to rescue a princess. There are some surreal twists in its over-the-top story, including a new villain and an "aftergame" (instead of afterlife) that takes place in Underwhere and Overthere. Gameplay often invokes *Super Mario Bros.*, with some settings and character graphics and RPG story and gameplay elements reminiscent of *Paper Mario*. There are even turn-based battles in the aftergame. The one-up mushroom turns your sprite Mario into a truly gigantic avatar, but this Super Mario is a blown-up image of a highly pixilated old-school sprite-like Mario from earlier 8-bit games. The result is a blocky abstraction of Mario-ness, a comic idea of the character as a digital image. *Super Paper Mario* was originally developed for the GameCube and was only shifted to the Wii just before its release. You mostly use the Wiimote held sideways in two hands, so that it resembles the old NES controller, but you can also use it (with the fairy-like "Pixl" cursor-characters) to point at the screen and reveal hidden doors or other secrets, and you can shake the controller to get extra points at times; otherwise, there's little in the game that's any more specifically connected to the Wii than to the GameCube.

The real innovation of the Wii game, the thing that sets *Super Paper Mario* apart, is not Wiimote-specific at all, but it's the kind of innovative design the general atmosphere surrounding the Wii has apparently encouraged. The player can push the A-button to flip from two to three dimensions. When you do, a portal, a cut-out door, appears in the flat backdrop, rotates with your character, and the setting flips to a 3-D view. So rows of blocks that were impassible in side-scrolling platform mode are now revealed as only one block deep and you can find a way around them. What looked like a distant backdrop of mountains flips to reveal itself as a close-up narrow ramp that you can climb onto and use to cross behind a chasm. Enemies or coins are revealed hidden behind pipes or rocks or blocks once you see them in 3-D, or, conversely, you discover you can just swerve around an oncoming enemy rather than jump over or on top of him, once he is seen in perspective. You can only stay in the third dimension for a limited time without losing health, so you play mostly in 2-D, always knowing that things are not as they appear. Your characters, however, remain 2-D cutouts (sometimes they twirl around to reveal their flatness), more like playing-card images than modern avatars. The rhythm of gameplay is determined by your decisions to flip and flip back from one perspective to another. The game's website exploits the hybrid aesthetic to the full: "Old school gaming goes 3-D!," it reads.

This crude slogan, though it's clearly reductive of game history and of the range of pleasures of playing *Super Paper Mario*, indicates something very important about the connection between platform and game in this case: not the use of advanced motion-sensor technology but the general self-consciousness about game history that Nintendo has leveraged to its advantage with the Wii, the sense of controlling a deep video game canon and of what that in turn affords—always-available multiple perspectives on game design and gameplay. A couple of decades ago, a scholar might have called this attitude "postmodern"—the leveling referentiality, infinite citability, mixing of surface textures in an aesthetic based on "bricolage" and "pastiche." But in the present moment of Web 2.0, fan fiction, file sharing, social networks, mashups, machinima, and wikimedia, such strategies and aesthetics are simply every-day, vernacular forms of expression—which should go some way toward explaining the easy and vast popularity of the Wii. (Old-school gaming goes n-dimensional!)

A much-anticipated new game designed for the Wii (not yet released as I write, but previewable in gameplay videos), *Super Mario Galaxy*, will apparently exploit the platform's unique features more extensively than any current game, such as the Wiimote's ability to allow the player to control objects with direct pointing. Miyamoto sees the game as part of the Wii's strategy of attracting new gamers. It makes comically-shaped planetary bodies, asteroids and planets, and so on, the "platforms" on which Mario runs and jumps, toying with perspective, a planetary-level zoom, so that Mario appears to be running on spheres at one moment and, with a zoom in, appears to be running across the larger plane of the planet's surface. A planet can be room-sized or world-sized, depending on a quick shift in perspective, making *Super Paper Mario*'s flipping from 2-D to 3-D look like a conceptual run-through for *Galaxy*. Gameplay will be two-handed, involving the nunchuck for moving Mario and the Wiimote for pointing a small star-cursor at objects (coins, stars, rocket enemies with Mickey-mouse-style arms) in order to hold them, redirect them or collect them; the same cursor will direct Mario's running and jumping. At least one reviewer sees *Super Mario Galaxy* as a game for the hardcore gamer, in contrast with most of the titles so far made available for the Wii.[14] But the company clearly sees it as bridging between various kinds of gamers while building the Wii base, appealing to new gamers as well. The cartoon galaxy looks remarkably like previews of Will Wright's *Spore*, as we'll see in the next chapter, and it's also reminiscent of the general settings of *Katamari Damacy*— perhaps indicating that a retro-looking space setting has in recent years emerged as a new meme for indicating "innovative" or "creative" game design.

But old-school gaming (signified by Mario's iconic presence) goes n-dimensional on the Wii overall, not just in any one game. The whole point of the console from the beginning was to have a system on which one could play Nintendo's back-catalogue, a way to access the canon as a database, as it were. Niintendo CEO Satoru Iwata reportedly wanted the Wii to "play every Nintendo game ever made."[15] The most effective application when it comes to that particular goal is the Virtual Console, a channel on the Wii that amounts to a kind of iTunes Store for old games. The Virtual Console is itself like a game for collectors: you purchase (or otherwise acquire) Wii points to spend at the store, either on cards at retail outlets or with a credit card online; a classic 1980s title may cost 500 or 1000 points for a download ($5 or $10). By May 2007 there were ninety-five games available. Titles included games originally for much earlier systems, including N64, NES, SNES (as well as some games licensed from other companies, Sega, for example), so that it was theoretically possible to turn the Wii console into an emulator of the Nintendo universe, or at least a subset of it. The goal is to recreate the feel of gameplay in the classic era, but on a "revolutionary" new system. Of course, this must be accomplished through facsimiles, through emulation: the original code needs tweaking at times to make the games playable on the Wii, some button-commands are switched around, and aspect ratios are sometimes altered. But the overall experience thereby constructed is one of access to game history, a porting of the cultural aura of the old-school fun of Nintendo from a time when "Nintendo" was almost synonymous with "video games" for the general public. It will be theoretically possible, eventually, to play through the *Mario* canon from *Donkey Kong* to *Super Mario Galaxy*—in fact to virtually toggle back and forth from, say, *Super Mario Bros.* to *Super Paper Mario*, making the flippable dimensions of the latter game seem like a specific instance of the larger general effect of the Wii as a platform: every-day multidimensionality.

## Culture wares

Game console technologies help to determine the meaning of video games inspired and constrained by those technologies, but the material technologies of production and reproduction can only come together with the forms of expression they support in the arena of culture, which is where meanings get made. As Montfort and Bogost point out, a "platform is a perspective," an abstraction, a way of conceptualizing a system for delivering a video game to the game player. In this sense, any platform is a "virtual console"—a cultural construct as much as a hardware and software construct. When a product hits the sweet spot as the Wii has done, it's likely the result of specific technologies and specific applications coming together, at just the right time, in a way that enables such a cultural platform to take shape at the crossroads of marketing efforts by the producers and acts of constructive reception on the part of consumers and (if you're particularly lucky) loyal fans.

The Wii was designed to leverage Nintendo's cultural capital in order to profit from gaming's "futures." Miyamoto tells the story of the invention of the Wii in 2003 as a meeting of engineers and designers discussing "the future of video games" (Hall). They debated technical features for the console, he says, but they also sought to design the system so that it would appeal to (and sell to) "moms," a way of referring to the non-gamer market (and a source of untapped income). So "the future of video games" was framed by the company not so much in terms of technology but in terms of "basic concepts and goals," presumably including abstract design goals but also perhaps goals concerning Nintendo's public image and the image of gaming in the larger culture. Miyamoto has also said that the Wii was designed to overthrow the stereotype of the antisocial video game player; again the goal was not technological but cultural. He mentions as his inspiration a 1993 book originally titled, *Game Over; How Nintendo Zapped an American Industry, Captured Your Dollars, and Enslaved Your Children*. The book contains a photograph of a zombie-like child whose face is lit by a game screen. It seemed important to "break out of that image," the designer says, to "break free from that stereotypical definition of what a gamer is, because until we do, we'll never truly be part of the national or worldwide culture."[16] When asked by the interviewer what he'd like the new image of the gamer to be, Miyamoto pointed to the photos being used in the company's campaign for the Wii, pictures of older people and children, a large number of them female, all standing and moving around, having active fun. So the mission to reposition videogaming in the larger culture happens to coincide with the nimble-dinosaur strategy for dominating the largest niche of potential video gamers: casual gamers interested in fun, including women in particular.

The truth is, this has been Nintendo's particular marketing strategy for many years and the Wii campaign has just returned to it and updated it. Looking back at the rollout of the Game Boy in 1991, David Sheff wrote (in the same 1993 book that Miyamoto says inspired in its negative portrayal his new vision of the gamer) that, as Nintendo's "target audience," which at the time were male preteens, became "saturated," it naturally pursued a new customer demographic. He quotes Nintendo PR executive Peter Main on the company's longtime strategy to escape from the "narrow base" and historic cliché of the player as an 8–13-year-old male.[17] Sheff suggests that younger girls became part of the new targeted demographic in a big way with the Game Boy (ironically enough, given the name), in part because "more powerful systems by competitors had distracted some of Nintendo's formerly loyal boys" (292). His own bias is clear in the assumption that gamers are mostly girls or boys (the "enslaved . . . children" of his book's title). Shifts in the perception of gamer demographics to match reality had been underway for at least a decade by 2003, when the Wii was designed. The stereotypical video game player, if he ever really existed in quite such numbers as marketers believed, was being displaced from various directions, replaced by older male (and some female) hardcore gamers, as well as by casual gamers (often women, often playing on cellphones or the Internet). In the 1990s the press focused a good deal on the untapped potential market of the "girl gamer." Barbie-themed games and even a pink PlayStation were one result, but the relative success among women of handhelds, especially the Game Boy and the DS, and the incredible popularity of Will Wright's *Sims* games (especially for PC) and MMORPGs such as *World of Warcraft* with a broader demographic, including adults and women, has forced a general recognition that things are more complicated in terms of games and gender and that the older stereotypes are often being perpetuated by the games industry and a certain hardcore contingent of players but do not reflect actual player demographics or interests, considered statistically. By one count, even several years ago, almost forty percent of active gamers in the U.S. are women.[18]

One interesting feature of the Wii ad campaign is its avoidance of simpleminded pink-hardware essentialism, even in the face of a good deal of popular talk and journalism about the Wii's being "for girls." One notorious example of this kind of journalism (and talk) was a promotional story in *Glamour* magazine (UK) in advance of the Wii's release, showing two models on the couch ready for a girls' night Wii party including cocktails and the Wii ("Want a night to remember?") (http://www.ukresistance.co.uk/2006/11/nintendo-wii-is-definitely-meant-for.html). Its list of "5 reasons why every girl needs a Wii" starts with "Because isn't it about time we had something he wants, but can't get his hands on?" The piece inspired virulent sexist comments on the Internet; it may have been based on marketing materials sent to the magazine by Nintendo, but, at any rate, it's one indicator of how far the "for girls" idea was threatening to some, even before the November 2006 release date. In retrospect, what's most prescient about the piece is the idea that the Wii is made for parties, for making gameplay a fun social activity. This has continued to be an important feature in the reception of the platform, and one that has no obvious correlation to gender. All platforms now allow for LAN (local area network) parties or group play of some kind, but in this context the Wii is part of a larger trend towards a more specific kind of "party:" the increasing popularity of highly social forms of game meant for group play and taking turns performing (ideally for an audience of other players). These would include especially *Guitar Hero, Dance Dance Revolution, Donkey Konga* and other similar musical games. Like Karaoke, and pre-video-game party games from the previous century such as *Twister*, these games are designed to promote social interaction around relatively casual, shorter bursts of gameplay.

Another media object will serve to demonstrate how layered and complicated the cultural references to gender can get in the midst of a campaign as charged as the Wii's. Months before the release, back in fall 2006, a 1.25-minute video that first appeared on the cable TV channel originally dedicated to games and aimed at male viewers, *G4*. A parody of the acclaimed Apple PC vs. Mac ads ("Hello, I'm a PC"), the spot represents the consoles as two women, the PS3 a sturdy, bespectacled, serious type, and the Wii a skinny blonde in a bikini and spiked heels who writhes her way through the dialogue like a stripper. The Wii likes go-carts ("vroom-vroom") and catches a prop red shell straight out of *Mario Kart*; the PS3 is interested in "World War II combat, karaoke, and tackle football." The Wii is "just as cute as a button" and "peppy," whereas the PS3 is "educated and worldly." The PS3 is "expensive" ("good things cost good money"); the Wii is "cheap. And fun." The spot ends with a picture of the system and the slogan, "Wii: very very fun."

Presumably someone at the male-targeted cable channel made this video in which game consoles are represented as what they have historically in fact been—objects of male desire. In that context the spot at first appears to favor the Wii: it's just sexier. But, as the sometimes confused comments on the web in response to the video revealed, the spot actually reveals (or gets caught in) its own misogynistic ambivalences, since the sexy and cute Wii is also clearly the stereotypical bimbo or slut, dumb as well as "peppy." Presumably the hardcore male gamer would want to seduce the Wii but would want his console to be all the things the PS3 woman declares *she* is (serious, educated, expensive worldy, knowledgeable about World War II). PS3 woman would seem to actually speak for him, perhaps an unconscious projection of the homosocial ethos of much of hardcore gaming. At any rate, the relatively masculine PS3 is in no danger of being taken for a "girl's" console. Some on the web (presumably Sony fans) assumed that the video was made by a "Nintendo fanboy." Others objected to the sexism of the film, or just to the derogatory implications that the Wii was "stupid" or "easy." Most interestingly, some people speculated that Nintendo was itself behind the video—despite the G4 brand in the corner—that it was a stealthy viral marketing ploy masquerading as a fan video on a cable channel, carefully timed to appear two months or so in advance of the product release.

That scenario is not very likely in this case, any more than Nintendo would have supplied copy to the *Glamour* writer for that different use of stereotypes. But in a viral media ecology where such things *might* happen, the effect is more or less the same, either way. The atmosphere surrounding the new console was only made more highly charged by such paratextual events, planned or not. The video made its way around the Internet, and buzz was generated. One imagines that at least Nintendo might not have been especially opposed to these kind of secondary and perhaps fan-created semi-viral pitches to, on the one hand, (female) non-gamers, or, on the other hand, to (male) hardcore gamers. But the company's official ad campaign was very different in tone. It aimed the console at an iconically "multicultural," "global"— "mass"— audience, while appearing to recognize that an important feature of that audience is its relative feminization. It's now widely assumed that the non-stereotypical, non-hardcore gamer is the most desirable target for new games and new platforms. The Nintendo campaign seems to understand that this relatively untapped audience is usefully imagined as gendered "feminine," whatever its actual sexual demographics, according to the same logic that sees hardcore gamers as gendered "masculine." The Wii has not been sold explicitly to women. Instead Nintendo has carefully represented gameplay as a space that's friendly to girls and women and old people as well as a slice of the 18–34-year-old male demographic. The first wave of TV ads show, as Miyamoto wished, people of different ages, standing and in motion. None of them looks like a serious or hardcore gamer, even those (a minority of those shown) play-ing FPS (first-person shooters) or action-adventure games. They're represented in each case as having fun.

The TV ads feature a team of two Japanese men in suits, Nintendo employees, presumably, driving up in a tiny Smart car, arriving unexpectedly at various locations in America, knocking on the door or walking into the yard, holding up a Wiimote and saying "We [or 'Wii'] would like to play." Then, over a soundtrack of electro-Japanese world music with a techno-beat, a mont-age sequence of fun gameplay ensues. At the end, the men say farewell, put on their dark sunglasses, and drive off into the sunset as the two "i"'s in the Wii logo bow quickly, Japanese-style. In the first spot the suited team (looking like Men in Black) arrives at a big-city high-rise, where they play *Zelda: Twilight*

*Princess* and what looks like *Metroid Prime 3: Corruption* with a trio of twenty-somethings: a white man, a black man, and a white woman. (The woman stands and watches and cheers, but she never takes a turn with the controller. In other ads girls and women do play.) Other ads show, for example, two bearded men in a rural setting (they have cows and chickens roaming around) playing sports and driving, and animal-themed games (one appears to be playing *Rayman Raving Rabbids*); a corporate boardroom, where a somber all-male board make Miis and begin to break out in laughter as the grumpy CEO's Mii gets funny hair (including a girl's pigtails) but then bowls a strike in *Wii Sports* while all his workers cheer; a white suburban family, girls and boys, who play *WarioWare: Smooth Moves*, wiggling and dancing around with the Wiimote; a matching ad but with a Mexican American family in Los Angeles; a multigenerational white family making Miis and laughing at the results (in this ad the Mii of one of the Japanese visitors gets a little girl's hairstyle); and a longer compilation-ad with clips from all of the other ads and ending with the two suited men, standing onstage before a cheering crowd, saying loudly "Wii would like to play!"—now a charged manifesto.

The campaign's message is clear in the compilation ad's title: "Wii for All," though it should more precisely read "Wii for all non-hardcore casual gamers, including old people and women." In this way, very much like the nineteenth-century gift-book annuals, the Wii is a platform aimed at a relatively feminized, middle-class segment of the marketplace, but it also imagines that marketplace as a potential "mass" audience, in terms of revenue possibilities and the audience's mainstream sensibilities. Instead of good taste in art and literature, however, the Wii as a platform promises to bestow upon its purchasers the gift of access to gaming in terms of simple fun.

Of course this is to speak only about Nintendo's side of the campaign. How fans and consumers are actually reacting is hard to determine—beyond sales figures, that is. Whether actual demographics match expectations (raw sales numbers certainly do) is another story. As the reaction to the *Glamour* article evinced early on, there is plenty of anecdotal evidence out on the web of a backlash among hardcore gamers against the perceived "lightweight" qualities of the system and its games. This is the loaded subtext of the *IGN* Editor Matt Casamassina's reassuring his audience in his video review that *Super Mario Galaxy* is "one of those games for the hardcore crowd," different from the "mainstream-y" or "non-gamer-y" games most closely associated with the Wii.

He clearly feels uncomfortable saying how much he enjoyed the game, but admits that it has made him a "believer" in the Wii as a platform. All the complexities of the reception of Nintendo's new platform are evident behind these remarks, taken in context. In fact, the platform, the Wii as a social construct, is being defined and in a real sense produced by these remarks and thousands of others like them. This is a perfect example of how a platform exists as a social text, defined by the particulars of its own reception.

Robert Darnton speaks of book history as a "circuit" running from creation to production to distribution to reception. Video games have a parallel (though different) cycle through which they circulate—and any particular phase of the cycle can affect the meaning of the game at any time. Even long after it has left the publisher, for example, a game's meaning can be shaped by attitudes toward gameplay, form, or fans emanating from the parent company and evident in its history of interactions with the public. The porting of an earlier game in a franchise to a new console, acting as an emulator as well as innovative platform, affects the reception and meaning of the old game (*Super Mario Bros*, say) as much as it affects the reception and meaning of new games (such as *Super Mario Galaxy*). The existence of the Wii and its Virtual Console, and the creation of easy links among a range of historical Mario games, inevitably changes the way we play the older Mario games, whether or not any individual act of gameplay is fully conscious of these changes. The overall reception history of the *Mario* franchise is materially changed by that port. And the way the Wii is received (and constructed by its cultural reception) will help to determine the meaning henceforth of *Super Mario Bros*, and *Super Mario Galaxy*, and any other game played on that platform. Platform is a dynamic function at any given time of the producing company, marketing campaigns, competing systems, ready fan culture, game history—the whole complex of determining factors that give Nintendo's Wii, for example, a special kind of social or cultural aura. Ultimately, this constructed cultural aura *is* the platform, and it is just as significant a part of the meaning of any video game as are its characters, narratives, gameworld, rules, and structures of gameplay.

Just as textual studies must be prepared to examine the institutions of treaty-making and attitudes toward the land in Aboriginal culture in New Zealand, for example, in order to understand the meanings and histories of particular texts of treaties, so studies of video games must look at the larger cultural phenomena that give meaning to a new platform like the Wii. A new method of steel-plate engraving in the 1820s can be connected to the meaning of a poem printed in a book, but only if we take into account various mediating factors: the publishers' attempts to market poetry to a newly populated female reading public by way of gift-book annuals, and the cultural forces of class and gender that helped determine the market for reproductions of fine art at the same time. Similarly, the Wiimote, with its simple, intuitive, gestural interface, can be connected to the meaning (not just the mechanics) of a new *Metroid* or *Zelda* or *Mario* game, but only if we realize the complicated mediating factors at work (including gender, in this case, as well), factors that define the platform on which the game is played. Platform must be understood as a (cultural) "perspective," as a culturally-constructed system that combines but is larger than the sum of the parts: hardware, software, and social contexts.

In late May 2007, moviegoers in the U.K. were watching the advertisement reel before showings of *Pirates of the Caribbean: At World's End* during its opening weekend. The ads were interrupted by a woman calling for her son, Steve. She found him sitting down front, loudly challenged him to a rematch of *Wii Tennis*, and Steve and his mother then played the game live in front of the theater with the Wii screen projected onto the big screen.

This was actually a viral marketing campaign by a company called CommentUK, in conjunction with Carlton Screen Advertising, with five teams of performer-pairs doing the act across Britain in nine different theaters over two weekends. The Marketing Director behind the campaign said in advance of the ads: "We expect to reach thousands of cinema goers over the next two weeks . . . we feel sure that the word of mouth viral effect of the activity will have a positive impact for the brand."[19] No doubt he's right, although online comments after the fact varied and included complaints about the invasion of viral marketing into every facet of life. But by the logic of viral marketing, these complaints only contributed to the buzz, and others were surely impressed with the game and its platform when they saw it displayed in such a literally theatrical, larger-than-life setting.

*Figure 5.1*  Actors playing at playing the Wii in a London cinema. Used by permission of CommentUK.

It's hard not to think in this circumstance of Winsor McCay and his vaudeville Gertie the Dinosaur show, virtual-reality experiments like The Cave, and holodeck dreams in general. But a moment's reflection reminds us that in this case the difference is that people are literally gaming as well as performing gaming, playing a sports simulation on an existing game platform; only the scale, the size of the screen, and the audience, and the set-up by the actors who become players, has changed. The living room or *home* theater is the real targeted performance venue for the advertised platform, but the Wii is about playing games in public, in social settings, with the player standing (or sitting) in front of a screen (usually a smaller television screen) and interacting somatically, bodily, with the game, waving her arms, jumping around, making a game happen. Making a move requires physical movement (beyond pushing buttons). There's a good reason the Nintendo ads (and the gallery of short candid-looking "Wii Experience" videos at the Wii website) always show players actively playing more than they show whatever's on the screen. Despite all the talk of its being intuitive and natural, the Wii's interface is anything but transparent. On the contrary, it is very carefully engineered, in every sense. In designing a marketing campaign to appeal to the non-hardcore niche, Nintendo has designed a platform that self-consciously embraces the idea that the player's moves, the player's body, are central components of the system. This perspective on gameplay may be at once the most old-school and the most revolutionary feature of the Wii as a platform. Either way, the fans and players will eventually decide.

# Chapter 6

# Anticipating *Spore*

This chapter is about a game that isn't finished yet. As I write, Maxis/
Electronic Arts' *Spore* is reportedly "complete," but is still being refined in
testing stage, in preparation for its release in 2008. However, thousands of
people around the world have seen previews of it in various forms, from
trailers and screen shots on the web to personal demos by its creator, Will
Wright, a charismatic star among game designers.[1] Other celebrities, such as
the actor Robin Williams and the experimental musician Brian Eno, have
helped to demonstrate the game (Eno is composing its generative music soundtrack).[2] It has been the subject of numerous articles and lectures and has won
several key industry awards already, just based on the demos and videos and
lectures and word of mouth. I've chosen to discuss *Spore* in advance because it
makes such a compelling case of how a video game can change the conversation
and influence the future of the form just through previews and advance press.
In fact *Spore*'s pre-marketing—the unprecedented intensity of its preview representations, and the conceptual discussions and theorizing by Wright and
others—mirrors the kind of evolutionary dominance that is the central theme
of the game. *Spore* has claimed the competitive position of leader, as the "future
of video games," without anyone ever having played the game as a whole. As I
researched this chapter and the months passed with delays in the release
schedule (as I write, it's slated for mid 2008), it became clear that I would not
get to play *Spore* before the book was published; it also became clear that even
in pre-game mode *Spore* was already dominating its niche in the media
environment, modeling (in theory) a concept of gaming that was already having
an influence on how people thought of the meaning of video games. So this
chapter is about *Spore*'s "pre-game" stage, a cultural phenomenon in its own
right. Though I base what follows on preview materials, and the final game may
of course differ in crucial ways from what I've so far been led to expect (you
who are reading this will know), my focus is precisely on what we are being led
to expect from *Spore* in this pre-release stage, and that's nothing less than a

theoretical model of one future for video games: as the generative output of an ongoing process of collaborative "editorial" world-building.

## Sporenography

In May 2005 (coincidentally around the same time that *Spore* went into initial production),[3] Take Two Interactive and Rockstar Games, the publisher and notorious developers of the critically acclaimed and widely demonized *Grand Theft Auto* series, announced a new third-person action adventure game. The new game would be set in a reform school, Bullworth Academy, instead of a fictional American city, and you'd play as a "troublesome schoolboy" in a disheveled uniform instead of a gangster on the streets.[4] Predictably enough, *Bully* was soon attacked in the press, especially by conservative activist-attorney Jack Thompson, who had wrangled with Rockstar over previous games, based mostly on this simple advance description, under the assumption that the player's character would be the bully of the title, that the game would train kids in violent behavior and glorify bullying. When the actual game was released in October 2006, it was revealed to be quite a bit more interesting, and more morally ambiguous, than expected. The main character, 15-year-old Jimmy Hopkins, mostly goes on missions in which he can fight bullies and defend the weak. Interestingly, the mission-based storyline is in keeping with the troubled position of CJ in *GTA: San Andreas*, who is caught up in the gangster life from the beginning encounter with corrupt police, seemingly prey to social forces beyond his control; playing *Bully* as Jimmy, you are faced with choices about how much to participate in the school's culture of bullying. Resisting the bullying life becomes one possible motivation for successful gameplay. In the end, the game's most subversive feature for many critics, and one likely reason it was assigned the T (for Teen) rating, was not the schoolyard violence but that it allowed for same-sex make-out scenes between Jimmy and another boy.

My point is that the early attacks on the game as glorifying violence and (at the last minute) homosexual activity, while perhaps inevitable given Rockstar's history (especially the infamous "Hot Coffee" mod for *GTA: San Andreas* that allowed your character to have sex with a prostitute), happened before anyone had actually played the game or even seen it played through. The public debate was staged based entirely on press-release descriptions of the game and then on preview screenshots, hearsay, blog posts, cultural buzz. It's not out of the question, of course, that the game was deliberately pre-marketed and titled by Take Two Interactive in order to provoke such advance controversy, which is rarely a bad thing for video game sales. At any rate, the horizon of expectations within which *Bully* was received was largely established before the fact of the game, in collaboration with the press and an activist lawyer, in a space we might think of as the preliminary paratextual arena, really more pre-text than paratext. Game critics who later played and often praised the game did so in the context of this arena, in unavoidable reaction to the attacks.

To some extent every game comes into the world pre-marketed and pre-viewed, its reception prepared for it in one way or another in this arena of public expectations. The paratextual effect of previews and demos is to create an initial threshold into the game, a defined space in which the meanings of the game can be partly predetermined, pre-played out in public. *Harry Potter* books are one fairly rare exception of this happening in the print world, and of course extensive early campaigns are mounted for some movies, and, less often, musical albums, but to a much greater extent video games depend on their preview phase, and on the overlapping networks of fan and casual online communities that are waiting to see and interpret previews, to generate buzz, pre-orders, and a cultural context, vectors along which the larger social meanings of the game will continue to unfold once it is released. Especially for those video games deemed important in some way, either marked by technical or design innovations, or just sequels in well-known franchises, the reception history begins well before the release date. And it can end there, too, as was brought home by the recent case of another Rockstar sequel, *Manhunt 2*, against which attorney Jack Thompson again brought suit; the controversy resulted in countersuits and settlements, as well as in the game's being banned in the U.K. and elsewhere. It first received an Adults Only rating in the U.S. Take Two modified the game in late summer 2007 to receive the milder M rating.

*Manhunt 2* and *Bully* were attacked based on the reputation of the developers and other games in the same series or by the same company. At the other end of the market, in an entirely different genre, the reverse effect can be seen, as a kind of presumptive halo hovers over Will Wright, perhaps the most revered game creator in America, the only one to truly rival the fan-adoration attached to Japanese masters such as Shigeru Miyamoto. Wright's reputation as the creator of *The Sims* (2000), the best-selling PC game in history and a franchise highly regarded by many adults as well as children, women as well as men, offers a pre-text for a positive reception. So advance notice in 2005 of a new "god game" code-named "Sim Everything" created widespread excitement. By now, anyone with an interest in video games has seen at least one of the many preview video demos released during the past two years of what is now called *Spore*, and all are out there on the web, on YouTube or linked to from specific conference sites. This is quite apart from the official trailers created by Maxis and Electronic Arts to preview the game. As is the case with most widely anticipated video games, dedicated fansites have come online along with the official websites, and links to available videos are distributed and redistributed everywhere. The official *Spore* website (www.spore.com) is arguably the *least* significant location on the web when it comes to news about the game. A quick search of YouTube alone as I drafted this paragraph produced 2700 results— many of them of course duplicate versions or clips of longer videos, but still an impressive number for an unreleased game. The most significant are videos showing Will Wright's gameplay demos at major events over the past two years, such as GDC (Game Developers' Conference), GDC Europe, and E3 (Electronic Entertainment Expo), and the special demo and lecture in conjunction with composer Brian Eno for the Long Now Foundation (made available online by ForaTV). Some are linked to journalism, such as the interview and short demo at the *New Yorker* Conference, "2012: Stories from the Near Future," with John Seabrook, who also authored a long profile of Wright and *Spore* for the magazine, not usually considered a venue for writing about video games.[5] Mostly the journalism follows in the wake of one of Wright's demos, often providing narrative descriptions of what it was like to watch him play the game. This wealth of demo videos, despite the fact that in most of them Wright shows off the same basic features of the game, and often makes many of the same remarks, gives viewers and fans a sense that they have experienced something of the game before the game. The journalism serves as paratextual framing for the vicarious experience offered in the preview videos. A dedicated fan who has bookmarked *Planet Spore*, for example, or *Total Spore*, or the relevant section of *Gamespot* and other sites that track the latest game news, can come to feel that he or she knows the game, has a stake in it, long before playing it. Previews work best when they seduce the fan into believing he or she is getting a taste of the game itself. But in the end, real fans know better. Such preview materials are a form of marketing, of course, and they aim to whet the appetite, to build anticipation for the desired experience while ironically ending up as a substitute for that deferred experience. So in that sense the *Spore* previews have aptly been named in one blogger's keyword-tag "Sporenography."[6]

The most conventional kind of preview video for an unreleased game is the trailer, which often imitates cinematic trailers in structure and formal effects, using specialized animations rather than in-game shots. Trailers are part of the category of cinematics to which many cutscenes also belong—of the game but not in it. Some game trailers are actually shown in theaters and on TV, but most are also distributed and viewed on the web, first from publishers' or production companies' sites and then—if successful—on gamer magazine and review sites, fansites, YouTube, and blogs. Trailers are often little movies, with cinematic production values, rendered and mixed from various sources but sometimes including demo videos or cutscenes. Of greater interest to potential players is the video of actual gameplay, what the game engine is capable of, complete with indicators and meters, heads-up displays of various kinds, the real interface of the game as it is played. Sometimes these are released by game companies and sometimes by authorized early reviewers. But a whole media ecosystem of previews, both stills and video, exists below the level of these official forms. The more dedicated a fan one is, and thus the more time one spends immersed in game sites and blogs and scans the media flow on a regular basis, including social networks of other fans and using RSS (rich site summary, or really simple syndication) subscriptions, the more likely one is to encounter such preview materials. One of the more interesting examples is the posting of screen grabs and text descriptions of gameplay based on what can be glimpsed on the screens of developers' workstations running in the background during video interviews for a making-of preview film. Like spies, fans are looking at screens within screens for the latest "intelligence" about a forthcoming game. Details about new maps and settings, as well as armor, weapons, and vehicles, were cherry-picked in this way from the making of *Halo* videos, for example, by fans who glimpsed the game in development, peering over the shoulders of interviewees, into the very offices and on to the desktops of the designers. It seems unlikely that the makers of the interview video would have been unaware of the titillating effect these brief vicarious glimpses would have among the dedicated fans out there, waiting for such advance intelligence. In this context, simply leaving the screens on in the background of the preview video, and thus revealing tantalizing views of bits of gameplay, could well have been an act of viral marketing.

Compared to this kind of advance marketing, the *Spore* previews have been relatively sparse and have been remarkably consistent in their formal structure. Yes, there was a first official *Spore* trailer in 2006, complete with fast-moving action animations and a catchy soundtrack with a beat. It opens with a parody of the usual science-fiction game trailer: a lightning storm. But in this case we zoom in not on a cybersoldier on a cliff, say, but into and down under the ocean, where cells are reproducing. The film then runs through the basic structure of the game in time-lapse form, from the beginning in a microscopic world of cells, to more complex, evolved cartoon creatures, who eventually move on to land, eat, mate, fight, form tribes and civilizations, build cities, increase their use of tools, eventually get into flying saucers for interstellar colonization, provoke planetary battles, invasions, or peaceful envoys, abduct local animals and terraform barren planets, explore innumerable quirky planets in the larger *Spore* universe, some inhabited by other equally quirky life forms with which you interact. It makes a good short movie, with the kind of cinematic camera angles and edits, wipes and dissolves, that users have come to expect from such films—in this case exemplified, for example, by the first-person point of view "shot" as "you" climb out of the water onto the land, only to confront other competitive creatures (one of whom jumps up in your face) and by the extreme wide-angle view to which the digital "camera" pulls back as your flying saucer zooms off into the galaxy at the last minute, the stars quickly dissolving into the original primordial soup as a background against which the *Spore* logo appears. Like the famous science film by Charles and Ray Eames, *The Powers of Ten*, which Will Wright repeatedly cites as a primary influence on *Spore*, the trailer visually links the cellular level with the cosmic level in a kind of fractal zoom. The starry skies at one end resemble the teeming ocean at the other. Writer Steven Johnson has identified the perspectival link between the Eames film and *Spore* as what he calls "the Long Zoom."[7] *Spore* is structured around massive shifts in scale across the evolutionary and cosmic spectrum, but with every level ultimately connected to the whole, and the trailer demonstrates this wordlessly in one long climactic "edit."

Pre-rendered using CGI (computer-generated image), this trailer looks more like a new animated feature or the opening credits for *The Simpsons* or *Futurama* than like captured gameplay footage. A more recent trailer (July 2007: *Spore Evolution*) is deliberately closer to the structure of gameplay and uses actual in-game video. One fan immediately edited the new footage together with in-game footage from a 2005 demo in order to demonstrate the improvements in every level.[8] Significantly, the first official trailer was not chosen for the comparison. The new 2007 trailer is much less cinematic, simply showing in-game scenes from each of the evolutionary stages of the game—Cell, Creature, Tribe, Civlization, and Space—divided by five icon screens, and a detailed look at the creature editor. You get to see the latest version of the interface display, which resembles the read-out panels of *The Sims* but in this case gauges "DNA points" for example, and the soundtrack seems to be Brian Eno's generative music. However well made, even this kind of official trailer, though preferable to the pre-rendered cinematic teaser that came before, is ultimately of less interest to serious game fans than a video of someone actually playing the game, the less staged-looking the better. And what characterizes true hardcore "Sporenography" are the demos by Will Wright, the auteur himself, in the role of pitchman-player, the god of the god game, clearly having a lot of fun with his creation.

Wright's demos at developers' or industry conferences are headline events in the world of games, drawing huge crowds including journalists who report on the talk and what it reveals about the game. The result has been a series of fairly long videos on the web of Wright speaking in his characteristic geeky style—part eclectic theorizing (ranging from astronomy to educational theory to sociology), part "how I did it" narrative, part demonstration of the game. In the videos, Wright stands at a podium or sits at a table with his laptop in front of him and the large screen behind him. When he demonstrates *Spore*'s creature editor and makes a charmingly whimsical dinosaur-like creature, then watches it come to life and begin walking around, blinking its eyes, making noises and jumping as the crowd erupts in laughter, it's hard not to think yet again of master showman Winsor McCay in front of his screen containing Gertie the Dinosaur, as I described him in chapter 4. Wright is similarly theatrical, a low-key vaudeville ringmaster engaging in improvisational patter that sounds spontaneous every time he repeats it, serving as mediator between the AI (artificial intelligence) on the big screen and his audience, both live and (eventually) out on the Internet, who are surely imagining themselves in his position as player/interactor.

One routine, exactly like a vaudeville gag, that Wright uses repeatedly is to move his creature into a competitive environment where a larger predator inevitably menaces it. As the background music changes and Wright's creature runs away, as if spontaneously (he says "oops"), the crowd always responds with laughter. Another set piece that gets a big laugh is the demonstration of mating, in which his dinosauric creature courts and then actually mounts a female in a large nest as the soundtrack switches to lounge music and (in one demo) pink hearts swirl around the nest. This comic "sex scene," the most explicitly "Sporenographic" of the preview materials, is reminiscent of the winking cartoon tone of the hot tub scenes in *The Sims*, a connection many in the demo audience will get immediately. It's no accident that one demo featured Robin Williams editing a creature. His manic stand-up and funny spontaneous reactions entertained the crowd, of course ("I think the program's going: 'No! this is not right!'"), while lending special celebrity status to the demo itself, but this would have been true for any talented comic. Williams in particular is already established in the public mind as the voice of numerous witty animated characters (some more successful and more beloved than others), so his performance piggybacked on the associations of his voice, helping to bring the *Spore* creature to life and enhancing its character in a recognizable way. *Spore*'s universe aims to be the kind of caricatured self-conscious cartoon in which Williams might act.

Every *Spore* demo is an effectively timed performance. Like any good demonstration, Wright's shows appear to involve spontaneous gameplay but he always hits his mark, in the theatrical sense. The demo is a performance of gameplay, which like gameplay itself walks a line between the predetermined and the emergent. But in this case the effect is enhanced by the audience's sense that they are watching a legendary creative director become just another player like themselves. And conversely, the demo demonstrates how *Spore* aims to make every player a version of the creative genius Will Wright is known to be. Over and over again in almost every demo and interview Wright has said that he wants players of *Spore* to feel more like George Lucas than Luke

Skywalker, J. R. R. Tolkien rather than Frodo Baggins. What he doesn't say is that in all the pre-release publicity he himself models the ideal of the auteur-player, the closeness of the two roles when it comes to the ideal player of *Spore*.

It's significant that Wright cites a film director and an author who are famous for creating massive, fully-formed fictional universes. Like a modern film director, the player-auteur is part author and part meta-*editor*, someone who imagines possibilities within a fictive universe and then structures and restructures the media object in order to enable those possibilities to emerge. Wright has explained that in watching people play *The Sims*, his team actually graphed the "gameplay landscape" as player data, based on the kinds of goals a player could try to achieve (material success or social success), visualizing across three dimensions thousands of players' acts of gameplay, as he says, allowing developers to "formally capture" how the players move within the "possibility spaces" of the game.[9] The result is a cube-shaped data visualization graph, a literal map of the possibility space of the game (imagined along predetermined vectors). Actual gameplay emerges within that space, as more or less improvised moves made within the constraints of the grid. One telling moment during Wright's talk at the 2007 South by Southwest conference came when he showed a slide of *Grand Theft Auto III* and remarked comically: "Here's *GTA*: I spent my entire time creating a character, a semi-homeless person hanging out with my homeboys and doing tricks on my bike."[10] Well, of course he did. Only the inventor of *The Sims* could turn even the gangster action game into a social sandbox. He repeatedly reminds people that he was educated in a Montessori school, where student-driven exploratory projects were the norm. In all of these anecdotes, what comes across is the importance of games as "possibility spaces." Refusing missions in order to hang out and do bike tricks is a way of testing the limits of possibility in *Grand Theft Auto*. How far can you push it before you are no longer playing the game, just playing in its world? Is the generic label, "sandbox game," a contradiction in terms? Is a simulation game really more toy than game, lacking in the necessary rules, objectives, integral competition? Wright is happy to call his games "modern Montessori toys,"[11] and he's clearly unfazed by the invidious distinction. At the very least, he wants to push the question—what *is* a game?—to the point where it breaks and reveals something new. The question itself offers a challenging grid of possibilities within which to explore the definition of games.

As we've seen, AI programming for games takes place as an imagined grid of possible interactions, and this way of thinking is crucial for developing the range of HCI (human-computer interface) interactions that are central to video games of all kinds: playing against NPCs (non-player characters), anticipating and reacting to moves by AI in various forms, making moves in response to other moves, rules, and structures of play, against and in cooperation with either other human or AI players, or even programmed features of the game-world. From looking for authorial presence in *Myst*, to interacting with NPCs in *Halo*, to trying to understand the motives of Grace and Trip in *Façade*, a good deal of videogaming is about seeking out and interacting with "alien" (artificial, programmed, remote) forms of intelligence. No wonder space exploration is the ultimate level of *Spore*, which developers have called a metagame containing a history of genres, stepping the player through a series of levels modeled on styles of gameplay from *Pac-Man* (Cell) to, say, *Masters of Orion* or *Star Wars* (Space). As Wright has said, the game has a "T"-shaped structure:[12] you level-up from cellular to creature to tribal and civilized phases according to fairly linear, vertically arranged goals; but at the top, when you gain the ability to travel in space, suddenly you can branch out horizontally, as it were, in a potentially endless search for new worlds and new life forms with which to interact. The ultimate "possibility space" is space.[13]

## SETI and *Spore*

The one source of inspiration for *Spore* always recognized by Will Wright is a short film about outer space and imagining its scale, *The Powers of Ten* (1977), by the famous team of architect-designers, Charles and Ray Eames. When the film appeared recently on YouTube, it was apparently thanks to a *Spore* fan; the video was tellingly tagged: "Spore Eames Universe Cool." The entire film is one long zoom—or, rather, one long zoom out and one zoom back in—taking the viewer from the human scale (a picnicking couple lying beside the shore of Lake Michigan) and then up and out to the continental, global, solar system, galaxy, and universe scales. Then the camera zooms back in from outer space until it finally delves into the cells of the man on the picnic blanket, down to the level of subatomic particles, quarks, and then back up to the idyll in the park. At each stage the scale is increased or decreased algorithmically, by powers of ten. The viewer of the film is made aware of the shifting orders of magnitude that make up the universe, what Steven Johnson calls "the long zoom," and one can imagine the Montessori-trained game designer wanting *Spore*—his "Sim Everything" game—to possess a similar power to educate players about relative scales in the universe through a kind of simulated hands-on experience.

Just the act of choosing as a point of departure and inspiration a 30-year-old science film made by architects and designers reveals a great deal about Will Wright and about *Spore*. What has not been noticed about *The Powers of Ten* as an influence on *Spore* is how much the film's visual design resembles mid-twentieth-century computerized interfaces (it was made for IBM, after all), including game interfaces. The main frame of the film is surrounded by a margin in which numbers display the level of viewing dynamically in both words and exponential notation. You remain aware of this simple heads-up display while watching the aerial and satellite and outer space scenes shift in the center of the screen, a modern cybernetic control system mediating between you and the images of the film. Lines and boxes even appear superimposed on the images, to mark the space in schematic ways. The changing exponential numbers tell you where you are on the imaginary map and indicate the relative sizes of objects in view, but also record acceleration and make explicit the algorithmic nature of the film, whose motion graphics are the output following from the simple mathematical rule of its title.

The film's brightly colored picnic scene, with its iconic objects—snacks and books and magazines (with covers about science and time) and clock—and sleeping doll-like man and woman, viewed from high overhead, may feel like a scene from *The Sims*; but the gamelike qualities of this film, or the qualities that in retrospect can be seen as anticipating today's games, run much deeper— from the literally algorithmic structure to the self-conscious interface, to the basic fact that the film as a whole *is* a "sim"—and we know it. The artificiality of the framing interface reminds viewers that they are, of course, watching an animated, simulated zoom. The "camera" cannot go where it appears to in the film. Except for the picnic scene itself, almost everything in the film is a contrived special effect of hand-drawn animation. This includes most significantly the zoom itself, as well as the cellular or stellar bodies, equally invisible beyond one end of the human scale and the other. The whole experience of seeing is simulated with the help of technology. One published photograph documenting the making of *The Powers of Ten* shows one half of the actor-couple, the man alone, on the picnic blanket, lying in a field behind a building, with the Eameses behind him on the set, Ray shooting photographs in the background and Charles shooting aerial views from a "cherry-picker" at the top of a tall crane emerging from the truck.[14] But, of course, this photo provides a further framing that echoes the long zoom of the film, revealing a perspective outside of—not edited into—the final film. Like Dziga Vertov's groundbreaking film, *Man with a Movie Camera* (1929),[15] this photo of the filming reminds us self-consciously of the work of making the movie, even though in this case the photo was not incorporated into the finished work. The "making of the *Powers of Ten*" photo calls attention to the act of simulation that produces the film's god's-eye perspective as it zooms out into space and down into the cell (and, below that, the atom). One essay on the film reminds us that "[m]ost of the images on the screen are color photographs of artwork. In this way the entire film is indirect, reflexive: photos of photos, photos of composites, or photos of original paintings based on scientific photos."[16] The film is a "journey that can be taken only thanks to images created with the help of expert handwork informed by mapping, calculation, and photography" (108). *The Powers of Ten* works in part by engaging viewers in the act of playing along with what we know is a simulation, seeing where the rule-based algorithms will take the creatures embedded in the simulated environment. No wonder the film inspired *Spore*. It could just as well have inspired *The Sims*. When I watch it now on my computer, rather than on a movie or TV screen, I can use the slider-controller to pause or move back and forth among the levels, moves that feel natural in the era of ubiquitous video game interfaces.

One of the games that Will Wright compares to *Spore*'s Tribe level, where creatures are organized into social groups that engage in rituals, and coopera-tive or competitive interaction, is *Populous* (1989), an early example of the strategy game as a god game. Created by the innovative designer Peter Molyneux (whose *Black and White* is perhaps the definitive god game, though less well known than *The Sims*), *Populous* allows the player to play god, shaping civilizations from prehistoric to Medieval, through battles, building campaigns, and cultural development, as well as changing landscapes and terrain. What strikes me most about published screenshots of *Populous* on Amiga, however, is the awkwardly busy interface design, in which an open book (of maps, includ-ing a cardinal direction indicator) is connected by a series of bars or pipes to the 3-D game landscape-map, with "pop-up" castles and houses and other features, laid out as if on top of a board game with symbolic token indicators. There's a certain family resemblance between this boldly artificial design and *The Sims*'s vertical lines with "spotlight" circles and other indicators, as well as roofless dollhouses laid out on a neighborhood grid, by which you control and get feedback on your character. It's hard to explain to someone unfamiliar with sim-play that the narrative content is ultimately not the point, so much as tweaking and monitoring the algorithmically-controlled simulation itself, the emergence of conditions and behaviors (and conditioned behaviors) out of a series of relatively simple rules or calculations. Wright's crediting *The Powers of Ten* is significant (among other reasons) because the cybernetic interface of most sim games—framing or heads-up displays for monitoring health, posses-sions, location, evolution, and the development of one's creatures across multiple levels of time and space—can be seen anticipated in the Eameses' mid twentieth-century science-education film.

It's also likely that the general design-ethos of Eames Studios indirectly informed Wright's conception of *Spore*. As one reporter put it when connect-ing the film with the game, "The Eames[es] wanted to bring good design to the masses; Wright wants to empower the masses to be good designers."[17] The most famous objects produced by the Eameses were pieces of molded plywood furniture, especially two iconic chairs: the leather and plywood lounge chair, and the more basic wood low chair. The sculptural biomorphic forms of these and other pieces were not themselves adopted by "the masses," but they influenced bent-wood school chairs and office furniture everywhere from the1950s to the 1970s. The Eames chairs (which ended up in New York's Museum of Modern Art, Chicago's Art Institute, and other collections around the world) symbolized a kind of organic modernism that was the hopeful, optimistic face of mid-century technological expansiveness, an attitude which arguably culminated in the framing of the American Apollo program, a hopeful modernism that connected life on Earth with the whole cosmos, homey molded plywood objects, sea shell collections, abstract expressionist painting, and dreams of interstellar flight in—oddly enough—similarly curvy, biomorphic spaceships. *Spore*'s logo, and the icon on the default start screen, is a curved abstract spiral galaxy and the game's "retro" cartoon aesthetic references the context of "organic" modernism, beginning with the 3-D bean- or lozenge-shaped bodies of creatures one edits from eggs by dragging and pulling them into shape like lumps of modeling clay. But the larger context of this aesthetic includes, for example, *The Jetsons*, Dr. Seuss landscapes, home-of-tomorrow magazine layouts from the early 1960s, mass-market kidney bean and amoeba-shaped furniture, science-fiction movie sets and the props and costumes of *Lost in Space*, the generally curvilinear mid-century "space-age" modernism that was everywhere in middle-class homes and public spaces throughout the 1960s and early 1970s.

Will Wright is a trailing-edge baby boomer, born in 1960, the same year the first modern SETI experiment (Search for Extra Terrestrial Intelligence) was performed at Cornell University, using a giant radio telescope to listen for signs of intelligent life amidst the general noise of outer space. Like many his age (who were repeatedly told in no uncertain terms: "You will Go to the Moon"[18]), Wright is personally fascinated by space exploration. He collects artifacts of Soviet space technology and cites SETI as an influence on *Spore*. The culmination of the era of mid-twentieth-century optimism about the possibilities of space exploration, SETI is closely bound up with mainstream science fiction of the past century, and marks a move away from *War of the Worlds* visions of invasion, or at least marks a significant variation on it, more in tune with *Star Trek, Close Encounters of the Third Kind*, and *ET*. But with SETI, space exploration became not only friendlier, it became more computational and abstract, since what one is exploring is the information grid, signals sent out from among what astronomer and astrobiologist, SETI activist, and TV host Carl Sagan famously referred to as "billions upon billions" of stars. Many of those, statistically speaking, are likely to have their own solar systems, some of which might include planets that could sustain life. Indeed, Sagan's poetic descriptions on TV and in print of what drives SETI are part of the context out of which *Spore* imagines the universe of interstellar space as the ultimate "sandbox," potentially teeming with "living things and intelligent beings and spacefaring civilizations."[19] In one passage in his book, *Cosmos*, Sagan suggests that, seen from a distance, a galaxy more closely resembles "a collection of lovely found objects—seashells, perhaps, or corals, the productions of Nature laboring for aeons in the cosmic ocean" (3). In arguing that space exploration is fundamental to our species, Sagan unselfconsciously represents it as an act of collecting, a vision of cosmic aesthetic appreciation and play.

Will Wright clearly extends this vision in his latest ludic simulation of human desire. During his demo of *Spore* at TED 2007, he zooms out on an extreme wide view of the large spiral galaxy within which ultimately most of the game takes place, and then watches it spin. You usually see such views, he says, in static images, but "when you actually bring it forward and start animating it, it's actually kind of amazing—what a galaxy would look like fast-forwarded," at about one million light years/second. The result spins on the giant screen behind him as Wright, sounding like Carl Sagan, comments on "this wonderful sparkling thing with the disc slowly rotating. . . ." Having seen the demo, we don't forget as he says this that we're looking at a very high-level view of the teeming gameworld of *Spore*, a literal representation of the game's socially constructed universe.

The SETI search for intelligent life was from the start a numbers game, a game of probability in which scientists were intent on enhancing the odds through design. In the public imagination, it represented a sense of wonder and curiosity, even a playful social impulse as idealized in Sagan's image of collecting the "found objects" of the galaxy, a passage that could have inspired the final levels of *Katamari Damacy* as well as *Spore*. The culmination of SETI was the Arecibo broadcast sent out in 1974, aimed at a star cluster on the edge of the galaxy, 21,000 light years away. The less-than three-minute message was a remarkable encoded binary file, a series of ones and zeroes, which, when decoded, would represent a totem-pole- patterned image of cartoon-like graphics including the Arecibo telescope itself, our solar system, a stick-figure human, and a double-helix strand of DNA. The point of *Spore*—and of SETI—is not really collecting objects (though one does that); it's using constructed and collected objects as vehicles for a search for intelligent life in the (game) universe. *Spore* is structured to increase the odds of encountering other forms of intelligence, and I think this is where its most significant design feature may emerge (assuming the game turns out to play as it has been described and demoed).

It's clear from the previews that space exploration in *Spore* could involve a good deal of cartoon violence. Wright has referred to the creature level of the game as a "third-person eater" (e.g,, at the South By Southwest Conference 2007), and spears and other weapons are among the early implements you can edit and deploy in the Tribe level. War seems a highly likely form of

*Figure 6.1* Arecibo image.

city-to-city interaction in the Civilization level, where a tank is even incorporated into the level's logo. Later, in the Space level of the game, flying saucers have tractor beams for abducting life forms and (presumably) other objects, and laser canons for blasting cities and their planets from orbit. Competition, colonization, and domination (in the evolutionary sense) are built into the game, since finding food, fighting off predators, competing with other cities, ultimately terraforming uninhabited planets and staking claims to them, spreading throughout the universe, will apparently be central goals. In this way *Spore* shares features with games that inspired it, god games such as *Populous* and *Black and White*, and empire-building strategy games from *Civilization* (which culminates in space colonization) to *Masters of Orion*—which has been called a classic of the "4X" genre: "explore, expand, exploit, exterminate."[20] Clearly, *Spore* makes room for more playful and peaceful explorations of alien civilizations as well, the equivalent of Wright's doing tricks on his bike with his friends in *Grand Theft Auto* instead of going on violent gangster missions. Nevertheless, one's carefully created civilization would stand in danger of being blasted to stardust by the first competing spaceship to come along, like a newly-created character in *World of Warcraft* being killed in the first ten minutes ("pwned!") by the proverbial anonymous 14-year-old, were *Spore* a live MMOG (massively multiplayer online game).

That's one reason Wright has instead designed it as what he calls a "Massively Single-Player Game." That is, *Spore* will exist in a proliferation of parallel universes, copies on players' computers, but all of which will be potentially shaped and populated by content made by massive numbers of other players, uploaded by them to *Spore* servers to be downloaded by all. Distributed content creation and asynchronous content sharing, a kind of time-shifted social interaction that the developers call the "pollination process," will be the true spine of the game.[21] As I play *Spore* I'll be able to encounter other players' creatures, cities, planets, and interact with them in my copy, killing them, cooperating with them, whatever, without altering the player's own copies of their creatures and objects and worlds. And I'll be able to pollinate the *Spore* universe with my own creations. The servers will supply constantly updated "Metaverse" statistics telling me, for example, that my planet in a particular galaxy has been blown up by another player (or many other players), and presumably giving particulars of the encounter; but this destruction will be visited only on copies of my planet; it will still be there in my game the next time I play. Wright has said that this model offers the best of both kinds of game, the benefits of playing online—"all the people building the world collectively together"—but without the drawback that "the fourteen-year-old can kill you or that you've invested all this time in your planet and somebody comes along and blows it up."[22] This pollination system connects *Spore* to *Katamari Damacy* or *Pokémon*, even, as you collect other people's stuff, collect encounters with numerous odd-morphology creatures and planets (there will even be data "cards" associated with the creatures, and a *Sporepedia*, according to Wright). It also attempts to improve upon what was already a strength of *The Sims* games: their generations of player communities who shared sims, wardrobes, buildings, real estate lots, and (thanks to a feature deliberately built in to *The Sims* 2) machinima stories enacted in the gameworld.

Indeed, Wright says explicitly that *The Sims* community sites gave him the idea for *Spore*'s model of asynchronous content creation and sharing, including tens of thousands of fan-made movies and stories as well as NPC characters and objects. But to me it's striking how much the pollination model also resembles SETI's strategy for finding signs of intelligent life. In *Spore* you play with characters and objects created earlier and uploaded to the server by a virtually infinite number of players out there in the distributed game universe; your interactions are asynchronous, time-shifted. SETI is about asynchronous interaction with alien forms of intelligent life. The distributed network of SETI radio telescopes listens for signals emanating from the vastness of space, an inherently time-shifted endeavor, since any trace of a signal that reaches Earth would have been sent out eons ago. In both cases, SETI and *Spore*, the ultimate goal is to find and interact with exotic forms of intelligence—in one case, literally interstellar aliens; in the other case, unseen other players and their creatures and creations. In both cases you begin by searching for patterns of (made) meaning amidst the noise of random background data, shaped and meaningful versus raw and empty worlds. Like *Spore*, SETI leveraged the available network to create a wider grid of possible interactors. The SETI@home project allows anyone to put their personal computer to use processing interstellar data; begun in 1999, it has attracted millions of volunteers whose computers become in effect part of the SETI grid.

Analogously, *Spore* wants to put users to work making content, creating the very signs of intelligent life that they and other players hope to discover in the game after downloading new content. In *Spore*, you may engage in a heated battle between your spacecraft and a fortified city on an alien planet, but you are actually playing against another player, asynchronously, maybe days or weeks after the city and its inhabitants were created and uploaded.

Like SETI, this requires a certain exploratory faith and a willingness to play along with the time-shifted discursive situation created by the server-to-PC shared-content model. This model is crucial in the end because it greatly increases the odds of discovering intelligent life in the *Spore* universe—since a massive number of other players, other creators, will be continuously uploading fresh content, including NPCs, for you to discover. Instead of live chat, whether text or voice, or live online interaction of any kind, players will communicate more in the SETI way, by sharing (and sometimes blowing up) what they've made, edited, and then "broadcast" out to the eager (game)

*Figure 6.2* Screenshot from Space level of *Spore*.

and bringing it out into the world. Historically, this kind of editing has involved reconfiguring a verbal work—a poem, say—starting either from an author's manuscript or from earlier versions, in response to perceived needs of a new audience, the work's shifting horizon of expectations or reception. An editor takes the raw material of a work and shapes it, adapting its appearance (or interface), among other changes, in order to allow it to prosper in a specific media-environment out in the world, a process not unlike the way natural selection "edits" DNA during evolution.

As everyone knows, most media today, from recorded music to video and film, are based on creative acts more like editing and re-editing (sampling and capturing, or distorting and remixing, for example) than like authoring as creation-out-of-nothing, which is the sense in which the Romantic poets understood the term "author." In the world of digital media, the act of creation is more often than not a form of editing. Anyone who has modded a game knows this firsthand, because they've probably used a "level editor," a software program for editing other programs or digital objects, usually with a graphical user interface not unlike *Spore*'s creature editor, with buttons to select, tables to check, and menus to pull down, and dragging and dropping (and sometimes, still, though less commonly, code-writing by hand). These editors allow the user, thanks to object-oriented programming, to make something new by altering or recombining existing bits of code. This is the computer-science sense of editor: a software tool for reconfiguring other software, text, images, programs. It includes, for example, binary hex editors, markup editors, text editors (including familiar commercial word processors), graphical image editors, and digital video editors. In games, besides level editors, there are sometimes specialized map or campaign editors, as well as character editors. Sometimes these editors are released by the game developers themselves, essentially a version of software used to make the game, and sometimes they are written by users intent on mods.

This highlights an important point: game editors are places where the roles of designer and user, creator and player, converge. Actually, at the dawn of the cinema, a director was often also the film's editor, in the hands-on sense, the person who cut and rearranged the segments of a film. Nowadays, at the dawn of digital cinema production, this is again true in a more figurative sense. When Will Wright says that he wants *Spore* players to feel more like George Lucas than Luke Skywalker, we should remember that Lucas came into film as a science-fiction fan and technophile. He has worked with a wide range of digital media, including games, but also including digitally created artificial actors for his films not unlike the creatures in *Spore* (think of Jabba the Hutt in the *Star Wars* universe, who began as a physical puppet and became a CGI effect). As with an increasing number of directors these days, he must think like and oversee many programmers and compositors, CG effects specialists and digital media editors, as much as traditional camera operators, lighting specialists, and script editors. It's telling in this regard that Wright says he wants his players to feel like George Lucas—but actually to perform the computer-generated work of a Pixar animator. *Spore* Producer Caryl Shaw has characterized the game as having "editors all along the way" (GDC 2006), and Wright has said that a key question for the development team was "how do we make these tools, these editors . . . just as fun as the game itself?" (TED 2007).

From the creature editor to terraforming in space, the *Spore* player will be editing content, playing with it interactively in conjunction with other players' content, and then—and this is the crucial step—re-editing in a series of looped, recursive responses. The second creature I build, and the third, will presumably be adapted by me, as editor, to the conditions experienced by the first (which include the conditions of other players' creatures and environments). So, for example, I might build an armored lizard that fares well in early levels but is too slow to compete with most creatures at the Civilization level. Having learned this limitation the hard way (perhaps my creature was chased down by fleet-footed bipeds wielding spears), I would go back to the drawing board (more or less literally) to recast the next creature. Or a city I build might take on a new skyscraper style in aesthetic imitation of an "NPC city" I encountered on someone else's planet (as it appeared in my game), thus altering the urban landscape of my own planet. Editing in digital environments is typically recursive in this way. It almost always involves tweaking in response to feedback, just as classic computer programming involves writing code, compiling the program, debugging, and rewriting. The process of playing *Spore* is a process of building up what Wright calls "this huge database of content," using editors and the overarching feedback-system of the game's distributed universe (TED 2007).

## Editing as universe-building

Readers who have followed me through earlier chapters will not be surprised that I see this kind of digital editing in the context of the long history of textual editing, which has traditionally been at the heart of textual studies. I want to make it clear from the outset that I have no interest in reducing *Spore* to a mere semiotic text or an instance of *textual* editing. On the contrary, the central role of dynamic editing in a game such as *Spore* excites me precisely because it teaches us something about the textual practices in which I've been trained, offers a fresh perspective on my own discipline. Textual studies has a good deal to learn from video games, beginning with what is at stake in textual forms of editing nowadays, which increasingly take shape in digital spaces. Textual editions are. I think. moving towards a model that resembles the editable universe of video games, at least in concept, though most humanist scholars are still unaware of this—perhaps because so few of them (so far) play games, and because they are so invested in the cultural seriousness of their scholarly editions, which they see as opposed to the stereotypical image of games as trivial entertainments. But a gamespace is very much like an edition (and vice versa), when both are properly understood.

In traditional textual studies, the scholarly editor worked toward one of two general goals for editions, to be published in the form of codex books (often multiple volumes for each edition). He or she might create a "diplomatic edition" (from the root-word behind "diploma," here meaning an accurate copy), a facsimile representation of a historical document, whether manuscript or typeset book, by placing photos alongside editorial transcriptions and explaining the relationship between the two using various notes and lists of variants and other forms of scholarly apparatus. Or he or she might create a "critical edition," sifting and comparing many different "witnesses" or textual instantiations of a given "work" (multiple editions and copies of *King Lear*, for example) in order to establish their relationship, on analogy with a family tree, and then emending a base text in various ways, inserting readings from other witnesses or speculating about an author's intention in order to correct errors. The goal in the critical edition would be to produce an eclectic text, pieced together by the editor to represent a reconstructed lost original version of a work or an ideal version of the work that never existed in the world (but which the author presumably wanted to exist). The scholarly edition, even in these traditional forms, it should be noted, has always been a reconfiguration of the work in question. The special apparatus at the back of the book or along the foot of the page is a kind of heads-up display, a formal interface revealing the operations that the editor has undertaken on the materials and prompting the user to undertake her or his own operations on the materials. The editor puts the texts together in a new way in order to allow readers to see the work in a new way, enabling both to contribute to the ongoing reception history of the work.

With the advent of digital textuality, especially, textual studies scholars have tended to conceive of editions even more explicitly in this way, arguing that editions should exploit the computer's potential to model and simulate scholarly discourse as a kind of collaborative universe-building, the social act of making (or re-editing) the meanings of our works of cultural expression. The Modern Language Association's recent volume of essays on *Electronic Textual Editing* (2006) exemplifies this trend.[26] The foreword by leading traditional theorist G. Thomas Tanselle cautions that "The computer is a tool, and tools are facilitators; they may create strong breaks with the past in the methods for doing things, but they are at the service of an overriding continuity, for they do not change the issues that we have to cope with" (3). But Tanselle's traditional view is implicitly qualified by a number of the essays in the collection, starting with the first, by Dino Buzzetti and Jerome McGann, which suggests how radically different the "breaks with the past" might be in digital editions.[27]

Buzzetti and McGann in effect propose that the social text can be rendered in machine-readable as well as human-readable code, citing McGann's *Rossetti Archive* as an example (70). The texts and other materials in that archive are encoded in XML and aggregated in a way that allows users to combine and recombine them along various axes, including the kinds of social determinants that D. F. McKenzie argued should be part of any edition. In such an edition, the literary work (a poem, for example) becomes a grid within which various possibilities are made realizable for different users, and the edition becomes a system for simulating and tracking multiple interpretive possibilities. The authors even use an interplanetary metaphor to explain this new form of edition: the material objects, manuscripts and published editions and so on, "orbit" around the construct named for the sake of convenience by the title of a poem. The work is thus not a self-identical thing but a "gravity field" (70). Rather than edit texts as stable objects, textual studies scholars should "reconstruct" the history of "makings and remakings"—in other words, edits and re-edits making up the social text (71). Those "remakings" include what all future users will do inside the space represented by the edition, objects orbiting one another, held together by the gravity field of the work.

Or, to zoom in from space to Earth: the literary or cultural work can be thought of as a world of meaningful objects that evolve and mutate as people reconfigure them over time. Editing the work therefore is a form of prompting evolutionary change based on user-generated mutations, and the whole edition is a programmed environment in which to enable and record textual evolution, a dynamic simulation of the ongoing textual history of a work to which the edition itself contributes, a space for realizing McKenzie's "social text" as an ecology of collaborative reconfigurations, charted and managed by networked software. Buzzetti and McGann: "Our aim is not to build a model of one made thing; it is to design a system that can simulate the system's realizable possibilities—those that are known and recorded as well as those that have yet to be (re)constructed" (72). The modeling system is already in many cases replacing the traditional edition in advanced textual studies work, at least in theory. Rather than converting a traditional scholarly edition into a digital facsimile or archive of digital texts, many textual studies scholars are conceptualizing the digital edition as something more like a dynamic database, where granular digital objects of various kinds, marked up or tagged in different ways, can be processed and (re)configured according to the needs of a potentially infinite number of users, each one of which in effect re-edits at a higher level the archived, edited materials. Visualizations of the data would in this case be normal features of the edition's interface. Digital textual scholarship becomes in this way of working a matter of creating space within which ongoing combinatorial operations can take place and be tracked and recorded, rather than one-time formations of static "definitive" editions.

Take for example one modest early case study—the scholarly universe of the NINES project, under the direction of Jerome McGann. NINES is a Networked Infrastructure for Nineteenth-Century Electronic Scholarship, a federation of scholars working in British and American nineteenth-century studies, editors of electronic archives and digital editions, and library specialists, supported by a team of software developers at the University of Virginia building a suite of critical and editorial tools. Chief among these software tools is Collex, an open-source "collection-builder" and "exhibit-builder," essentially an editor that allows a user to search for and find peer-reviewed texts, images, critical essays, and records of library holdings, pulling them together, dragging and dropping them into a new collection, combined with critical commentary and analysis of their own, resulting in a new form of scholarly publication that can be in turn submitted to the NINES board for scholarly review and possible online publication. Like other social software, Collex produces user-generated tag clouds and is based on sharing one's collections with others of like mind and interest. It employs a Web 2.0 model for scholarly purposes, leveraging the advantages of social networking software to shape shared content. Collex treats the peer-reviewed objects in NINES—to date over 175,000 texts and other objects, manuscript, print, images, and records of holdings in libraries and collections all over the world—as modular components, data that can be searched and collected, tagged and sorted, combined and recombined in different ways by different users.

This new model of an alternative to the scholarly edition in digital space is conceptually related to the database, certainly, but when it comes to how it is created and used, I think it also has a great deal in common with video games. Once the initial environment is in place and materials are being vetted by the board for inclusion, any user acts as an editor in this space, someone who imagines possibilities within a paratextually rich and socially constructed universe and then (re)constructs the editorial space in order to enable those possibilities to emerge. It's fitting then that *Ivanhoe*—a game of literary interpretation—is another of the software tools available through NINES. Such scholarly alternatives to editions, as they have traditionally been conceived, provide an integrated space for users to share their editorial contributions, an asynchronous network of user-edited content-objects contributing to the whole universe of textual possibilities. In other words, such experiments are, I think, moving textual studies several key steps closer to the underlying structural principles of today's most innovative video games.

Throughout this book I've argued that video games can be useful models for textual scholarship. They are already highly developed systems for simulating possibility spaces, for recording and tracking how users reconstruct or re-edit a broadly paratextual universe of meaningful performances. Understood in this way, a video game such as *Spore* is already a more vivid formal, procedural realization of D. F. McKenzie's theory of the social text than any scholarly edition to date. Today's textual studies scholars would do well to spend more time playing and studying and learning from video games, since models for the kinds of tools they seek "descend to us through our culture in games and role-playing environments."[28] Video gamers already know in the most practical, mundane ways that meanings are social and collaboratively constructed, that they reside not in self-contained objects, narratives, plots, or dramatic arcs, but in procedurally-enabled dynamic interactions, cooperative and competitive, improvised in conjunction with other "intelligences," even if those interactions take place with time-shifted AI creatures (or whole planets), left like Arecibo messages for the universe of other players to search out, collect, evolve and re-form, eventually to be re-edited by others, in the ongoing game that is itself the collaborative process of making the meanings of video games.

# Notes

## Introduction

1  D. B. Weiss, *Lucky Wander Boy* (Harmondsworth: Penguin, 2003), 87.
2  Talmadge Wright, Eric Borea, and Paul Breidenbach, "Creative Player Actions in FPS On-Line Video Games: Playing Counter-Strike," *Game Studies: The International Journal of Computer Game Research*, 2.2 (December 2002): www.gamestudies.org/0202/wright/.
3  Espen Aarseth, "Computer Game Studies, Year One," *Game Studies*, 1.1 (July 2001): www.gamestudies.org/0101/editorial.html.
4  Rune Klevjer, "In Defense of Cut-Scenes," in Frans Mäyrä (ed.), *Computer Games and Digital Cultures* Conference Proceedings, Tampere (Finland:Tampere University Press, 2002); reprinted: www.uib.no/people/smkrk/docs/klevjerpaper.htm.
5  McKenzie Wark, *GAM3R 7H3ORY*, Version 1.1: www.futureofthebook.org/gamertheory/, 1.007; I cite the online "preprint" (by chapter and section or lexia number) but it was also published in book form by Harvard University Press, 2007.
6  Gonzalo Frasca, "Ludologists love stories, too: notes from a debate that never took place" (2003): www.ludology.org/my_articles.html.
7  Markku Eskelinen, "The Gaming Situation," *Game Studies*, 1.1 (July 2001): www.gamestudies.org/0101/eskelinen/.
8  Stuart Moulthrop, "From Work to Play: Molecular Culture in the Time of Deadly Games," in *First Person: New Media as Story, Performance, and Game*, ed. Noah Wardrip-Fruin and Pat Harrigan (Cambridge, MA and London: MIT Press, 2004), 56–69.
9  Ian Bogost, *Unit Operations: An Approach to Videogame Criticism* (Cambridge, MA and London: MIT Press, 2006), xii, 52.
10  Toril Moi, ed., *The Kristeva Reader* (New York: Columbia University Press, 1986), 111.
11  For an introduction to textual studies, its history, and controversies, compare D. C. Greetham, *Textual Scholarship. An Introduction* (New York: Routledge, 1994); G. Thomas Tanselle, *Textual Criticism and Scholarly Editing* (Charlottesville, VA: Bibliographical Society of the University of Virginia, 2003); and Jerome McGann, *A Critique of Modern Textual Criticism* (Chicago, IL: University of Chicago Press, 1983).
12  David Greetham, "Textual Scholarship" in Joseph Gibaldi, ed., *Introduction to Scholarship in Modern Languages and Literatures* (New York: MLA, 1991), 101–37 (103–4).

13 "What is Textual Scholarship?" in *A Companion to the History of the Book*, ed. Simon Eliot and Jonathan Rose (Malden, MA and Oxford: Blackwell, 2007), 21–32 (25).

14 Henry Jenkins, *Fans, Bloggers, and Gamers: Exploring Participatory Culture* (New York and London: NYU Press, 2006), 137.

15 See Henry Jenkins, *Convergence Culture: Where Old and New Media Collide* (New York and London: NYU Press, 2006); Steven Johnson, *Everything Bad is Good For You: How Today's Popular Culture is Actually Making Us Smarter* (New York: Riverhead Books, 2005).

16 William Gibson, *Spook Country* (New York: Putnam's, 2007), 344.

17 McKenzie Wark, *GAM3R 7H3ORY*, 1.005.

18 William Gibson, interviewed in documentary film, *No Maps for These Territories*, directed Mark Neale (Chris Paine and 907, 2001).

19 William Gibson, *Neuromancer* (New York: Ace Books, 1984), 6.

20 For insight into this wider cultural fantasy of disembodied information, see N. Katherine Hayles, *How We Became Posthuman: Virtual Bodies in Cybernetics, Literature, and Informatics* (Chicago, IL: University of Chicago Press, 1999).

21 *Make Love, Not Warcraft*, episode 147, *South Park*, aired October 4, 2006. On occasion in the chapters that follow I refer to *World of Warcraft*, but that phenomenally popular game and the genre it represents, MMORPGs, demands a more extensive and dedicated treatment of its own than I have the space or in-game experience to provide here.

22 *Summoner Geeks* is a cross-platform phenomenon, a viral video available on YouTube and elsewhere using 3-D animated game characters voiced by geeky teen players. It appears to have begun life as a 1996 audio recording of a comedy sketch by the troupe *Dead Alewives*; it was first made available as an "Easter egg" or hidden extra for fans in a game, *Summoner* (2000) (Wikipedia).

23 Jerome McGann, *The Romantic Ideology: A Critical Investigation* (Chicago, IL: University of Chicago Press, 1983).

24 Matthew G. Kirschenbaum, *Mechanisms: New Media and the Forensic Imagination* (Cambridge, MA and London: MIT Press, 2007).

## 1 The game of *Lost*

1 Lynnette Porter and David Lavery, *Unlocking the Meaning of LOST: An Unauthorized Guide* (Naperville, IL: Sourcebooks, 2006), 22–23.

2 Mark Cotta Vaz, *The Lost Chronicles: The Official Companion Book* (New York: Hyperion, 2005), 78.

3 As Porter and Lavery point out, this connection was emphasized when *Lost* was parodied in a *Mad TV* sketch; in it the castaways stumble upon Jeff Probst, the creator and host of *Survivor*, in their jungle, and find that they are contestants on the reality show (*Unlocking the Meaning of LOST*, 139).

4 Porter and Lavery, 23.

5 Steven Johnson, *Everything Bad is Good For You: How Today's Popular Culture is Actually Making Us Smarter* (New York: Riverhead Books, 2005), 62–115.

6 www.lostisagame.com/. The site's Pynchonesque creator identifies himself only as "all_games" and says he's "a 50 yr. old marketing executive with an addiction to LOST" (www.lostisagame.com/about.htm#theory1).

7 Dan Hill on his City of Sound blog ("Why Lost is Genuinely New Media," March 27, 2006) refers to *Lost* as an example of "meta-media," an accurate enough term. Hill (a designer) includes a graphical visualization of the media objects surrounding a single episode of *Lost*: www.cityofsound.com/blog/2006/03/why_lost_is_gen.html.

8 Aldous Huxley, *Island* (1962; New York: Perennial Classics, 2002), 1.

 9 Gerard Genette, "Introduction to the Paratext," *New Literary History* 22.2. (Spring 1991), 26179. And *Paratexts: Thresholds of Interpretation*, trans. Jane E. Lewin (first publ. 1987 as *Les Seuils*; Cambridge: Cambridge University Press, 1997). See especially pp. 344–403 (on "epitext").

10 Genette, "Introduction to the Paratext," quotes Claude Duchet's explicit remarks on advertising in this context (n3).

11 The analytical distinctions between *paratext, epitext* (from *epi-* meaning "in addition to"), and *peritext* (from *peri-* meaning "around or about") are clearer when it comes to codex books of the modern era than they are for more complex multi-media productions.

12 Gary Troup, *Bad Twin* (New York: Hyperion, 2006), 254. The novel has a tiny *Lost* logo on its dust jacket and its copyright page contains not only the usual disclaimer that this is a work of fiction, but also an admission that "the author himself is a fictional character."

13 *Lost: The Video Game*, Gameloft, S.A.: www.gameloft.com/lost-mobile-game/.

14 The image—although it was a legitimate parody in my opinion—has since been removed from the blog and the artist apparently wishes to remain anonymous.

15 Steven Johnson, *Everything Bad is Good for You*, 42–3.

16 Jules Verne, *The Mysterious Island* (New York, Penguin [Signet Classic], 1986).

17 The ultimate source for this device is *Robinson Crusoe*, which early on spends many pages describing the castaway's salvaging of useful objects, including weapons, from the wrecked ship, an inventory of objects Crusoe will later use to solve problems on his island.

18 The traditional school of textual studies is most often associated with W. W. Greg, Fredson Bowers, and G. T. Tanselle. Tanselle articulated the importance of author-ial intentions in a number of writings, but especially a 1976 essay, "The Editorial Problem of Final Authorial Intentions," in *Studies in Bibliography* (1976), 167–211; reprinted in *Selected Studies in Bibliography* (Charlottseville, VA: University of Virginia Press, 1979), 309–53.

19 Jerome McGann, *Radiant Textuality: Literature After the World Wide Web* (New York: Palgrave Macmillan, 2001), 228–31. And on the example of games, see chapters 8–9 of *The Scholar's Art: Literary Studies in a Managed World* (Chicago and London: University of Chicago Press, 2006).

20 Matthew Kirschenbaum, *Mechanisms* (Cambridge, MA: MIT Press, 2008). Kirschenbaum's "forensic" method takes in the actual programs and hardware of the games he studies, just as traditional textual studies looks typesetting and paper formats.

21 The first volume in the *Platform Studies* series will be *Video Computer System: The Atari 2600 Platform*, by Nick Montfort and Ian Bogost (MIT Press, forthcoming 2008). See http://platformstudies.com.

22 Stephen Greenblatt, *Hamlet in Purgatory* (Princeton, NJ: Princeton University Press, 2001), 43–5.

23 Kate Arthur, "Dickens, Challah, and that Mysterious Island," *New York Times*, May 25, 2006 (E1), 1.

24 On the background to the production and publication of *Our Mutual Friend*, see Peter Ackroyd, *Dickens* (New York: HarperCollins, 1990), 938–68; his account of the famous Staplehurst disaster, on which my summary is based, is on pp. 958–64.

25 Robert L. Patten, "The Composition, Publication, and Reception of *Our Mutual Friend*," *The Dickens Project*, http://humwww.ucsc.edu/dickens/OMF/patten2.html.

26 Jay Clayton, *Charles Dickens in Cyberspace: The Afterlife of the Nineteenth Century in Postmodern Culture* (Oxford: Oxford University Press, 2003), 199.

27 Celia Pearce, "Productive Play: Game Culture From the Bottom Up," in *Games and Culture* 1.1 (January 2006), 17–24: http://games.sagepub.com: 10.1177/1555412005281418.

28 Henry Jenkins, *Textual Poachers: Studies in Culture and Communication* (New York: Routledge, 1992). See also *Fans, Bloggers, and Gamers: Exploring Participatory Culture* (New York and London: NYU Press, 2006), and *Convergence Culture: Where Old and New Media Collide* (New York: NYU press, 2006).

29 Steven Johnson, *Everything Bad is Good For You*, 169.

30 Matt Hills, *Fan Cultures* (London and New York: Routledge, 2002), refers to this general phenomenon as hyperdiegesis, "the creation of a vast and detailed narrative space, only a fraction of which is ever directly seen or encountered within the text . . ." (137).

31 Henry Jenkins, "Transmedia Storytelling," *MIT Technology Review*, (January 15, 2003): www.technologyreview.com/articles/03/01/wo_jenkins011503.asp.

32 Daniel Terdiman, "Online game rising from the dead," *CNet News*, (May 18, 2006): http://news.com.com.

## 2 Collecting *Katamari Damacy*

1 Some collectors convert their knowledge or "subcultural capital" into cultural capital in general and, of course (on eBay, for example), monetary capital. But some refuse to do so. See Nathan Scott Epley, "Of PEZ and Perfect Price: Sniping, Collecting Cultures, and Democracy on eBay," in *Everyday eBay: Culture, Collecting, and Desire*, ed. Ken Hillis, Michael Petit, and Nathan Scott Epley (New York and London: Routledge, 2006), 151–65 (159–61)

2 Namco Bandai, *Katamari Damacy* (2004); *We Love Katamari* (in Japanese: "Everyone Loves Katamari Damacy," 2005), both for Sony Play Station 2; *Me and My Katamari*, for Play Station Portable (Japan, 2005; U.S., 2006).

3 For an example of the giant snowball gag, see *Betty Boop in Snow White* (1933); the "fight cloud" is a staple in Andy Capp comics, for example. The sequel, *We Love Katamari*, includes a snow level where you actually roll up a giant snowball, with skiers, trees, and other objects sticking out of it, or that the King of All Cosmos admits at one point that *Katamari Damacy* was "not very original" since it copied snowball rolling. Other parallels include games such as *Super Monkey Ball* and 3-D variations on *Pac Man* such as *Pac n Roll*. The game itself contains witty references to dung beetles.

4 Thankfully, the "story vs. game" debate now seems to have receded in game studies but was for a year or two around 2003 a central area of contention. See *First Person; New Media in Story, Performance, and Game*, ed. Noah Wardrip-Fruin and Pat Harrigan (Cambridge, MA: MIT Press, 2004), especially section II, "Ludology," with contributions from ludologists Markku Eskelinen (36–44) and Espen Aarseth (45–55); Stuart Moulthrop's salutary essay in the same section argues for attention to the social facets of gameplay. Janet Murray, often the target of ludology during the debate, summarized her position in "The Last Word on Ludology vs. Narratology in Game Studies," part of her keynote address, DiGRA, Vancouver, 2005. For an overview of the terms involved in the debate, see Gonzalo Frasca, "Simulation versus Narrative: Introduction to Ludology," in *The Video Game Theory Reader*, ed. Mark J. P. Wolf and Bernard Perron (New York and London: Routledge, 2003), 221–35.

5 Rob Fehey, "Focus on: Katamari Damacy Creator Keita Takahashi," *gamesindustry .biz*, (October 13, 2005): www.gamesindustry.biz/content_page.php?aid=12233.

6 Takahashi's notion of punk-rock fun—as playfully nihilistic or mundanely parodic play about play itself—is a useful supplement to the cognitive-challenge model

put forth by Ralph Koster in his *A Theory of Fun for Game Design* (Scottsdale, AZ: Paraglyph Press, 2005).

7  Espen Aarseth, "Genre Trouble: Narrativism and the Art of Simulation," in *First Person: New Media as Story, Perfoamance, and Game*, ed. Noah Wardrip-Fruin and Pat Harrigan (Cambridge MA and London: MIT Press, 2004), 45–55 (47–8).

8  McKenzie Wark, *GAM3R 7H3ORY*, Version 1.1: www.futureofthebook.org/gamertheory/, 4.076–100 (cited in the text by lexia number).

9  Jean Baudrillard, *The Gulf War Did Not Take Place*, trans. Paul Patton (Bloomington and Indianapolis, IN: Indiana University Press, 1995).

10  Matthew Kirschenbaum, *Mechanisms* (Cambridge, MA: MIT Press, 2007), 37–41.

11  William Gibson, "My Obsession: I thought I was immune to the Net. Then I got bitten by eBay," in *Everyday eBay: Culture, Collecting, and Desire*, ed. Ken Hillis, Michael Petit, and Nathan Scott Epley (New York and London: Routledge, 2006), 19–30 (21).

12  Introduction to *Everyday eBay: Culture, Collecting, and Desire*, ed. Ken Hillis, Michael Petit, and Nathan Scott Epley (New York and London: Routledge, 2006), 2–3.

13  Mary Desjardins, "Ephemeral Culture/eBay Culture: Film Collectibles and Fan Investments," in *Everyday eBay: Culture, Collecting, and Desire*, ed. Ken Hillis, Michael Petit, and Nathan Scott Epley (New York and London: Routledge, 2006), 31–43 (33).

14  Walter Benjamin, "Unpacking My Library: A Talk About Book Collecting" in *Illuminations*, ed. Hannah Arendt (New York: Schocken Books, 1969), 59–67.

15  Johan Huizinga, *Homo Ludens: A Study of the Play Element in Culture* (originally published 1938; Boston, MA: Beacon Press, 1950), 8, 10.

16  D. B. Weiss, *Lucky Wander Boy* (New York: Penguin, 2003), 259.

17  Matt Hillis, "Transcultural *Otaku*: Japanese Representations of Fandom and Representations of Japan in Anime/Manga Fan Cultures," delivered at *Media in Transition 2: Globalization and Convergence* conference, (May 10–12, 2002), MIT: http://web.mit.edu/cms/Events/mit2/Abstracts/MattHillspaper.pdf.

18  William Gibson, "Modern Boys and Mobile Girls," *Guardian Unlimited, The Observer*, (April 1, 2001): http://observer.guardian.co.uk/life/story/0,6903,466391,00.html.

19  See Chris Kohler's *Power Up: How Japanese Video Games Gave the World an Extra Life* (Indianapolis, IN: Brady Games, 2004).

20  See a range of essays in *Pikachu's Global Adventure: The Rise and Fall of Pokémon*, ed. Joseph Tobin (Chapel Hill, NC: Duke University Press, 2004).

21  Chris Kohler, "Square Enix Gives Fans What They Want; Same Old Thing," *Wired*, (May 15, 2007): www.wired.com/gaming/gamingreviews/news/2007/05/square_enix.

22  www.cannonspike.com/CamFan/miscellaneous/japan2003/arcades.htm.

23  On this aspect of the *Arcades Project*, see Judith Pascoe's *The Hummingbird Cabinet: A Rare and Curious History of Romantic Collectors* (Ithaca, NY and London: Cornell University Press, 2006), 15–18.

24  See the detailed study and textual reconstruction, produced before the *Arcades Project* was readily available, in an English translation by Susan Buck-Morss, *The Dialectics of Seeing: Walter Benjamin and the Arcades Project* (Cambridge and London: MIT Press, 1990).

25  Walter Benjamin, *One Way Street*, in *Reflections: Essays, Aphorisms, Autobiographical Writings*, ed. Peter Demetz (New York: Schocken Books, 1978), 61–94 (79, 78).

**3  The *Halo* universe**

1  *Halo Zero* at Doberman Sofware: www.dobermansoftware.net.

2  "David," "Observations on *Halo 2*," (November 18, 2004), *Buzzcut: Critical Video game Theory*: www.buzzcut.com/article.php?story=20041118174143932.

3  On the Cortana Letters, see the archive at the fansite Bungie.org: http://halosm.bungie.org/story/cortanaletters.html.

4  For the view from inside the creation of the ARG, see Jane McGonigal, "Why I Love Bees: A Case Study in Collective Intelligence Gaming," in *Ecologies of Games*, ed. Katie Salen (Chicago, IL: McArthur Foundation, forthcoming, Spring 2008). See also the dedicated wiki: http://bees.netninja.com/staticwiki/beewiki/FrontPage.

5  Burt Helm, "Bungie's Leap into the Big Leagues," *Business Week Online* (December 23, 2004): www.businessweek.com/smallbiz/content/dec2004/sb20041223_1735_sb038.htm.

6  Henry Jenkins, *Convergence Culture: Where Old and New Media Collide* (New York and London: NYU Press, 2006), 27.

7  42 Entertainment's mission statement, accessed Fall 2006: www.42 entertainment.com/.

8  Henry Jenkins, "Get a (Second) Life," blog post, (January 10, 2007): www.henryjenkins.org/2007/01/get_a_second_life.html.

9  Rune Klevjer, "The Way of the Gun: The Aesthetic of the Single-player First Person Shooter," published in Italian as "La via della pistola. L'estetica dei first person shooter in single player," in *Doom. Giocare in prima persona*, ed. Matteo Bittanti and Sue Morris (Costa & Nolan, Milano, 2006); reprinted: www.uib.no/people/smkrk/docs/wayofthegun.htm.

10  Stewart Brand, "Spacewar: Fanatic Life and Symbolic Death Among the Computer Bums," *Rolling Stone* (December 7, 1972); reprinted: www.wheels.org/spacewar/stone/rolling_stone.html.

11  Physical light guns could point at screens by the 1930s, but these were not full-fledged, computer-based video games.

12  I can no longer find this remark printed on the Bungie company history pages, where I first saw it; but a similar joke about another game being "*Minotaur* in a tube" remains: www.bungie.net/inside/content.aspx?link=HistoryOfBungie_p2.

13  "Taito Men Talk Legendary Games," *Edge Magazine* (October 2005); reprinted: www.edge-online.co.uk/archives/2005/10/taito_men_talk.php.

14  Ian Bogost, *Unit Operations: An Approach to Video Game Criticism* (Cambridge, MA and London: MIT Press, 2006), 67.

15  Preview video, "Inside *Halo 2*," retrieved from Bungie.org fansite: http://halo.bungie.org/misc/makingofhalo2mirrors.html.

16  McKenzie Wark, *GAM3R 7H3ORY*, Version 1.1: www.futureofthebook.org/gamertheory/, 6 (cited in the text by lexia).

17  *This Spartan Life*, episode 4: www.thisspartanlife.com/episodes.php.

18  The Powerpoint slides and presentation notes, "The Illusion of Intelligence: The Integration of AI and Level Design in Halo," on the fansite Bungie.org http://halo.bungie.org/misc/gdc.2002.haloai/talk.html.

19  1up Show video, interview with Frankie O'Connor and Bryan Garrard, at San Diego Comicon 2006 (July 28, 2006): www.1up.com.

20  D. F. McKenzie, *Bibliography and The Sociology of Texts*, The Panizzi Lectures 1985 (London: The British Library, 1986).

21  Espen Aarseth, "Genre Trouble," in *First Person: New Media as Story, Performance, and Game*, ed. Noah Wardrip-Fruin and Pat Harrigan (Cambridge, MA and London: MIT Press, 2004), 45–55 (52).

22  Jerome McGann, "From Text to Work: Digital Tools and the Emergence of the Social Text," *Romanticism on the Net*, 41–2, (February–May 2006): www.erudit.org/revue/RON/2006/v/n41-42/013153ar.html, paragraphs 37, 38.

23 Daniel Terdiman, "Shakespeare Coming to a Virtual World," *C/net*, October 19, 2006: http://news.com/Shakespeare+coming+to+a+virtual+world/2100 -1043_3-6127294.html. Still in the early stages of development, this MMO is planned around the Wars of the Roses and the world of *Richard III*.

24 Will Wright and Brian Eno, "Playing With Time," *The Long Now Foundation, Seminars About Long Term Thinking*, (June 26, 2006): http://blog.longnow.org/2006/06/26/will-wright-and-brian-eno-playing-with-time/; available from the Foundation as an MP3 download: http://media.longnow.org/seminars/salt-0200606-wright-and-eno/salt-0200606-wright-and-eno.mp3 and from Fora TV as a video: http://fora.tv/fora/showthread.php?t=451.

25 Find *Ivanhoe* (including an automated demo) at: www.patacriticism.org/ivanhoe/.

26 Clive Thompson, "*Halo* 3: How Microsoft Labs Invented a New Science of Play," *Wired* 15.09 (September 2007), 140–92.

## 4 The game behind *Façade*

1 *Façade* is available as a free download from http://interactivestory.net. The site also contains a number of significant documents on the game, starting with the user guide, *Behind The Façade* (draft, August 7, 2005), which I have used extensively in writing this chapter. Among other honors, *Façade* was given the Grand Jury Prize at the Slamdance Independent Games Festival 2006.

2 Markuu Eskelinen, "The Gaming Situation," *Game Studies* 1.1 (2001): www.gamestudies.org/0101/eskelinen/. The term "interactor," which contains a pun on "actor," ultimately comes from Neal Stephenson's novel, *The Diamond Age; Or, A Young Lady's Illustrated Primer* (New York: Bantam Spectra, 1995), and is used by Janet H. Murray to describe the ideal player of an interactive drama in her extremely influential book, *Hamlet on the Holodeck: the Future of Narrative in Cyberspace* (Cambridge, MA: MIT Press, 1997).

3 Espen Aarseth's response to Janet Murray's "From Game-Story to Cyberdrama," in *First Person*, 2–11 (10); a hybrid form of story-game already dominates mainstream video games in the present. On hybrid and impure game forms, see Rune Klevjer's arguments in "In Defense of Cutscenes," in *Computer Games and Digital Cultures*, ed. Frans Mäyrä, Conference Proceedings, Tampere (Finland: Tampere University Press, 2002); reprinted: www.uib.no/people/smkrk/docs/klevjerpaper.htm, which I take up below.

4 The other theorist of immersive narrative for the developers of *Façade* is Brenda Laurel, whose *Computers As Theater* (Boston, MA: Addison-Wesley, 1993), which applies Aristotle to interface design, among other things, has been widely influential.

5 Janet Murray's talk and preliminary Powerpoint slideshow, "The Last Word on Ludology vs. Narratology," DIGRA 2005, Vancouver, Canada: www.lcc.gatech.edu/~murray/digra05/.

6 Andrew Stern on Grand Text Auto blog, (May 23, 2007): http://grandtextauto .gatech.edu/2007/05/23/transparency-in-the-behavior-of-and-interface-to-npcs/.

7 Brenda Bakker Harger, "Behind *Façade*: An Interview with Andrew Stern and Michael Mateas," *Iowa Review Web* (June–July 2006): www.uiowa.edu/~iareview/mainpages/tirwebhome.htm.

8 Evan Shamoon, interview with Matteas and Stern, "Type What You Feel," *Games For Windows* 6 (May 2007), 32–4 (34).

9 Seth Schiesel, "Redefining the Power of the Gamer," *New York Times*, (June 7, 2005): www.nytimes.com/2005/06/07/arts/07arti.html?ex=1181966400&en=56189 81f6a477f55&ei=5070.

10 Ernest Adams, "You Must Play *Façade*, Now!" *Gamasutra*, (June 28, 2005): http://gamasutra.com/features/20050728/adams_01.shtml.

11 Video of the TV story is linked to from *Façade's* home site: http://interactivestory.net#press.

12 *Behind the Façade*, esp. 6–7, 10–11.

13 In an email exchange with me (June 2007), Chloe Johnston, the voice actor who "played" Grace, described the highly artificial process of recording the dialogue, revealing for example that she and her co-actor playing Trip "were conscious of the pauses that are necessary to insert the names. And we had some sense of the way people would be responding, so we definitely finished sentences and used cadences that were not entirely naturalistic."

14 Will Wright, "Playing with Time," SALTT seminar podcast with Brian Eno (The Long Now Foundation). The remark I've quoted was in response to a question by host Stewart Brand: "Why is 'play' the common verb, here?"

15 For example, in their own *Behind the Façade*. Edward Albee, *Who's Afraid of Virginia Woolf?* (New York: Scribner Classics, 2003).

16 Emil Roy, "*Who's Afraid of Virigina Woolf?* and The Tradition," in *Critical Essays on Edward Albee*, ed. Philip C. Kolin and J. Madison Davis (Boston, MA: G. K Hall, 1986), 87–94.

17 Linda Ben-Zvi, " 'Playing the cloud circuit': Albee's Vaudeville Show," in *The Cambridge Companion To Edward Albee*, ed. Stephen Bottoms (Cambridge: Cambridge University Press, 2005), 178–97 (179).

18 Viola Spolin, *Improvisation for the Theater: A Handbook of Teaching and Directing Techniques* (Evanston, IL: Northwestern University Press, 1983).

19 What Spolin calls "blocking" and is sometimes called "denying" another player's "offer," refusing to play the "yes, and . . ." or "yes, but . . ." game, is arguably more like hacking or using a cheat in a game, refusing to play within the given constraint, like simply killing "noobs" in a MMORPG instead of engaging them *en masque* and answering their questions, for example. I owe this and other insights from within the Chicago improv community and about *Façade* as improv to conversations with Doug Guerra, who played *Façade* from the beginning and was the first to demonstrate it to me.

20 Jesper Juul, *Half-Real: Video Games Between Real Rules and Fictional Worlds* (Cambridge, MA and London: MIT Press, 2005), 1.

21 Shamoon, "Type What You Feel," *Games For Windows*, 33.

22 *Star Trek: The Next Generation*, season 1, episode 1: "Encounter at Farpoint" (1987).

23 *Star Trek: The Next Generation*, season 6, episode 8: "A Fistful of Datas" (1992).

24 *Star Trek: Voyager*, season 4, episode 18: "The Killing Game," two parts (1998).

25 See for example Bertolt Brecht, "Uber experimentelles Theater," *Schriften zum Theater* (1), *Gesammelte Werke* (Frankfurt am Main: Surkamp, 1967), XV, 285–305.

26 Gonzalo Frasca, "Video Games of the Oppressed; Critical Thinking, Education, Tolerance, and Other Trivial Issues," in *First Person*, 85–94.

27 Stuart Moulthrop, "From Work to Play: Molecular Culture in the Time of Deadly Games," in *First Person: New Media as Story, Performance, and Game*, ed. Noah Wardrip-Fruin and Pat Harrigan (Cambridge, MA and London: MIT Press, 2004), 56–69 (65).

28 Rune Klevjer, "In Defense of Cutscenes": www.uib.no/people/smkrk/docs/klevjerpaper.htm.

29 Though some games have taken on explicitly political or social or economic content, with interesting results, for example, Ian Bogost's *Persuasive Games*: www.persuasivegames.com/.

30 Karl Kroeber, *Make Believe in Film and Fiction: Visual versus Verbal Storytelling* (New York: Palgrave Macmillan, 2006), 49.

31   Though you cannot reconfigure the more fundamental story arc that the "drama manager" AI program always works to effect. Agency is thus structured, literally plotted, by combined human and machine authorship.

32   Andrew Stern, blog post on Grand Text Auto, May 16, 2007.

33   John Astington, *English Court Theatre, 1558–1642* (Cambridge and New York: Cambridge University Press, 1999), 109.

34   Stephen Orgel, "Acting Scripts, Performing Texts," in *Crisis in Editing: Texts of the English Renaissance*, ed. Randall McLeod (New York: AMS Press, 1988), 251–94 (253).

35   See Stephen Orgel, "What is a Text?" in *Research Opportunities in Renaissance Drama* 24 (1981), 3–6.

36   Jerome McGann, "The Monks and the Giants," in *Textual Criticism and Literary Interpretation*, ed. McGann (Chicago, IL: University of Chicago Press, 1985), 180–99 (191).

37   I'm grateful to Andrew Stern for his feedback on this chapter. He confirmed for me (in email, June 15, 2007) that Grace nearly repeats her line for dramatic emphasis. He also pointed out that the reverse order in which Trip appears first to close and then to open the door is likely a glitch in the stageplay generation process, rather than in the game itself. (Which explains why I didn't notice it while playing: Trip probably opened and then closed the door as expected.) Of course, as a textual-studies scholar, I'm fascinated by that very discrepancy—between performance from the "script" of the game's program and the textual production of a post-hoc "script" of that performance.

## 5  The Wii platform

1   Robert Darnton, "What is the history of books?" in *The Book History Reader*, ed. David Finkelstein and Alistair McCleery (New York: Routledge, 2002), 9–26 (11).

2   Jerome McGann, *Radiant Textuality: Literature After the World Wide Web* (New York: Palgrave Macmillan, 2001), 64.

3   Richard Altick, *The English Common Reader* (Chicago, IL: University of Chicago Press, 1967), 362; and William St. Clair, *The Reading Nation in the Romantic Period* (Cambridge: Cambridge University Press, 2004), 230.

4   Paula R. Feldman, *The Keepsake for 1829* (New York: Broadview Press, 2006), introduction, 9.

5   As Terence Hoagwood, Kathryn Ledbetter, and Martin M. Jaconsen show in the essay on "Production of *The Keepsake* for 1829," in their edition of *L.E.L.'s "Verses" and The Keepsake for 1829*, Romantic Circles: www.rc.umd.edu/editions/lel/, one could order the annual in either an octavo version (for 13 shillings) or by special order in the larger, deluxe royal octavo version (for 2 pounds, 12 shillings, 6 pence). The plain-proof images of the illustrations were available from the publisher, who produced them for 2 pounds, 2 shillings.

6   Unless otherwise indicated, Nintendo company history, game history, and technical specifications throughout this chapter are based on materials shipped with the console or the *Nintendopedia*: www.nintendopedia.org, David Sheff, *Game Over: How Nintendo Zapped an American Industry, Captured Your Dollars, and Enslaved Your Children* (New York: Random House, 1993), and Chris Kohler, *Power-Up: How Japanese Video Games Gave the World an Extra Life* (Indianapolis, IN: BradyGames [DK Publishing], 2004).

7   Kenji Hall, "The Big Idea Behind Nintendo's Wii," interview with Shigeru Miyamoto and Ken'ichiro Ashida, *Business Week Online*, (November 16, 2006): www.businessweek.com/technology/content/nov2006/tc20061116_750580.htm?chan =search.

8  Martin Fackler, "Putting the We back in Wii: Nintendo changes direction, and it appears to be paying off," *New York Times* (June 8, 2007).

9  Sales statistics for April 2007 based on NPD Group numbers as reported on Chris Kohler's *Wired* blog, (May 17, 2007): blog.wired.com/games/2007/05/april_npd_sales.html. Japanese sales figures as reported by Reuters, June 6, 2007.

10  Stephen Totilo, "Shigeru Miyamoto, Design Guru, Says Wii Can Destroy Gamer Stereotype," *MTV News*, (May 26, 2006): www.mtv.com/news/articles/1532607/20060526/index.jhtml.

11  The "two-pronged" strategy is described by Martin Fackler, "Putting the We back in Wii," *New York Times* (June 8, 2007).

12  Matt Casamassina, "Miyamoto Talks Righty Link," *IGN*, (September 20, 2006): http://wii.ign.com/articles/733/733762p1.html.

13  Chris Kohler, *Power Up*, 61; Kohler's knowledgeable history of Japanese video games is rich with the kind of details called for by platform studies. On sales of *Super Mario Brothers*, he cites a white paper by Computer Entertainment Software Association.

14  Matt Casamassina, *IGN Weekly* video, E3 2007: http://www.ign.com.

15  According to Miyamoto in Kenji Hall, "The Big Ideas Behind Nintendo's Wii."

16  Stephen Totilo, "Shigeru Miyamoto, Design Guru, Says Wii Can Destroy Gamer Stereotype," *MTV News*, (May 26, 2006): www.mtv.com/news/articles/1532607/20060526/index.jhtml.

17  Peter Main quoted in Sheff, *Game Over*, 292.

18  Aleks Krotoski, *Chicks and Joysticks: An Exploration of Women and Gaming*, Entertainment and Leisure Software Publishers Association whitepaper (U.K., September, 2004), 10: www.surrey.ac.uk/~psp1ak/publications.htm. On the cultural contexts for the "Girl's Game" movement, see the early collection, *From Barbie to Mortal Kombat*, ed. Henry Jenkins (Cambridge, MA: MIT Press, 1998), and Jenkins' own 2001 conference presentation on the topic, "Further Reflections": http://culturalpolicy.uchicago.edu/conf2001/papers/jenkins.html.

19  www.commentuk.co.uk/nintendo_wii.html. The idea has occurred to others, as witnessed in a fan-created video of people playing Wii Sports in an empty theater: http://kotaku.com/gaming/clips/wii--now-playing-in-theatres-224022.php.

## 6  Anticipating *Spore*

1  As I prepared to send this chapter to press, the first report by a player of the "completed" (but not "finished") game was published by Sam Kennedy on the game review site, 1up.com: www.1up.com/do/previewPage?cId=3162206.

2  For an extended discussion of the conceptual and formal connections between Eno's kind of generative music and Wright's idea of generative content for games, see their joint presentation (introduced by Stewart Brand) at the SALTT Seminar for the Long Now Foundation, "Playing with Time," (June 26, 2006): www.longnow.org/projects/seminars/. The full video is available at Fora TV: http://fora.tv/fora/showthread.php?t=451.

3  According to a paper by Eric Todd, a Senior Developer, *Spore*'s concept development began around Fall 1999; it went into preproduction (including extensive prototyping) in Spring 2003 and actual production in June 2005. It's now slated for release in the second quarter of 2008. "Preproduction Through Prototyping," Game Developers' Conference 2006; Powerpoint presentation retrieved from Spore Revolution: www.sporerevolution.com/gdc_2006/index.html.

4  On the history of the controversy surrounding *Bully*, see Clive Thompson, "*Bully* for You," *Wired News*, (October 9, 2006): www.wired.com/gaming/gamingreviews/commentary/games/2006/10/7192.

5  Besides the numerous demo videos, previews, and trailers, descriptions of *Spore* and the theories behind it have been made available through conventional print journalism, for example, Steve Morgenstern, "The Wright Stuff," *Popular Science* 8.9, (February 2007): www.popsci.com/popsci/technology/f1a18906612a0110vgnvcm1000004eecbccdrcrd.html; and John Seabrook, "Game Master," *The New Yorker*, (August 9, 2007): www.newyorker.com/archive/2006/11/06/061106fa_fact.

6  Michael Mowhertor's post on Kotaku: http://kotaku.com/gaming/the-sims/spore-explained-to-new-yorker-crowd-260666.php.

7  Steven Johnson, "The Long Zoom," *The New York Times Magazine*, October 8, 2006, 50–55; *The Powers of Ten*, Charles and Ray Eames (Santa Monica, CA: Eames Office, 1977).

8  Posted by Maikeru06 on www.gametrailers.com, July 22, 2007: "*Spore* E3 2K5 and 2K7 Comparison."

9  The cube-graph was shown on a slide during Will Wright's and Brian Eno's joint SALTT Seminar for the Long Now Foundation, "Playing with Time," June 26, 2006: www.longnow.org/projects/seminars/.

10  Will Wright's keynote address South by Southwest Conference, Austin, TX, (March 13, 2007); video retrieved from *Spore Revolution*: www.sporerevolution.com/.

11  See Wright's presentation and demo at TED 2007, where he also called *Spore* "a philosophy toy": www.ted.com/speakers/view/id/128.

12  Wright repeatedly describes the T-shaped structure in interviews and demos. See for example Steve Morgenstern, "The Wright Stuff," *Popular Science* 8.9 (February 2007): www.popsci.com/popsci/technology/f1a18906612a0110vgnvcm1000004eecbccdrcrd.html.

13  Caryl Shaw, Producer for *Spore*'s "pollinated content" system, makes this explicit: "The possibility space [in the Space level of the game] is as immense as space itself," in her GDC 2006 presentation, "Building Community Around Pollinated Content in Spore"; audio retrieved from Gamasutra: www.gamasutra.com/features/20060523/gamapodcast_01.shtml.

14  Diana Murphy, ed., *The Work of Charles and Ray Eames: A Legacy of Invention* (New York: Harry N. Abrams, 1997), 18.

15  The affinity between Vertov's self-conscious "database" style and later digital film-making is discussed by Lev Manovich, *The Language of New Media* (Cambridge, MA: MIT Press, 2002), 239–43.

16  Philip and Phylis Morrison, "A Happy Octopus: Charles and Ray Learn Science and Teach it with Images," in *The Work of Charles and Ray Eames: A Legacy of Invention* (New York: Harry N. Abrams, 1997), 105–117 (108).

17  N'Gai Croal, "Now, May the Force Be . . . Us," *Newsweek*, May 23, 2005, 68.

18  I'm a year older than Wright and remember, for example, among many books and films (and film-strips) of the type in the Apollo era, *You Will Go To The Moon*, by Mae B. Freeman and Ira Freeman, illus. Robert Patterson (New York: Random House, 1971).

19  Carl Sagan, *Cosmos* (New York: Ballantyne, 1980), 3.

20  Wikipedia, "Masters of Orion" (July 2007).

21  My pre-release understanding of this content-sharing system is based on Wright's demos and interviews as well as *Spore* developer Caryl Shaw's GDC 2006 presentation, "Building Community Around Pollinated Content in Spore"; Powerpoint presentation retrieved from Spore Revolution: www.sporerevolution.com/gdc_2006/index.html; audio retrieved from *Gamasutra*: www.gamasutra.com/features/20060523/gamapodcast_01.shtml.

22  Mark Saltzman, "The Game of Life: Will Wright Gives Us an Early Look at

*Spore*," *Austin Chronicle*, (March 1, 2007): www.austinchronicle.com/gyrobase/Issue/story?oid=oid:451615.

23  I found the image of a slide containing the early version of the levels of *Spore* at www.spore.es: www.spore.es/imagenes/otras/150.jpg.

24  Will Wright (introduced by John Seabrook), "Gaming 2012," *New Yorker* conference: www.newyorker.com/online/video/conference/2007/wright.

25  See "Preproduction Through Prototyping," Game Developers' Conference 2006; Powerpoint presentation by Spore developers retrieved from Spore Revolution: www.sporerevolution.com/gdc_2006/index.html.

26  John Unsworth, with Lou Burnard and Katherine O'Brien O'Keeffe, ed., *Electronic Textual Editing* (New York: MLA, 2006),

27  Dino Buzzetti and Jerome McGann, "Critical Editing in a Digital Horizon," in John Unsworth, with Lou Burnard and Katherine O'Brien O'Keeffe, ed., *Electronic Textual Editing* (New York: MLA, 2006), 53–73.

28  Jerome McGann, *Radiant Textuality: Literature After the World Wide Web* (New York: Palgrave Macmillan, 2001), 164.

# Selected bibliography

Aarseth, Espen J. *Cybertext: Perspectives on Ergodic Literature*. Baltimore: Johns Hopkins University Press, 1997.

Aarseth, Espen J. "Computer Game Studies, Year One," *Game Studies*, 1.1 (July 2001): www.gamestudies.org/0101/editorial.html.

Aarseth, Espen J. "Genre Trouble: Narrativism and the Art of Simulation," in *First Person: New Media as Story, Performance, and Game*. Edited by Noah Wardrip-Fruin and Pat Harrigan. Cambridge MA and London: MIT Press, 2004.

Ackroyd, Peter. *Dickens*. New York: HarperCollins, 1990.

Adams, Ernest. "You Must Play *Façade*, Now!" *Gamasutra* (June 28, 2005): http://gamasutra.com/features/20050728/adams_01.shtml.

Albee, Edward. *Who's Afraid of Virginia Woolf?* New York: Scribner Classics, 2003.

Albee, Edward. "Computer Game Studies, Year One." *Game Studies* 1.1 (July 2001): www.gamestudies.org/0101/editorial.html.

Altick, Richard. *The English Common Reader*. Chicago: University of Chicago Press, 1967.

Arthur, Kate. "Dickens, Challah, and that Mysterious Island." *New York Times* (May 25, 2006): E1.

Astington, John. *English Court Theatre, 1558–1642*. Cambridge and New York: Cambridge University Press, 1999.

Baudrillard, Jean. *The Gulf War Did Not Take Place*. Translated by Paul Patton. Bloomington and Indianapolis, IN: Indiana University Press, 1995.

Benjamin, Walter. "Unpacking My Library." In *Illuminations*. Edited by Hannah Arendt, translated by Harry Zohn. New York: Schocken Books, 1969, pp. 55–67.

Benjamin, Walter. *Reflections: Essays, Aphorisms, Autobiographical Writings*. Edited by Peter Demetz. New York: Schocken Books, 1978.

Benjamin, Walter. *The Arcades Project*. Translated by Howard Eiland and Kevin McLaughlin. Cambridge, MA and London: Belknap Press of Harvard University Press, 1999.

Ben-Zvi, Linda. " 'Playing the cloud circuit': Albee's Vaudeville Show," in *The Cambridge Companion To Edward Albee*. Edited by Stephen Bottoms. Cambridge: Cambridge University Press, 2005, pp. 178–98.

Bogost, Ian. *Unit Operations: An Approach to Videogame Criticism*. Cambridge, MA and London: MIT Press, 2006.

Bogost, Ian. *Persuasive Games*: www.persuasivegames.com/.

Bottoms, Stephen, ed. *The Cambridge Companion To Edward Albee*. Cambridge: Cambridge University Press, 2005.

Brand, Stewart. "Spacewar: Fanatic Life and Symbolic Death Among the Computer

Bums." *Rolling Stone* (December 7, 1972); reprinted: www.wheels.org/spacewar/ stone/rolling_stone.html.

Brecht, Bertolt. *Gesammelte Werke*. Frankfurt am Main: Surkamp, 1967. Vol. XV.

Buck-Morss, Susan. *The Dialectics of Seeing: Walter Benjamin and the Arcades Project*. Cambridge and London: MIT Press, 1990.

Buzzetti, Dino and Jerome McGann. "Critical Editing in a Digital Horizon." In *Electronic Textual Editing*. Edited by John Unsworth, with Lou Burnard and Katherine O'Brien O'Keeffe. New York: MLA, 2006, pp. 53–73.

Casamassina, Matt. "Miyamoto Talks Righty Link," *IGN* (September 20, 2006): http://wii.ign.com/articles/733/733762p1.html.

Casamassina, Matt. *IGN Weekly* video, E3 2007: http://www.ign.com.

Clayton, Jay. *Charles Dickens in Cyberspace: The Afterlife of the Nineteenth Century in Postmodern Culture*. Oxford: Oxford University Press, 2003.

Croal, N'Gai. "Now, May the Force Be . . . Us." *Newsweek* (May 23, 2005): 68.

Darnton, Robert. "What is the history of books?" In *The Book History Reader*. Edited by David Finkelstein and Alistair McCleery. New York: Routledge, 2002, pp. 9–26.

"David," "Observations on *Halo 2*," *Buzzcut: Critical Video Game Theory* (November 18, 2004): www.buzzcut.com/article.php?story=20041118174143932.

Desjardins, Mary. "Ephemeral Culture/eBay Culture: Film Collectibles and Fan Investments," in *Everyday eBay: Culture, Collecting, and Desire*. Edited by Ken Hillis, Michael Petit, and Nathan Scott Epley. New York and London: Routledge, 2006, pp. 31–43.

Eames, Charles and Ray Eames. *The Powers of Ten*. Santa Monica, CA: Eames Office, 1977.

*Edge Magazine*. "Taito Men Talk Legendary Games," (October 2005), reprinted: www.edge-online.co.uk/archives/2005/10/taito_men_talk.php.

Eliot, Simon and Jonathan Rose, eds. *A Companion to the History of the Book*. Malden, MA and Oxford: Blackwell, 2007.

Epley, Nathan Scott. "Of PEZ and Perfect Price: Sniping, Collecting Cultures, and Democracy on eBay," in *Everyday eBay: Culture, Collecting, and Desire*. Edited by Ken Hillis, Michael Petit, and Nathan Scott Epley. New York and London: Routledge, 2006, pp. 151–65.

Eskelinen, Markku. "The Gaming Situation." *Game Studies* 1.1 (July 2001): www.gamestudies.org/0101/eskelinen/.

*Façade* (2005): http//:interactivestory.net.

Fackler, Martin. "Putting the We back in Wii: Nintendo changes direction, and it appears to be paying off." *New York Times* (June 8, 2007): C1.

Fehey, Rob. "Focus on: Katamari Damacy Creator Keita Takahashi," *gamesindustry.biz* (October 13, 2005): www.gamesindustry.biz/content_page.php?aid=12233.

Feldman, Paula R. *The Keepsake for 1829*. New York: Broadview Press, 2006.

Finkelstein, David and Alistair McCleery, eds. *The Book History Reader*. New York: Routledge, 2002.

Frasca, Gonzalo. "Simulation versus Narrative: Introduction to Ludology," in *The Video Game Theory Reader*. Edited by Mark J. P. Wolf and Bernard Perron. New York and London: Routledge, 2003.

Frasca, Gonzalo. "Ludologists love stories, too: notes from a debate that never took place" (2003): www.ludology.org/my_articles.html.

Frasca, Gonzalo. "Video Games of the Oppressed; Critical Thinking, Education, Tolerance, and Other Trivial Issues." In *First Person: New Media as Story, Performance, and Game.* Edited by Noah Wardrip-Fruin and Pat Harrigan. Cambridge, MA and London: MIT Press, 2004.

Freeman, Mae B. and Ira Freeman, illus. Robert Patterson. *You Will Go To The Moon.* New York: Random House, 1971.

Genette, Gerard. "Introduction to the Paratext." *New Literary History* 22.2 (Spring 1991): 261–79.

Genette, Gerard. *Paratexts: Thresholds of Interpretation.* Translated by Jane E. Lewis. Cambridge: Cambridge University Press, 1997.

Gibson, William. "Modern Boys and Mobile Girls." *Guardian Unlimited, The Observer* (April 1, 2001): http://observer.guardian.co.uk/life/story/0,6903,466391,00.html.

Gibson, William. *Neuromancer.* New York: Ace Books, 1984.

Gibson, William. *Pattern Recognition.* New York: Putnam's, 2003.

Gibson, William. "My Obsession: I thought I was immune to the Net. Then I got bitten by eBay," in *Everyday eBay: Culture, Collecting, and Desire.* Edited by Ken Hillis, Michael Petit, and Nathan Scott Epley. New York and London: Routledge, 2006, pp. 19–30.

Gibson, William. *Spook Country.* New York: Putnam's, 2007.

Greenblatt, Stephen. *Hamlet in Purgatory.* Princeton: Princeton University Press, 2001.

Greetham, David C. *Textual Scholarship. An Introduction.* New York: Routledge, 1994.

Hall, Kenji. "The Big Idea Behind Nintendo's Wii," interview with Shigeru Miyamoto and Ken'ichiro Ashida. *Business Week Online* (November 16, 2006): www.businessweek.com/technology/content/nov2006/tc20061116_750580.htm?chan=search.

*Halo Zero*, Doberman Sofware, www.dobermansoftware.net.

*Halo: Combat Evolved*, Bungie/Microsoft, for Xbox, PC (2001); *Halo 2* (2004).

Harger, Brenda Bakker. "Behind *Façade*: An Interview with Andrew Stern and Miichael Mateas." *Iowa Review Web* (June–July 2006): www.uiowa.edu/~iareview/mainpages/tirwebhome.htm.

Hayles, N. Katherine. *How We Became Posthuman: Virtual Bodies in Cybernetics, Literature, and Informatics.* Chicago: University of Chicago Press, 1999.

Helm, Burt. "Bungie's Leap into the Big Leagues," *Business Week Online,* (December 23, 2004): www.businessweek.com/smallbiz/content/dec2004/sb20041223_1735_sb038.htm.

*Improv Encyclopedia*, http://improvencyclopedia.org.

Hillis, Ken, Michael Petit, and Nathan Scott Epley, eds. *Everyday eBay: Culture, Collecting, and Desire.* New York and London: Routledge, 2006.

Hills, Matt. *Fan Cultures.* London and New York: Routledge, 2002.

Hills, Matt. "Transcultural *Otaku*: Japanese Representations of Fandom and Representations of Japan in Anime/Manga Fan Cultures." *Media in Transition 2: Globalization and Convergence* conference, MIT, (May 10–12, 2002): http://web.mit.edu/cms/Events/mit2/Abstracts/MattHillspaper.pdf.

Hoagwood, Terrence, Kathryn Ledbetter, and Martin M. Jaconsen, eds. *L.E.L.'s "Verses" and The Keepsake for 1829.* Romantic Circles: www.rc.umd.edu/editions/lel/.

Huizinga, Johan. *Homo Ludens: A Study of the Play Element in Culture*, 1938. Boston: Beacon Press, 1950.

Huxley, Aldous. *Island*, 1962. New York: Perennial Classics, 2002.

Jenkins, Henry. *Convergence Culture: Where Old and New Media Collide.* New York and London: NYU Press, 2006.

Jenkins, Henry. *Fans, Bloggers, and Gamers: Exploring Participatory Culture*. New York and London: NYU Press, 2006.

Jenkins, Henry. *From Barbie to Mortal Kombat*, ed. Henry Jenkins. Cambridge, MA: MIT Press, 1998.

Jenkins, Henry. *Textual Poachers: Studies in Culture and Communication*. New York: Routledge, 1992.

Jenkins, Henry. "Transmedia Storytelling." *MIT Technology Review* (January 15, 2003): www.technologyreview.com/articles/03/01/wo_jenkins011503.asp.

Johnson, Steven. *Everything Bad is Good For You: How Today's Popular Culture is Actually Making Us Smarter*. New York: Riverhead Books, 2005.

Johnson, Steven. "The Long Zoom." *The New York Times Magazine* (October 8, 2006): 50–55.

Jones, Steven E. "The Book of Myst in the Late Age of Print." *Postmodern Culture* 7.2 (January 1997).

Juul, Jesper. *Half-Real: Video Games Between Real Rules and Fictional Worlds*. Cambridge, MA and London: MIT Press, 2005.

*Katamari Damacy*. Namco Bandai, for Sony Play Station 2 (2004); *We Love Katamari* (2005); *Me and My Katamari*, for Play Station Portable (Japan, 2005; U.S., 2006).

Kirschenbaum, Matthew G. *Mechanisms: New Media and the Forensic Imagination*. Cambridge, MA: MIT Press, 2008.

Klevjer, Rune. "In Defense of Cut-Scenes." In. *Computer Games and Digital Cultures* Conference Proceedings, edited by Mäyrä Frans,. Tampere, Finland: Tampere University Press, 2002; reprinted: www.uib.no/people/smkrk/docs/klevjerpaper.htm.

Klevjer, Rune. "The Way of the Gun: The Aesthetic of the Single-player First Person Shooter." In *Doom. Giocare in prima persona*. Edited by Matteo Bittanti and Sue Morris. Milan: Costa & Nolan, 2006; reprinted: www.uib.no/people/smkrk/docs/wayofthegun.htm.

Kohler, Chris. *Power Up: How Japanese Video Games Gave the World an Extra Life*. Indianapolis, IN: Brady Games, 2004.

Kohler, Chris. "Square Enix Gives Fans What They Want; Same Old Thing," *Wired*, (May 15, 2007): www.wired.com/gaming/gamingreviews/news/2007/05/square_enix.

Kolin, Philip C. and J. Madison Davis, eds. *Critical Essays on Edward Albee*. Boston, MA: G. K. Hall, 1986.

Koster, Ralph. *A Theory of Fun for Game Design*. Scottsdale, AZ: Paraglyph Press, 2005.

Kroeber, Karl. *Make Believe in Film and Fiction: Visual versus Verbal Storytelling*. New York: Palgrave Macmillan, 2006.

Krotoski, Aleks. *Chicks and Joysticks: An Exploration of Women and Gaming*, Entertainment and Leisure Software Publishers Association Whitepaper. U.K., September, 2004: www.surrey.ac.uk/~psp1ak/publications.htm.

Laurel, Brenda. *Computers As Theater*. Boston, MA: Addison-Wesley, 1993.

*Legend of Zelda: Twilight Princess, The*. Nintendo for the Gamecube and the Wii (2006).

*Lost*. ABC TV (September 2004)

*Lost: The Video Game*. (Mobile game for phones and iPod.) Gameloft, S.A. (2007).

McLeod, Randall, ed. *Crisis in Editing: Texts of the English Renaissance*. New York: AMS Press, 1988.

McGann, Jerome. *A Critique of Modern Textual Criticism*. Chicago, IL: University of Chicago Press, 1983.

McGann, Jerome. *The Romantic Ideology: A Critical Investigation*. Chicago, IL: University of Chicago Press, 1983.

McGann, Jerome, ed. *Textual Criticism and Literary Interpretation*. Chicago, IL: University of Chicago Press, 1985.

McGann, Jerome. *Radiant Textuality: Literature After the World Wide Web*. New York: Palgrave Macmillan, 2001.

McGann, Jerome. "From Text to Work: Digital Tools and the Emergence of the Social Text." *Romanticism on the Net*, 41–2 (February–May 2006): www.erudit.org/revue/RON/2006/v/n41–42/013153ar.html.

McGann, Jerome. *The Scholar's Art: Literary Studies in a Managed World*. Chicago, IL and London: University of Chicago Press, 2006.

McGonigal, Jane. "Why I Love Bees: A Case Study in Collective Intelligence Gaming." *Ecologies of Play*. Edited by Katie Salen. Chicago, IL: McArthur Foundation: forthcoming, 2008.

McKenzie, D. F. *Bibliography and The Sociology of Texts*. The Panizzi Lectures, 1985. London: The British Library, 1986.

Maikeru06. "*Spore* E3 2K5 and 2K7 Comparison." (July 22, 2007): www.gametrailers.com.

Manovich, Lev. *The Language of New Media*. Cambridge, MA and London: MIT Press, 2002.

Miller, Rand, Robyn Miller and David Wingrove. *The Book of Atrus*. New York: Hyperion, 1995.

Moi, Toril, ed. *The Kristeva Reader*. New York: Columbia University Press, 1986, 111.

Montfort, Nick. *Twisty Little Passages: An Approach to Interactive Fiction*. Cambridge, MA and London: MIT Press, 2003.

Montfort, Nick and Ian Bogost. *The Atari 2600 Platform*. Platform Studies. Cambridge, MA: MIT Press, forthcoming 2008.

Morgenstern, Steve. "The Wright Stuff," *Popular Science* 8.9 (February 2007): www.popsci.com/popsci/technology/f1a18906612a0110vgnvcm1000004eecbccdrcrd.html.

Morrison, Philip and Phylis Morrison. "A Happy Octopus: Charles and Ray Learn Science and Teach it with Images." In *The Work of Charles and Ray Eames: A Legacy of Invention*. New York: Harry N. Abrams, 1997.

Moulthrop, Stuart. "From Work to Play: Molecular Culture in the Time of Deadly Games," in *First Person: New Media as Story, Performance, and Game*. Edited by Noah Wardrip-Fruin and Pat Harrigan. Cambridge, MA and London: MIT Press, 2004, pp. 56–69.

Mowhertor, Michael: http://kotaku.com/gaming/the-sims/spore-explained-to-new-yorker-crowd-260666.php.

Murphy, Diana, ed. *The Work of Charles and Ray Eames: A Legacy of Invention*. New York: Harry N. Abrams, 1997.

Murray, Janet H. "The Last Word on Ludology vs. Narratology in Game Studies." Keynote address, DiGRA conference, Vancouver, 2005.

Murray, Janet H. *Hamlet on the Holodeck: The Future of Narrative in Cyberspace*. Cambridge, MA: MIT Press, 1997.

Murray, Janet H. "From Game-Story to Cyberdrama," in *First Person: New Media as Story, Performance, and Game*. Edited by Noah Wardrip-Fruin and Pat Harrigan. Cambridge, MA and London: MIT Press, 2004, pp. 2–11.

*Myst*, Cyan/Broderbund for Mac and PC (1993).

*Nintendopedia*: www.nintendopedia.org.

Nylund, Eric. *Halo: The Fall of Reach*. New York: RandomHouse, 2001.

Orgel, Stephen. "What is a Text?" *Research Opportunities in Renaissance Drama*, 24 (1981): 3–6.

Orgel, Stephen. "Acting Scripts, Performing Texts." In *Crisis in Editing: Texts of the English Renaissance*. Edited by Randall McLeod. New York: AMS Press, 1988, pp. 251–94.

Pascoe, Judith. *The Hummingbird Cabinet: A Rare and Curious History of Romantic Collectors*. Ithaca, NY and London: Cornell University Press, 2006.

Patten, Robert L. "The Composition, Publication, and Reception of *Our Mutual Friend*." *The Dickens Project*: http://humwww.ucsc.edu/dickens/OMF/patten2.html.

Pearce, Celia. "Productive Play: Game Culture From the Bottom Up." *Games and Culture* 1.1 (January 2006): 17–24: http://games.sagepub.com: 10.1177/ 1555412005281418.

Porter, Lynette and David Lavery. *Unlocking the Meaning of LOST: An Unauthorized Guide*. Naperville, IL: Sourcebooks, 2006.

Roy, Emil. "*Who's Afraid of Virigina Woolf?* and The Tradition," in *Critical Essays on Edward Albee*. Edited by Philip C. Kolin and J. Madison Davis. Boston, MA: G. K Hall, 1986, pp. 87–94.

Sagan, Carl. *Cosmos*. New York: Ballantyne Books, 1980.

Saltzman, Mark. "The Game of Life: Will Wright Gives Us an Early Look at *Spore*." *Austin Chronicle* (March 1, 2007): www.austinchronicle.com/gyrobase/ Issue/story?oid=oid:451615.

Schiesel, Seth. "Redefining the Power of the Gamer." *New York Times* (June 7, 2005): www.nytimes.com/2005/06/07/arts/07arti.html?ex=1181966400&en= 5618981f6a477f55&ei=5070.

Seabrook, John. "Game Master." *The New Yorker* (August 9, 2007): www.newyorker.com/archive/2006/11/06/061106fa_fact.

Shamoon, Evan. "Type What You Feel." *Games for Windows*, 6 (May 2007): 32–4.

Shaw, Caryl. "Building Community Around Pollinated Content in *Spore*." Audio retrieved from *Gamasutra*: www.gamasutra.com/features/20060523/gamapodcast _01.shtml.

Sheff, David. *Game Over: How Nintendo Zapped an American Industry, Captured Your Dollars, and Enslaved Your Children*. New York: Random House, 1993.

Spolin, Viola. *Improvisation for the Theater: A Handbook of Teaching and Directing Techniques*. Evanston, IL: Northwestern University Press, 1983.

*Spore*. Redwood City, CA: Maxis/Elecronic Arts. Forthcoming, 2008.

*Spore Revolution*: www.sporerevolution.com/gdc_2006/index.html.

St. Clair, William. *The Reading Nation in the Romantic Period*. Cambridge: Cambridge University Press, 2004.

*Star Trek: The Next Generation*, season 1, episode 1: "Encounter at Farpoint" (1987).

*Star Trek: The Next Generation*, season 6, episode 8: "A Fistful of Datas" (1992).

*Star Trek: Voyager*, season 4, episode 18: "The Killing Game," two parts (1998).

Stephenson, Neal. *The Diamond Age; Or, A Young Lady's Illustrated Primer*. New York: Bantam Spectra, 1995.

Stern, Andrew. Grand Text Auto blog, (May 23, 2007): http://grandtextauto.gate-ch.edu/2007/05/23/transparency-in-the-behavior-of-and-interface-to-npcs/.

*Super Paper Mario*. Intelligent Systems/Nintendo for the Wii (originally for the Gamecube) (2007).

Tanselle, G. Thomas. *Textual Criticism and Scholarly Editing*. Charlottesville, VA: Bibliographical Society of the University of Virginia, 2003.

Tanselle, G. Thomas. "The Editorial Problem of Final Authorial Intentions." In *Selected Studies in Bibliography*. Charlottesville, VA: University of Virginia Press, 1979, 309–53.

Terdiman, Daniel, "Online game rising from the dead," *CNet News*, (May 18, 2006): http://news.com.com.

Terdiman, Daniel. "Shakespeare Coming to a Virtual World," *C/net*, (October 19, 2006): http://news.com.com/Shakespeare+coming+to+a+virtual+world/2100-1043_3-6127294.html

Thompson, Clive. "*Bully* for You." *Wired News* (October 9, 2006): www.wired.com/gaming/gamingreviews/commentary/games/2006/10/7192.

Thompson, Clive. "*Halo* 3: How Microsoft Labs Invented a New Science of Play." *Wired* (September 2007), 140–92.

Tobin, Joseph, ed. *Pikachu's Global Adventure: The Rise and Fall of Pokémon*. Chapel Hill, NC: Duke University Press, 2004.

Todd, Eric. "Preproduction Through Prototyping," Game Developers' Conference, 2006; Powerpoint presentation retrieved from *Spore Revolution*: www.sporerevolution.com/gdc_2006/index.html.

Totilo, Stephen. "Shigeru Miyamoto, Design Guru, Says Wii Can Destroy Gamer Stereotype." *MTV News* (May 26, 2006): www.mtv.com/news/articles/1532607/20060526/index.jhtml.

Troup, Gary. *Bad Twin*. New York: Hyperion, 2006.

Unsworth, John, with Lou Burnard and Katherine O'Brien O'Keeffe, eds. *Electronic Textual Editing*. New York: MLA, 2006.

Vaz, Mark Cotta. *The Lost Chronicles: The Official Companion Book*. New York: Hyperion, 2005.

Verne, Jules. *The Mysterious Island*. New York: Penguin, 1986.

Wardrip-Fruin, Noah and Pat Harrigan, eds. *First Person: New Media as Story, Performance, and Game*. Cambridge, MA and London: MIT Press, 2004.

Wark, McKenzie. *GAM3R 7H3ORY*, Version 1.1: www.futureofthebook.org/gamertheory/.

Weiss, D. B. *Lucky Wander Boy*. Harmondsworth: Penguin, 2003.

*Wii Sports*. Nintendo for the Wii (2006).

Wolf, Mark J. P. and Bernard Perron, eds. *The Video Game Theory Reader*. New York and London: Routledge, 2003.

Wright, Talmadge, Eric Borea, and Paul Breidenbach. "Creative Player Actions in FPS On-line Video Games: Playing Counter-Strike." *Game Studies* 2.2 (December 2002): www.gamestudies.org/0202/wright/.

Wright, Will. Keynote address, South by Southwest conference. Austin, TX, (March 13, 2007): video retrieved from *Spore Revolution*: www.sporerevolution.com/.

Wright, Will. Presentation and demo at TED conference, Monterey, CA, 2007: www.ted.com/speakers/view/id/128.

Wright, Will. "Gaming 2012," *New Yorker* conference: www.newyorker.com/online/video/conference/2007/wright.

Wright, Will and Brian Eno. "Playing With Time." The Long Now Foundation, Seminars About Long-Term Thinking (June 26, 2006): http://blog.longnow.org/2006/06/26/will-wright-and-brian-eno-playing-with-time/; MP3: http://media.longnow.org/seminars/salt-0200606-wright-and-eno/salt-0200606-wright-and-eno.mp3; video: http://fora.tv/fora/showthread.php?t=451.

# Glossary

| | |
|---|---|
| ABL | a behaviour language |
| ADC | analog to digital converter |
| AI | artificial intelligence |
| ARG | alternate reality game |
| CGI | computer generated image |
| CI | collective intelligence |
| CRT | cathode ray tube |
| FPS | first-person shooter |
| HCI | human–computer interface |
| HUD | heads-up display |
| LAN | local area network |
| LED | light-emitting diode |
| MEMS | micro electro-mechanical system |
| MLA | Modern Language Association |
| MMOG | massively multiplayer online game |
| MMORPG | massively multiplayer online role-playing game |
| MOO | MUD object oriented |
| MUD | multi-user domain dimension or dungeon |
| NES | Nintendo Entertainment System in North America |
| NINES | Networked Infrastructure for Nineteenth-Century Electronic Scholarship |
| NPC | non-player character |
| RFID | radio-frequency identification |
| RPG | role-playing game |
| RSS | rich site summary, or really simple syndication |
| RTS | real-time strategy |
| SETI | Search for Extra Terrestrial Intelligence |

# Index